THE
CLASSIC
ITALIAN
COOKBOOK

JULIA DELLA CROCE

THE
CLASSIC
ITALIAN
COOKBOOK

A DK PUBLISHING BOOK

Project Editor
Lorna Damms
Art Editor
Sue Storey at Patrick McLeavey & Partners
Senior Editor
Carolyn Ryden
Senior Art Editor
Tracey Clarke
Managing Editor
Susannah Marriott
Deputy Art Director
Carole Ash
Photography
Clive Streeter
Home Economist
Lyn Rutherford
Production Controller
Manjit Sihra
Production Manager
Maryann Rogers
US Editor
Laaren Brown

All nutritional-information figures are approximate and are based on figures from food composition tables with additional data for manufactured products, where appropriate, not on direct analysis of prepared dishes. Nutritional information is given per serving based on the number of servings in parentheses. Use these figures as a guide only. Please note that KCal is an abbreviation for kilocalories, sometimes inaccurately called calories.

For my mother, Giustina Ghisu della Croce

First American Edition, 1996
2 4 6 8 10 9 7 5 3
Published in the United States by
DK Publishing, Inc.
95 Madison Avenue
New York, New York 10016
http://www.dk.com

Library of Congress Cataloging-in-Publication Data
Della Croce, Julia
Classic Italian cookbook / by Julia della Croce. --
1st American ed.
p. cm.
Includes index.
ISBN 0-7894-1061-3
1. Cookery, Italian. I. Title.
TX723.D42914 1996
641.5945--dc20
96-15191
CIP

641.5945
DEL

Reproduced in Italy by Scanner Services SRL
Printed and bound in Italy by A. Mondadori, Verona

CONTENTS

INTRODUCTION 6

ITALY'S CULINARY
HERITAGE 8

THE ITALIAN PANTRY 18
A vibrant photographic guide to the key ingredients essential for achieving authentic Italian flavor

Vegetables **20**
Fish **22**
Shellfish **24**
Meat **26**
Cheese **28**
Pasta, Grains, and Breads **30**
Aromatics **32**
The Pantry **34**
Sweet Flavorings and Fruit **36**

CLASSIC DISHES 38
An inspiring selection of some of Italy's most distinctive classic dishes

Antipasti **40**
Minestrone Invernale **42**
Pizza and Focaccia **44**
Linguine alle Vongole **46**
Risotto alle Verdure **48**

Pesce Lesso con Due Salse 50
Gallinelle e Polenta 52
Osso Buco alla Milanese 54
Vegetable Dishes 56
Tiramisù 58

RECIPES 60

Over 150 recipes, traditional and modern,
for celebrated dishes from all around Italy

Antipasti 62
Soups 72
Pasta 78
Beans, Rice, and Polenta 90
Fish and Seafood 98
Meat Dishes 110
Vegetable Dishes 126
Sauces 136
Desserts 142

MENU PLANNER 152

TECHNIQUES 156

A practical introduction to special
equipment and preparation techniques,
with step-by-step sequences

Equipment 158
Preparing Vegetables 160
Preparing Fish and Shellfish 162
Preparing Meat 164
Making Fresh Pasta 166
Making Polenta 169
Pizza and Focaccia Dough 170

INDEX 172

ACKNOWLEDGMENTS 176

GENERAL INTRODUCTION

During the course of writing this book, I have been asked what is meant by the title *Classic Italian Cookbook*. It is a question I have often asked myself, particularly in contemplating which recipes I should include. In formulating an answer, I offer a definition from the Random House Dictionary: "classic: of enduring interest, quality, or style…" The recipes in this volume have survived decades and even centuries, and are still much used in Italian cooking today. Their preparation is based on sound principles of using fresh ingredients of the highest quality, and turning them into a finished dish with the least amount of modification, thus preserving their inherent goodness and flavor.

Some writers of cookbooks would have us believe that any departure from the way things have been done for centuries defies authenticity. On the contrary, cuisine is a living art, affected by historical events, popular trends, and the introduction of new foods. While the names of dishes are unchanged, their preparation is typically lighter today than it was when people were more physically active. The current recognition of Italian food as one of the world's most healthy cuisines has been pleasing to those of us who have been nurtured on it. However, any reference to "the Italian diet" always leaves me cold. The Italian way of eating is much more than a sensible diet: It is a way of life.

History has proven that where there is a great civilization, there is great cuisine. The roots of Italian cooking are in the ancient Mediterranean cultures. Italy's first known inhabitants, the Etruscans, had a highly artistic and developed culture, amazingly advanced in agriculture. Over that are layers of influence from invading peoples, including the Romans, Phoenicians, Saracens, Goths, Normans, French, Spanish, and Austrians.

For centuries, there was a distinction between what the wealthy ate and what was eaten by the poor. Eating meat was a privilege reserved for very few until modern times, while the peasant class, with its close connection to the earth, had access to fruit and vegetables, and to the wild foods of the sea and forests. Thus, with even comparatively meager resources, the peasants developed rich cooking traditions. Through the courts and the religious communities, with their higher level of education and international connections, new foods and cooking ideas were gradually diffused. With the rise of the middle class at the time of the Renaissance, the concern for quantity was replaced with concern for quality. It is in the middle class that a meeting of *cucina ricca* ("the rich kitchen") and *cucina povera* ("the poor kitchen") took place, brought together by a common reliance on local resources. Over the centuries this blend evolved until finally it blossomed into what we know as the classic Italian kitchen – an exceptional embroidery of diverse cultural, economic, and historical influences. For the most part, great Italian food is found in the home. The

task of cooking is still generally left to women, but everyone understands the importance of good food. A case in point is my maternal grandfather, who was a gentleman farmer in Sardinia. An intellectual and a *padrone* who controlled much of the local land, he never did manual work. Nor did he do any of the routine cooking. Yet, every Sunday, he prepared the spit over the open hearth of the fireplace and roasted the lamb for the elaborate family lunch. My mother draws a vivid picture of him, dressed elegantly, sitting in front of the fire and patiently turning the lamb. Despite his limited repertoire, he was a passionate gourmet. Sixty years after his death, stories are still told in the family about his remarkable love of good food and wine.

Years ago when I was studying in Edinburgh, I would walk from one end of the city to the other to buy olive oil in the town's only Italian shop. I well remember those long treks in the chilly, blustery Scottish winter, but I felt as though every step was a step toward my roots, for in that bottle of deep golden oil were captured the sun, the earth, and the centuries of my ancestors' lives. It was a real treasure, and not only because the cost of the oil was as much as a week's rent in those days.

The celebration of food and wine for an Italian is a daily event overlaid with spiritual significance, not one reserved solely for special occasions. The love of good food, the intimate connection to the craft of growing and making it, the joy of eating and sharing it, is passed from generation to generation. What shall we name this phenomenon? Is this not "classic" — classic Italian food of enduring interest, quality, and style?

Julia della casa

ITALY'S CULINARY HERITAGE

THE MOST DEEPLY ROOTED aspect of Italian cooking is that of its regional differences. After all, it wasn't until 1870 that Italy became a nation. While the Roman Empire had unified the peninsula politically and with an official language, producing an atmosphere of universalism, its regions persisted in their local customs and provincial languages. In addition, each region has had its own embroiled history of foreign invasions and influences, which affected the culture and consciousness of its population.

After the fall of Rome, Italy had neither a capital nor a center, but was a country of many capitals and centers. Even now, every region, city, and village is still richly unique. This diversity is reflected in the cuisine. Each province and city has its own shape of pasta, its unique breads and pastries, its own selection of recipes. Italy's example shows that recipes are not created in a vacuum; they are the living records of the way in which a society lives, thinks, and feels. In these pages I hope to begin to convey the unique character of each region's food culture and its part in Italian cuisine as a whole.

While Italian guidebooks always begin a discussion of the regions with Piedmont and then proceed south, in the brief gastronomical tour that follows, I have begun with Tuscany because that is where Italian civilization and cuisine began. From there, I move on to Rome and the Greek-influenced south, which also predates the north in the development of cuisine. Last to appear are the Italian islands, Sicily and Sardinia, because their remoteness has made them particularly unique in gastronomical terms.

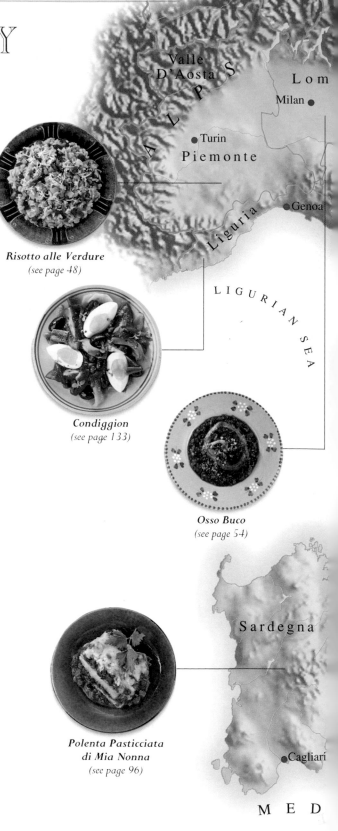

Risotto alle Verdure
(see page 48)

Condiggion
(see page 133)

Osso Buco
(see page 54)

*Polenta Pasticciata
di Mia Nonna*
(see page 96)

ITALY'S REGIONS
This map shows Italy's regions and marks key towns and cities. Above are dishes typical of particular regions that can be found in subsequent chapters.

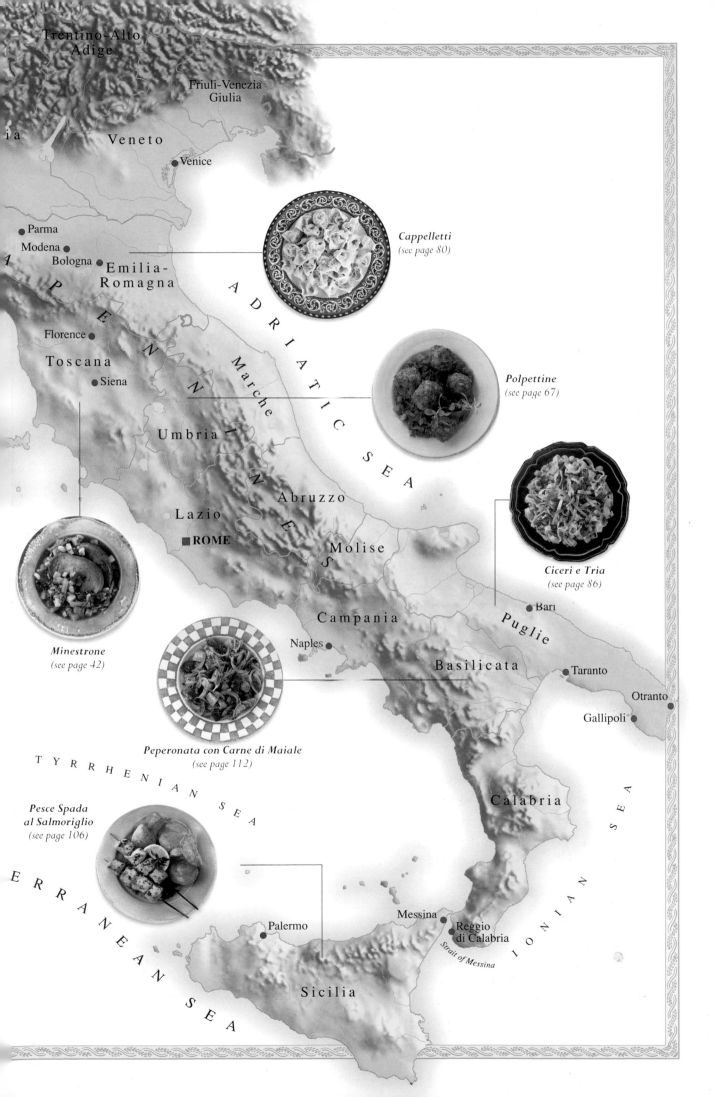

Trentino-Alto Adige

Friuli-Venezia Giulia

Veneto

Venice

Parma

Modena

Bologna

Emilia-Romagna

Florence

Toscana

Siena

Umbria

Marche

Cappelletti
(see page 80)

Polpettine
(see page 67)

Ciceri e Tria
(see page 86)

Abruzzo

Lazio

ROME

Molise

Campania

Naples

Basilicata

Bari

Puglie

Taranto

Otranto

Gallipoli

Minestrone
(see page 42)

Peperonata con Carne di Maiale
(see page 112)

TYRRHENIAN SEA

ADRIATIC SEA

Calabria

IONIAN SEA

Pesce Spada
al Salmoriglio
(see page 106)

Palermo

Messina

Reggio
di Calabria

Strait of Messina

Sicilia

MEDITERRANEAN SEA

APENNINES

TOSCANA (TUSCANY)

Minestrone (see page 42)

Tuscany is the heartland of Italy both in a geographic and a historical sense. Italian civilization began there. When Rome was no more than a muddy encampment, Etruscan civilization was already highly developed, and it is in Tuscany, ancient land of olive, wheat, and vine, where Italian cooking began. Tuscan cooking is uncomplicated and natural; lavish in its use of raw materials, but straightforward in its preparation. It relies on bread and pasta, seasonal fruit and vegetables, high-quality cheeses, cured meats, and olive oil produced by skilled artisans whose craft is a result of personal pride and centuries of know-how. The westernmost provinces look to the sea for many dishes, while in the hilly regions, shepherds still tend their flocks and make good rustic cheeses. In addition, Tuscans have earned for themselves the nickname of *mangiafagioli,* "bean-eaters." This is also the land of *bistecca alla fiorentina,* which has been one of the highlights of the Florentine table for a hundred years. In fact, it is not a beefsteak, but a rib of young Chianina beef. The Chianina is a huge, imposing breed of white cattle whose flavorful meat is tender, lower in cholesterol, and more digestible than other beef. A description of Tuscan cooking would not be complete without mentioning wine, a passion that began with the Etruscans, who developed techniques of viniculture. This is why Italians say that Tuscany was baptized in wine.

UMBRIA

*Polpettine all'Umbra
(see page 67)*

The culinary traditions of Umbria are tied to the mountains and valleys that dominate its landscape. The cooking, based on the region's superior olive oil, is honest and simple, flavored with local herbs, especially marjoram, fennel, and rosemary. A prevalent feature of the cuisine is the bountiful use of meats of both domesticated and wild varieties. There is beef, pork, kid, veal, and baby lamb, raised naturally on a diet of grasses, wild thyme, and sage. Hare and capon, many species of game birds, and river fish (mostly giant carp and trout) vary the menu. The most striking Umbrian dishes are the grilled and spit-roasted meats, such as the famous *arista,* tender roast pork loin scented with rosemary or fennel seeds, and *porchetta,* luscious whole roast suckling pig flavored with garlic and pepper. The finest *prosciutti* (hams) and dried and fresh sausages are also found here. Umbria produces several local pasta specialties of note: *ciriole alla ternana,* thick whole-wheat noodles that are served with various sauces, and *umbrici,* handmade spaghetti. The hills abound with wild mushrooms. Five varieties of truffles grow here and the black truffle is used generously in everything from risotto to pasta, meat, and fish dishes.

MARCHE (THE MARCHES)

The Marches have been held at one time or another by the Etruscans, the Greeks, the Romans, and the Gauls, but while each left its mark, none of these cultures has dominated. This is the most homogeneous region in terms of geography and natural resources. Fishing and agriculture are the area's only industries, and its cuisine reflects sea and land traditions equally. Local waters supply the spectrum of seafood, including shrimp, lobster, squid, cuttlefish, anchovies, sardines, sole, and turbot. All go into the celebrated local *brodetto* (fish soup), of which each town has its own version. Every category of food is well represented in the country cooking. There is excellent farmed meat and game of every description. The local olive oil, cured meats, sausages, and cheeses are laudable. The Marches are blessed with white truffles that rival the celebrated ones of Piedmont, and with wild mushrooms of many varieties, notably the incomparable *porcino*. An important feature of the cuisine is the unrestrained use of vegetables and fruit.

LAZIO

If anything, the cooking of Lazio is Etruscan in character: simple and earthy. The singular gastronomical legacy of ancient Rome is not what is eaten but how. Romans still love lavish displays of food and conviviality at the table. To enter a local trattoria today is to witness, in modern-day form, the legendary Roman penchant for the table as the locals eat their food with unrestrained gusto. The air is filled with voices, all speaking at once, and the aromas of multitudinous dishes. If the approach is unrestrained, so are the flavors. Lazio is partial to herbs and aromatics, including mint, rosemary, sage, tarragon (otherwise used infrequently in Italy, except in Siena), pepper, cloves, and cinnamon. The Romans likewise favor uncomplicated popular dishes (an old Roman saying goes, "the more you spend, the worse you eat"). Olive oil and lard are the preferred cooking fats. Characteristic dishes include a *fritto misto* of organ meats; pasta, bean, and rice dishes; stews and roasted meats, notably *abbacchio* (roasted, milk-fed baby lamb flavored with rosemary); and artichokes cooked in superb ways.

ABRUZZO

Abruzzo is rugged mountain country, though three of the provinces have access to a short strip of coastline. Consequently, there are three styles of cooking: that of the sea, the mountains, and the hinterland. Among the coastal region's favorite dishes are *scapece*, fried fish subsequently marinated in vinegar, and *fritto misto*, mixed fish fry. The cuisine of the mountains is founded on products derived from sheep, lamb, and pecorino cheese. The famous local pasta speciality is *maccheroni alla chitarra*, "guitar macaroni," named for the guitarlike instrument on which it is formed, served with *ragù*. The inland region produces high-quality crops. Superior cherries, pears, apples, peaches, and table grapes are exported all over Europe. The land is conducive to raising cattle, pigs, goats, and fowl, and the region's pork products are well known. One common feature of Abruzzese cooking is its use of cheese and hot red pepper.

MOLISE

Molise is the youngest region, having separated from Abruzzo in 1968, and relies primarily on agriculture and tourism. Wheat and olive oil are produced in relatively small amounts, though they are the staple ingredients, and excellent dried pasta is manufactured here. Having been tied to Abruzzo, the region has food traditions that are largely similar, with mountain, sea, and inland cuisines. Molise borders on Apulia to the south and, like its neighbor, produces vegetables of remarkable flavor. There are superb cured pork products and local cheeses. The countryside is more serene and wooded than that of Abruzzo, a fact that contributes to the excellence of Molisan honey. Unique dishes include handmade *fusilli*, served with fiery tomato sauce, and *caragnoli*, ribbonlike fried pastries glazed with honey.

CAMPANIA

The exodus of emigrants from Naples has made many of this region's dishes famous all over the world, especially pizza and pasta. The tomato, which thrives in the region's long, hot summers and friable, volcanic soil, is also emblematic of Campanian cooking. There is an inordinate appetite for cheese. Silky mozzarella from buffalo milk, creamy scamorza, and a host of other cheeses are familiar components in the region's prolific pizza and pasta dishes. They are also eaten as table cheeses. Neapolitans have been called *mangiamaccheroni*, "macaroni-eaters," by their compatriots since the turn of the century, when the pasta industry took hold and *maccheroni* became a cheap source of nourishment for the masses. The name was superimposed on another more ancient one, *mangiafoglie*, "leaf-eaters," for the fertile soil produces vegetables of legendary quality. It was here in the 1950s that the scientist Ancel Keys found the lowest rate of heart disease in the western world. Nonetheless, the Neapolitans have created a wonderful profusion of artful desserts and *gelati*, "ice creams."

Pizza Napoletana (see page 68)

BASILICATA

Peperonata con Carne di Maiale (see page 112)

Basilicata, which includes Lucania, derives its name from a Byzantine governor. Much of the region is barren, steep mountain land, and there are three agricultural zones that correspond to three different altitudes. Feudalism and oppressive taxation in the past have had their impact on the population, and if there is a Lucanian style of cooking, it is one of making the most of humble ingredients. This is accomplished with the help of hot peppers of various kinds, especially *peperoncini* (chili peppers) and even with ginger (a legacy of the Saracens), which is used with great enthusiasm. The pig and lard are of utmost importance in the diet. Basilicata's pork products have been famous since ancient times, when the Roman Apicius recorded the following recipe for Lucanian sausage: "Chop pepper, cumin, peverella, rue, parsley, sweet spices, bay berries, and mix with ground pork, pounding all together with Apicius's salt, fat, and fennel seeds; encase it in a long skin and hang it and smoke it."

PUGLIE (APULIA)

Ciceri e Tria
(see page 86)

The Greek presence is felt more in Apulia than anywhere else. Taranto, a city on its western coast, was once the capital of Magna Graecia. Other cities, including Gallipoli, Bari, and Otranto, are also of Greek origin. The region is divided into three distinct provinces, each of which has its own pronounced culinary style. Whatever the differences, these styles are profoundly Mediterranean, founded on olive oil and dependent on vegetables, grains, fruit, and seafood. Apulia is well known for its abundant produce, which supplies the region's large food industry. Olive oil, table grapes, figs, and almonds are of particularly high quality and meet the demands of the most capricious tastes. Being nearly surrounded by coastline, the region has an astonishing variety and quantity of fish and shellfish, which are found in the many seafood dishes of the provinces. There is little meat in the diet, but a variety of excellent sausage products and fine cheeses of both cow's and sheep's milk compensate for this. Bread is made in many different ways and shapes. Apulia is also serious pasta country. Locally manufactured dried pasta has found markets all over the world. Handmade specialties also abound throughout the provinces, including *orecchiette* ("little ears"), *strascenate* ("dragged ones"), and *cavatelli*. The popularity of pasta is proven by a saying: *"Criste mì, fa chiove le maccarrune, e le chianghe de le logge fatta ragù,"* which translates as "Jesus, make it rain macaroni and fill the porticos of [our] balconies with meat sauce."

CALABRIA

Calabria is a land of remarkable natural beauty, of pristine beaches and panoramic mountain views. At the toe of the geographical boot, it is a stone's throw from Sicily over the Strait of Messina. This region has the closest historical ties to Greece. Having been extensively colonized in the 8th century BC, Greek Calabria at its zenith was a state of legendary wealth and power, whose cities surpassed any others in Magna Graecia – even Athens – in splendor and luxury. In the course of its long and turbulent political history, it has been taken in turn by the Byzantines, the Saracens, the Normans, the Bourbons, and others in between. Today, Calabria is isolated, having suffered from centuries of feudal rule, and along with other poor regions of the Italian south, it saw a mass exodus of emigrants to North America and other countries in the late eighteenth and early nineteenth centuries. Despite the difficulties of farming the land, there is a congenial environment for vegetables and fruit. Citrus fruits are grown and widely exported. The eggplant finds Calabrian soil particularly hospitable, and there is a veritable eggplant cuisine as a result. Other noteworthy products are tomatoes, onions, and peppers. Seafood is abundant in the coastal areas, especially swordfish and tuna. Lamb and cheeses made from sheep's milk are significant local industries. There are occasional Sicilo-Arab touches in the cooking, but overall the cuisine is simple peasant food based on olive oil, pasta, and an abundant variety of vegetables.

EMILIA-ROMAGNA

Cappelletti (see page 80)

Emilia-Romagna is comprised of two parts, Emilia to the west, and Romagna to the east. Its population is known for its formidable eating. The Italian love of good food finds its quintessence here, for this is the land of parmigiano cheese (Parmesan), Parma prosciutto, balsamic vinegar from Modena, tortellini, and a tribe of stuffed pastas and other handmade egg pasta dishes, including *tagliatelle alla bolognese*. The variety and high quality of food in Emilia is the result of the rich soil of its extensive alluvial plain. This ideal agricultural land has placed Emilia ahead of all the other Italian regions in the production of wheat, tomatoes, and fruit, and enabled it to become a major exporter of other food products, including rice and dried porcini. The lush, verdant landscape also makes it ideal for dairy cattle, which provide the milk, cream, and butter that are at the foundation of many of the region's dishes. The pig is pampered here, as it is destined for the many exquisite sausages and hams. The east coast of the region faces the Adriatic, so there is also a seafood cuisine. Sturgeon, a valuable eating fish and the source of the even more precious black caviar, is caught in the Po River. What was said of Bologna by one Giovanni Schedel in the 15th century in his *Cronache* can be said of all of Emilia-Romagna to this day: "[It] is called the fat and the rich for the reason that it produces abundantly wheat, wine, and everything necessary to life."

LIGURIA

Condiggion (see page 133)

A narrow and mountainous arch of coastline hinged to the French Riviera, Liguria is, above all, connected to the sea. That is not to say that its cuisine is predominantly one of fish. Rather, the cooking compensates for the life of the sailor who has spent months at sea without fresh, home-grown foods. The Ligurians have been mushroom lovers since antiquity, and wild porcini and *ovoli* mushrooms thrive here. They are the most inventive vegetable cooks in all of Italy and make tarts of chard, spinach, and borage. Another influence on the cooking has been its Muslim past, which has endowed it with an affinity for elaboration. Thus, the *cappon magro*, "fast-day salad," is a towering, intricately designed pyramid of layer upon layer of boiled cauliflower, carrots, celery, green beans, artichokes, beets, potatoes, eggs, salt cod, bass, lobster, and shrimp. This is all arranged artfully on a bed of hardtack anointed with olive oil, and decorated with capers, anchovies, preserved mushrooms, pickles, olives, mullet roe, possibly oysters, and more shrimp; then dressed with *salsa verde*. Ravioli, filled with everything from ricotta to pumpkin or sweetbreads, are another specialty. While the spices that were trafficked through Genoa for centuries are ignored (a case of familiarity breeding contempt), the herbs that grow wild on the Ligurian slopes are used lavishly. Most famous of all the local dishes is *pesto*, a heady basil sauce served with noodles and in *minestrone*, which the Genoese claim to have invented. None of these dishes could exist without Ligurian olive oil, which is considered to be among the best in Italy.

PIEMONTE (PIEDMONT)

Risotto alle Verdure
(see page 48)

Piedmont is the land of butter, cheese, and milk. It is also considered to make the best wine in Italy, Barolo, derived from the Nebbiolo grape. The terrain is suited to cattle raising and the Piedmontese produce great cheeses, including tome and robiola. Fontina, which originated in Val d'Aosta, is also found here. It is the foundation of the region's famous *fonduta*, a cheese sauce flavored with truffles (Piedmont is the only region where the precious white truffle is found in abundance). Pasta is confined to two forms, *agnolotti* and *cannelloni*. *Agnolotti* are stuffed with truffles, rice, and meat, or sometimes with game (pheasant, hare, or quail). *Cannelloni* are thin crepes filled with veal, ham, and cheese, then topped with béchamel sauce. Rice, grown locally, appears in everything from appetizers to desserts, though it is best represented in risotto. The Piedmontese love garlic and believe in its healing qualities, as the local proverb "garlic is the pharmacist of the peasant" demonstrates. *Bollito misto* (mixed boiled meats) is the most famous meat dish, which at its most streamlined consists of capon, chicken, beef, veal tongue, and *cotechino* (a pork sausage), served with no less than three and up to five different sauces. Other unique local specialties include *bagna caôda*, vegetables dipped in an anchovy sauce, and *grissini*, crisp breadsticks stretched to an arm's length. Desserts are great in Piedmont, and each city has its own specialties. For example, Turin, the capital city, is famous for chocolates and caramels, Ovada for its *biscotti*.

VALLE D'AOSTA (VAL D'AOSTA)

This region is nestled between the French and Swiss Alps, which accounts for the fact that both French and German are spoken. Like the population, the cooking of the region is multinational at its roots. It ignores pasta, except for gnocchi made of cornmeal or potato, which are served with the splendid local cow's milk cheese, fontina. Like Piedmont, its southern neighbor, Val d'Aosta is a mountain culture. Butter and cheeses (tome, robiola, and, above all, fontina) are produced in the Alps. No olive oil is used. The mountains provide wild goat and boar, chamois deer—unseen in most other Italian regions — hare, marmot, and many species of game birds. The Alpine lakes have trout and the forests are full of chestnuts, raspberries, and *mirtilli*, a type of blueberry. Here, polenta in a porridge form is enriched with milk and fontina. Alternatively, it is cut into pieces after cooling and setting, then sent to the oven smothered with sweet butter and cheese. Meat broth, a highly important part of the cuisine, is the foundation of all manner of thick soups that are often fortified with rice or black bread. The Teutonic influence is perhaps most obvious in the consumption of *speck*, a type of smoked ham that is also very popular in Trentino-Alto Adige. With such hefty eating, there is good reason for the dearth of desserts.

LOMBARDIA (LOMBARDY)

Osso Buco (see page 54)

There are nine mostly agricultural provinces in Lombardy, with Milan being the only industrial one. Although it has been said that a unified Lombard cuisine does not exist, this is not quite true. French and German tastes and cooking techniques have influenced the local cuisine since the time of Austrian domination. Certain dishes have gained international repute. Take as an example *osso buco* with *risotto alla milanese* (braised veal shanks with saffron risotto), *costolette alla milanese* (breaded fried veal chops), or *panettone* (the light, sweet bread riddled with raisins and candied fruit). Gourmets all over the world love Lombardy's *bresaola*, delicate air-cured beef fillet; and its famous cheeses, grana, mascarpone, stracchino, Gorgonzola, and taleggio among them. Rice is king here, especially the variety grown locally for risotto. And who in Lombardy would make risotto without butter, the primary cooking fat since Roman times?

FRIULI-VENEZIA GIULIA

Friuli-Venezia Giulia is one of the least inhabited regions of Italy. During the course of its rocky history, waves of invading peoples, including the Romans, Venetians, and Hapsburg Austrians, have swept over it. Venetian tastes predominate here, but there are two influential culinary traditions, that of Friuli and that of Trieste. The food is mostly rough and hearty, though Venice superimposes some of its refinements in the first course with risotto, as does Austria in the pastry kitchen. Thick vegetable soups to which beans, rice, or barley are added are typical Friuli fare. Pork stew with cabbage and goulash are of the Trieste cuisine, which is a melting pot of Venetian, Hungarian, Greek, Austrian, Slavic, and Hebrew traditions. Polenta is the usual accompaniment to the sturdy game dishes typical of this mountain kitchen. Other foods of note are the sweet, lean ham of San Daniele, and Liptauer cheese, a combination of Gorgonzola and mascarpone, flavored with spices, leek, anchovies, and capers.

TRENTINO-ALTO ADIGE

Italian-speaking Trentino and German-speaking Alto Adige are distinct provinces with separate cuisines. The cooking of Trentino is a blend of Lombard and Venetian styles. Alto Adige, once the Austrian South Tyrol, is boldly Teutonic with a smattering of Slavic. Trentino cooking relies on polenta, meat, and game, and on *stoccafisso*, unsalted dried cod. There is an extraordinary variety of local mushrooms: 250 wild species from this region alone can be found in the Trentino market. Pork is central to the cuisine of Alto Adige and *speck*, a smoked ham flavored with juniper, garlic, bay, and pepper, is made from it, as are numerous sausages. Bread is baked with rye or barley and seasoned with caraway in the Slavic style. This is all heavy stuff, but the abundance of freshwater fish from the Adige River lightens the fare. The wine and beer is German in style, and it is interesting to note that there are at least five provincial colloquial words to describe various degrees of drunkenness, which is also atypical of the rest of the country.

VENETO

The cuisine of Venice and the Veneto is refined, with a touch of the exotic. Here we find sweet and sour, for example, a taste confined to those areas where there was strong Eastern influence. Venice was once a powerful city that supplied Europe with salt, spices, and goods from the Orient. Its markets are still spectacular and its cooking is an unidentifiable amalgam of its worldly and extravagant past. The most important foods are rice, polenta, beans, and *baccalà*, salt cod. No other region uses rice with such creativity and finesse. Pasta is not used much, except for *gnocchi*, to which the Veronese show homage with a yearly festival. The love of seafood does not overshadow a taste for meat, of which there is a great deal, often prepared in unusual ways – turkey with pomegranate comes to mind. It is not surprising that a land that traded in sugar should produce great sweets, and the Veneto does, in profusion. It is also noted for splendid wines, hence the saying that Venice is first a culture of water, then of wine.

SICILIA (SICILY)

Pesce Spada (see page 106)

Although the Greeks preceded the Saracens in Sicily, it was the latter who put a lasting mark on Sicilian cuisine. The island was under Arab rule for some two hundred years, and even after Norman occupation, the highly developed culture of Muslim Sicily continued to influence the life of the island. Unlike the culinary traditions of other regions, those of Sicily cannot be identified solely with either the peasant kitchen or that of the aristocracy. It is rather a case of a great cuisine arising from old traditions. Rare in Italian cooking, sweet and savory flavors are brought together in one dish, such as in *pasta con le sarde*, a macaroni pie in which sardines and salted anchovies are juxtaposed with fennel, pine nuts, and raisins. Also a legacy from the Arabs is a penchant for macaroni, which was introduced to the island in 1154 in the form of *itriyah*, hollowed-out pasta "strings," and a gift for pastry making.

SARDEGNA (SARDINIA)

Sardinian cooking is tied to pastoral traditions. It is one of utter simplicity and bold flavors. The primary elements are olive oil, lamb, bread, and sheep's cheese, which is exported worldwide. Despite the torrid summer climate, there is a great variety of vegetables; artichokes and tomatoes are especially sought after. Dates, figs, citrus fruit, pomegranates, cherries, plums, and nuts grow well and appear in a seemingly endless array of desserts and confections. Wild sage, rosemary, myrtle, bay, and mint perfume the honey of the island. Saffron, a legacy of the Catalan settlements of the 13th century, is used extensively. The quality of Sardinian breads is exceptional. The most famous bread is *pane carasau* in dialect, or *carta da musica* in Italian, so named for its incredible thinness and the crunchy sound it makes when being eaten. Sardinians like pasta, too. Unique to the island are two varieties made from semolina: *fregula*, crumblike soup pasta, and *malloreddus*, tiny saffron-tinted shells.

THE ITALIAN PANTRY

*To achieve the flavor and goodness of authentic Italian
cooking, every recipe should be approached with two
principles in mind. First, you should begin with impeccably
fresh ingredients. Second, these raw ingredients should be
combined with genuine Italian products, such
as aromatic extra-virgin olive oil, imported cheeses, or
cured meats. These pages will introduce you to
just some of the ingredients that are used to create
the flavors of true Italian cuisine.*

VEGETABLES

Italian vegetables are characterized by their flavor. This exceptional quality is the result of long growing seasons and the cultivators' skill. Vegetables are not grown for size or shape, but for flavor. They are allowed to reach maturity in their natural surroundings and are picked ripe, when their flavors are fully formed and most intense.

OTHER TYPICAL VEGETABLES
Carrots, celery, onions, leeks, turnips, zucchini and zucchini flowers, truffles, oyster mushrooms, cardoons, beets, pumpkin, cabbages, broccoli, fava beans, radishes, potatoes, cucumbers.

PEPPERS (Peperoni)
Sweet peppers may be green, yellow, red, or orange, elongated or squat and round. Green peppers are not fully ripened and are less widely used than the others, which have matured to full color, sweetness, and depth of flavor. There are also varieties of hot peperoni.

EGGPLANTS (Melanzane)
Introduced to Italy by the Saracens, eggplants are typically deep purple. Green eggplants are too bitter for use and have been picked when immature. Favor small or medium-sized specimens with smaller navels at the base (the male type), for these have fewer seeds. Indentations on the skin indicate overripeness.

PLUM TOMATOES
(Pomodori San Marzano)
The San Marzano or plum tomato is the ideal variety for cooking. These tomatoes have thin skins, thick fleshy walls, and relatively few seeds. To reach their peak of flavor, the tomatoes must ripen on the vine under the sun. Ripe tomatoes make the best sauces.

Skin should look taut and polished

Tips should be tight and closed

ASPARAGUS (Asparagi)
Asparagus, of which there are green, white, and purple Genoese varieties, must be eaten soon after picking. The stalks should be very crisp and moist. Avoid those with tips that have begun to bud, a sure sign that the stalks have lost their sugar.

Fat white asparagus

Lollo rosso

Arugula

SALAD LEAVES (Insalata)
Green salads are invariably eaten after the second course to refresh the palate. They are usually simple leafy salads, without croutons, nuts, or cheese, that include a variety of young, tender greens, both bitter and sweet for contrasting flavors. These might include radicchio, rucola (arugula), lollo rosso (red lettuce), young dandelion leaves, and scarola (escarole). The leaves should be vibrant and crisp.

Radicchio

ARTICHOKES (Carciofi)

Small artichokes are the most flavorful. When allowed to grow too large, the hairy inner choke overdevelops and the heart loses its tenderness and flavor. Avoid artichokes with leaves open like a dying rose, rather than lying sleek and tight against one another. Stems should be rigid and crisp.

MUSHROOMS (Funghi)

Intensely flavored, fleshy, and moist, porcini ("cepes") are the king of mushrooms. They grow as large as dinner plates in Italy, where they are sometimes grilled over an open fire like a steak. Other varieties include the common white or brown-capped (chestnut) mushroom, egg-shaped ovoli, and trompettes de mort.

Chestnut mushroom

Porcino
(Boletus edulis)

GREEN BEANS (Fagiolini)

If picked when still young, green beans are marvelously buttery and tender. If grown past their prime, the beans become starchy and hard, and the pods get tough and stringy.

FENNEL (Finocchio)

The bulb of the fennel is anisey and sweet, while the feathery leaves have a strong taste reminiscent of dill. Select the sweeter, rounder (female) bulbs and discard the tough stalk part. Wedges of bulb can be eaten raw or cooked.

Look for plump white bulbs without blemishes

Escarole

Red chicory

Spinach

CAULIFLOWER (Cavolfiore)

A member of the cabbage family, cauliflower has excellent nutritional properties. It is used cooked as a side dish, in pasta sauces, and as a raw salad vegetable. There are also green (romanesco) and purple varieties. The crown should be spotless and the stalk crisp.

MIXED GREENS (Erbe)

Cooked greens are an important part of the Italian diet. Such vegetables as spinach, Swiss chard, chicory, escarole, and cime di rapa (broccoli rape) are typically blanched, then sautéed with olive oil and garlic, pancetta, or beans. These greens are also used in pasta sauces, pies, soups, tarts, in stuffed pasta, and on focaccia. As a general rule, select unblemished, unwrinkled, and moist specimens.

FISH

The coastal regions of Italy have always relied on the daily catch from the sea to supplement the diet. Even in the northern and mountainous regions far from the sea, fish are procured from freshwater lakes and streams, and Italians always look forward to the fish course with exultant anticipation.

OTHER FISH AND SEAFOOD

Sole, gray mullet and mullet roe (bottarga), red snapper, salted herring, mackerel, cod, stoccafisso (unsalted dried cod), grouper, turbot, dogfish, scorpion fish, eel, carp, sturgeon, trout, perch, shad, and frog.

ANCHOVIES (Alici)
As anchovies have no scales, they need only be boned before cooking. Fresh anchovies can be boiled, made into patties, breaded and deep-fried, or, if very fresh, eaten raw with lemon.

The sea bass has gleaming silver scales with a darker back and white belly

SMALL FRY
No fish is too small to escape the Italian fisherman, even the tiny whitebait (bianchetti or pesciolini), which are infant sardines, and anchovies and goby (rossetto or guatto). These tiny fish are deep-fried, made into fritters, cooked into frittate, *"omelettes," and soups, boiled or, if just caught, eaten raw.*

Whitebait

SEA BASS
(Spigola or branzino)
The sea bass is a saltwater fish that migrates to rivers and lakes from spring until fall. It is fished from both salt and fresh water. Its delicate white flesh is firm and relatively free of bones, which makes it eminently suitable for boiling or poaching, though it is also delicious grilled over charcoal or baked whole.

The red mullet has extraordinarily delicate white flesh

RED MULLET (Triglia)
There are several species of red mullet, ranging in color from pink to true red; all are popular. Their size is small, but the flesh is exceptionally tasty. Typical cooking methods include grilling, frying, and baking in salt or parchment, or with tomato.

SARDINES (Sardine)
Fresh sardines, unlike the canned variety, are very delicate eating. They are a fatty fish, so little oil or butter is required to cook them. Sardines are typically breaded and fried, grilled, or baked. They may also be stuffed.

SEA BREAM (Pagro)
There are many varieties of sea bream, with dentex and porgy being the largest members of the family. Sea bream has fine, sweet, firm flesh and is excellent grilled, roasted, cooked in parchment with herbs, stuffed, and baked. It may be divided into fillets or used whole. Smaller fish are delicious simply fried.

Dentex

SALT COD (Baccalà)
The best salt cod is white and fleshy, not brownish and scrawny-looking. It must be soaked in cold water overnight, then rinsed before cooking. Once it was difficult to find outside ethnic markets, but it is now more readily available and may be sold boneless and skinless, which eliminates some preparation work (see page 163). It has always been an important staple food for many Mediterranean countries and is an enormously versatile ingredient.

FISH STEAKS
Swordfish (pesce spada), tuna (tonno), and monkfish (rana pescatrice or coda di rospo) are prized for their meaty, firm flesh, which makes them excellent for the grill. They are also suitable for breading, boiling, frying, and baking. Swordfish tends toward dryness so it is often marinated before cooking to improve its texture. The sweetest part of the tuna is the belly (ventresca). Monkfish is a far smaller fish and can be cooked whole (minus the head). It also appears in fish soups.

Swordfish   *Tuna*   *Monkfish*

SHELLFISH

$\mathbb{A}$ll manner of shellfish and cephalopods are prized for their briny flavor. As with other seafood, it is critical that they be impeccably fresh; mollusks and lobster should be bought and cooked live. The names of shellfish vary from region to region, which sometimes causes confusion.

OTHER TYPICAL SHELLFISH
Oysters, scallops, spiny lobsters (also called rock lobsters), sea urchins, sea dates, razor clams, snails.

Cooked mussel

Cuttlefish

Venus clams

MUSSELS (Cozze or mitili)
Smallish mussels are preferable to less tender large ones. Scrub them well to remove sand or grit, and cook them live, discarding any that fail to open.

CLAMS (Vongole or arselle)
Italian clams are tiny — much the same size as cockles — and are sweet and tender. They should be scrubbed and soaked (see page 163), and cooked alive.

CEPHALOPODS
The Italians are particularly fond of this category of seafood. Squid (calamari) can be the length of a finger or up to 1 foot (30cm) long. Tender, small ones are best deep-fried; larger ones should be boiled or baked. Cuttlefish (seppie) can be treated like squid. In Venice, their ink is used to flavor risotto and to tint pasta.
Octopuses (polipi) are large creatures and require lengthy cooking. However, the baby ones can be fried or cooked into a risotto or pasta sauce.

Spider crab

CRAB (Granchio)
Of all the types of crab found in Mediterranean and Adriatic waters, the spider crab (granseola) is the most prized. The favorite Venetian way to eat crab is to boil it, remove and shred the meat, combine it with lemon juice, olive oil, salt, and pepper, and then return to the shell for serving.

Squid

Cooked langoustine

SHRIMP (Gamberi)
Many types of shrimp are valued for their delicate meat. More of their briny flavor remains intact if they are cooked unpeeled. The dark intestinal vein must be removed before eating; the underside vein (the nervous system) is harmless. Langoustines (scampi) or Dublin Bay shrimp are a type of lobster. They may be up to 1 foot (30cm) long and have very sweet flesh. Treat them like shrimp or lobster in cooking, according to size.

Raw large shrimp

MEAT

Although there is relatively little meat in the course of an Italian meal, a great variety of it is used, including game and domesticated meat. All parts of the animal that are good to eat are used. Pork is especially valued for fresh and cured sausages, and for specialty cured meats *(salumi)*, such as prosciutto.

OTHER RAW AND CURED MEATS
Capon, turkey, chicken, goose, pheasant, wild boar, hare, kid, rigatino (lean smoked pancetta), culatello and speck (smoked hams), sweet and hot fresh sausages, luganega (smoked pork sausage), salt pork.

GAME

Quail

Guinea fowl

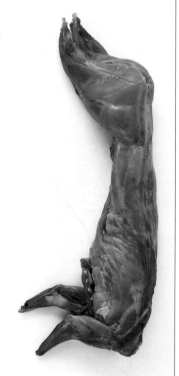

GAME BIRDS
Guinea fowl and small game birds, such as quail, thrush, partridge, sparrow, squab, woodcock, and snipe, are prized for their succulent, uniquely flavorful meat.

DUCK (Anatra)
There are two basic categories of duck: the large domesticated variety (shown here) and small wild birds, usually mallards. Look for young ducks, particularly for roasting, as they are much more tender.

RABBIT (Coniglio)
Domesticated rabbit has a mild flavor, similar to chicken, though it is more bony. Leaving the fur on until just before cooking keeps the flesh fresh and moist.

SALUMI (CURED MEATS)

MORTADELLA
A Bolognese specialty, mortadella *is made from finely ground pork and is riddled with peppercorns and pistachios. It is encased in a skin to form a huge sausage, then cooked.*

BRESAOLA
This salted, air-dried beef fillet dries out rapidly; eat it within 24 hours of slicing. It should be cut paper-thin and dressed with oil, lemon juice, and pepper.

PANCETTA
Pancetta, *unsmoked bacon, is used in cooking. It is formed from the belly section of the pig, which is rolled with salt and spices, such as cloves, cinnamon, and pepper. Unsmoked pancetta has a more subtle flavor than the smoked variety.*

Mortadella

Bresaola

Pancetta

MEAT CUTS

BEEF (Manzo)
Italian beef cuts are categorized as follows: "prime" cuts for quick grilling and sautéing, "choice" roasting cuts, and "select" cuts for long braising and stewing. Beef should be aged and nicely marbled, with firm, white fat.

LAMB (Agnello)
For roasting, Italians prefer pale-fleshed, buttery, tender baby lamb (the Romans call it abbacchio), or three-month-old, milk-fed lamb (agnello di latte). Older, red-fleshed lamb is typically stewed or braised.

VEAL (Vitello)
This delicately flavored, tender meat is highly prized in Italy. Veal calves are milk-fed and slaughtered from one month to one year of age while their flesh is still pale pink. Veal over six months (vitellone) is a deeper red.

PORK (Maiale)
Every part of this popular and versatile meat is eaten. For roasting, suckling pigs or prime cuts of older animals are used. Because of its natural sweetness, minced pork is often included in sauces and fillings.

VENISON (Cervo)
Venison and other meats from the roe-buck, fallow deer, and chamois are rich and gamy. Young animals have more tender meat. Venison should be hung for a week and marinated before cooking.

ORGAN MEATS (Frattaglie)
Meat and fowl organ meats are cooked with great imagination. Liver, kidneys, brain, lungs, spleen, tongue, sweetbreads (thymus glands), tripe (stomach), and chicken gizzards, crests, and wattles are all utilized.

COPPA (or Capocollo)
This cured pork product is made throughout Italy with various flavorings. The neck is boned, seasoned with salt, sugar, pepper, nutmeg, or cloves, encased, then marinated in white wine. It is hung and aged for three months.

SALAMI
The three main types are fresh salami, including cotechino and zampone, dry-aged salami, which encompasses numerous local types such as Milano and soppressata, and cooked and preserved salami, such as mortadella. All are made of pork.

PROSCIUTTO
Prosciutto crudo, "raw ham," is a salted, air-dried pork leg. The most renowned hams come from Parma and San Daniele. The best prosciutto crudo is fragrant, pale pink, and tender to the bite. Prosciutto cotto, "cooked ham," comes in many varieties.

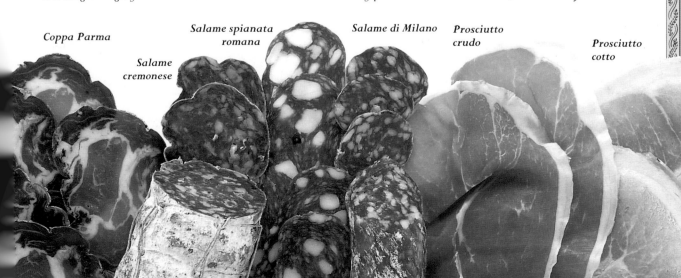

Coppa Parma

Salame cremonese

Salame spianata romana

Salame di Milano

Prosciutto crudo

Prosciutto cotto

CHEESES

The 450 cheeses produced in Italy are each a product of local geography, resources, history, and tradition. Every region and province has its own cheeses, which are made by hand by skilled cheese-makers whose craft has been passed down through the generations. Cheeses may be made from cow's, sheep's, or goat's milk.

OTHER TYPICAL CHEESES
Fior di Sardegna, asiago, canestrato pugliese, robiola, montasio, murazzano, pecorino toscano, pressato, ragusano, casolet, monte veronese, silter, branzi.

FONTINA
The signature cow's milk cheese of Val d'Aosta, fontina is also eaten in neighboring regions. It has a sweet, mild, and nutty flavor, and its excellent melting qualities make it suitable for fillings, toppings, and sauces, such as the famous Piedmontese fonduta. Fontina is also a table cheese.

CACIOCAVALLO
This is a drawn-curd cheese from the south, like provolone. It is made from the milk of cows raised on a diet of wild grasses and plants, which gives the cheese a distinctive aroma and flavor.

Toma

Provolone

Fontina

Caciocavallo

TOMA
A flat round cheese usually made of cow's milk and produced in the Alpine region of Val d'Aosta. After the cheese is formed, it is covered with mountain grasses and left to ripen, which imbues it with a pleasant flavor and aroma.

PECORINO
This famous cheese is made from sheep's milk. There are young, soft, tangy varieties suitable for use as table cheeses, and sharper aged, hard ones suitable for grating. Most pecorino exported abroad comes from Sardinia (pecorino sardo), Lazio (pecorino romano), and Tuscany.

PROVOLONE
A cow's milk cheese made all over Italy, provolone can be pear-shaped, spherical, oblong, or pig-shaped, dolce (sweet) or piccante (sharp). It is a good melting cheese and table cheese.

Young pecorino

Aged pecorino

GORGONZOLA
This superb, fermented, creamy cow's milk cheese, characterized by its blue veining and strong barnyard aroma, is a specialty of Lombardy. Young, runny Gorgonzola, dolce latte, is spread on bread or over hot polenta, or made into a pasta sauce. Aged Gorgonzola is highly aromatic and pungent, and is eaten as a table cheese.

Aged Gorgonzola

MOZZARELLA

A fresh, soft cheese made from buffalo milk (mozzarella di bufala), mozzarella can also be made from sheep's or cow's milk. It is meant to be eaten the same day as it is made; refrigerating spoils its flavor. It is the best melting cheese, suitable for topping southern-style baked dishes, and is sometimes smoked.

Markings of the basket in which it is left to drip dry

RICOTTA

Ricotta means "recooked," and is so named because it is made from whey released in the heating process of making other cheeses. It is a fresh, creamy cheese.
Ricotta salata is lightly salted, solid but tender, and is grated or served as a table cheese. Ricotta forte is made from salted, hardened sheep's milk ricotta and is aged for one month.

Ricotta

Mozzarella

Scamorza

MASCARPONE

A thick, fresh, naturally sweet cream cheese, mascarpone is used in cooking and in baking, particularly in sauces and creams. It is also the basis of many uncooked desserts, such as tiramisù.

Mascarpone

SCAMORZA

This is a flask-shaped cow's milk cheese from the south with a fairly low fat content. Italians like to serve it grilled with ham and mushrooms.

Grana

GRANA OR GRANA PADANO

Young grana is an excellent table cheese, while mature grana is suitable for grating. It is a cow's milk cheese in the parmigiano family, but aged for less time and produced in larger quantities. Emilia-Romagna, Lombardy, Piedmont, and the Veneto all produce this cheese.

TALEGGIO

A young, buttery cow's milk cheese from Bergamo in the mountains of Lombardy, taleggio can be eaten, with its distinctive orange crust, as a table cheese.

Parmesan

PARMIGIANO-REGGIANO

Parmigiano-reggiano (Parmesan) has been made in Emilia-Romagna for 700 years. It is a cow's milk cheese that is aged for at least one year. It has a rich straw color with an intense, complex flavor and moist, flaky texture. Only the authentic cheese has "parmigiano-reggiano" punched into the rind. This is an eating cheese as well as a grating/cooking cheese.

BREADS, PASTA, GRAINS, & BEANS

Grain and the products made from it have formed the bulk of the Mediterranean diet for 4,000 years. After the discovery of the "New World," beans, along with other vegetables, were adopted into the diet. Even now, these staple foods remain central to the cuisine.

OTHER STAPLE FOODS & BREADS
Farro (also called spelt; a type of wheat), barley, buckwheat, rye flour, fregula (large couscous), dried fava beans, peas, piadina (a flat griddle bread typical of Romagna).

GRAINS & BEANS

POLENTA
Fine cornmeal polenta and polenta taragna (buckwheat polenta) are essential staples, particularly in the northern region.

Carnaroli rice

Arborio rice

Vialone nano rice

RICE
Long-grain rice is used for boiling and in soups. Arborio, Vialone nano, and Carnaroli rice are used for risotto because they are uniquely suited to slow cooking in a small quantity of liquid: the large core of the rice remains somewhat firm, while the exterior becomes creamy, absorbing all the flavors.

BORLOTTI BEANS
The color of borlotti varies from mottled red to brown or blue-gray. They are used fresh or dried, in baked dishes and soup.

CANNELLINI BEANS
These are the most common Italian beans. They have a creamy texture when cooked. Avoid the canned product.

LENTILS (Lenticchie)
Earthy brown lentils do not require presoaking. They are much used for soups, stews, and baked dishes.

CHICKPEAS (Ceci)
Dried, rehydrated chickpeas have a wonderfully nutty flavor, far superior to the canned product.

BREADS

Grissini sticks

BREADS (Pane) AND FOCACCIE
Every Italian region has its own typical breads. They are made with refined wheat flour, whole-wheat, semolina, cornmeal, or rye, and may contain herbs, olives, or cheese. Focaccie, flat yeast breads, are eaten as antipasti or snacks.

Country loaf

Olive focaccia

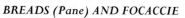

Rye bread

Corn bread

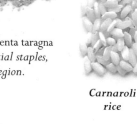

PASTA

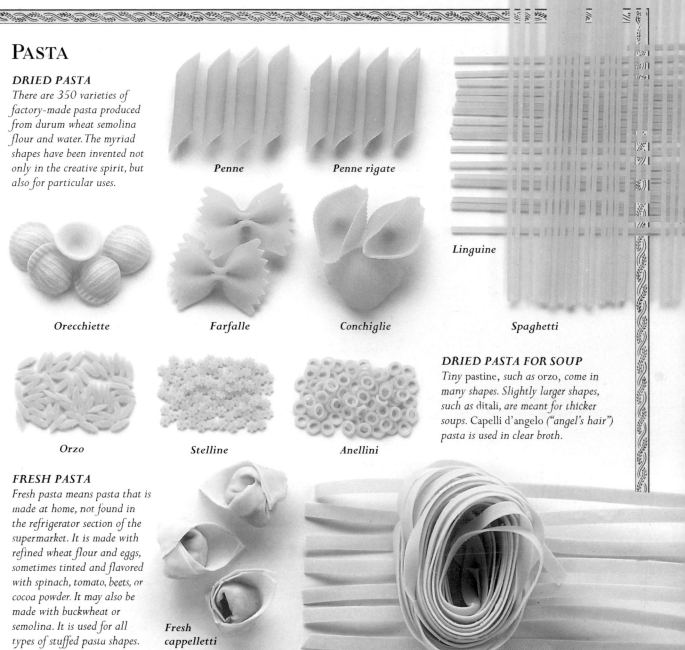

DRIED PASTA

There are 350 varieties of factory-made pasta produced from durum wheat semolina flour and water. The myriad shapes have been invented not only in the creative spirit, but also for particular uses.

Penne

Penne rigate

Linguine

Orecchiette

Farfalle

Conchiglie

Spaghetti

Orzo

Stelline

Anellini

DRIED PASTA FOR SOUP

Tiny pastine, such as orzo, come in many shapes. Slightly larger shapes, such as ditali, are meant for thicker soups. Capelli d'angelo ("angel's hair") pasta is used in clear broth.

FRESH PASTA

Fresh pasta means pasta that is made at home, not found in the refrigerator section of the supermarket. It is made with refined wheat flour and eggs, sometimes tinted and flavored with spinach, tomato, beets, or cocoa powder. It may also be made with buckwheat or semolina. It is used for all types of stuffed pasta shapes.

Fresh cappelletti

Fresh tagliatelle

SWEET BREADS

Sweet yeast breads studded with fruit, nuts, and spices are an ancient tradition. The dough is usually enriched with eggs, butter, or oil and may be flavored with flower waters. Celebration breads contain fillings, chocolate, or sweet wine.

Panettone

Pandoro flavored with Marsala

Sweet bread rolls

AROMATICS

A wide variety of herbs and spices is used in Italian cooking, but usually in small quantities, adroitly matched to bring out, not mask, the main ingredients. Most herbs are best used fresh when their flavors and scents are at their peak.

OTHER AROMATICS
Mustard, mace, coriander, cumin, sesame seeds, chives, myrtle leaves (Sardinia), celery leaves, tarragon (Siena), horseradish.

BASIL (Basilico)
An annual tropical herb related to mint, basil is highly aromatic, with a strong, sweet flavor. There are many varieties, some more pungent than others. Because of its intensity, it should not be used indiscriminately. Avoid dried basil.

Marjoram

Basil

FENNEL
The fennel plant, which flourishes as a wild and domestic plant in hot climates, has a sweet aroma and a flavor reminiscent of licorice. It provides seeds, bulb, and feathery leaves.

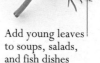

OREGANO (Origano)
The flavor and aroma of oregano are more bitter than those of marjoram. Its aggressive flavor limits its use in the kitchen, though it is found in certain southern dishes, such as pizza, and zesty pasta sauces.

Both fresh and dried oregano work well

MARJORAM (Maggiorana)
Marjoram has a taste similar to oregano, but is more complex and mellow in comparison. This herb is very versatile and successful in both its fresh and dried forms.

Add young leaves to soups, salads, and fish dishes

Pepper is best used freshly ground from the whole corns

Look for plump, firm cloves

SEA SALT (Sale)
Sea salt is a natural product made by evaporating sea water. It has a concentrated, intense flavor. Coarse salt is also natural.

PEPPER (Pepe)
Black pepper is the dried, mature, unhusked berry. White pepper is the inner center of ripe pepper berries and has less of a bite.

GARLIC (Aglio)
A member of the onion family, garlic has extraordinary health giving attributes. It is much used in southern Italian cooking. It should never be used in its bitter dried or powdered form. Avoid garlic that has begun to sprout.

JUNIPER (Ginepro)
The berries from an evergreen, juniper has a wild, musky scent and flavor, ideal for game. It should be crushed before use.

CHILI PEPPER (Peperoncino)
Whole or crushed chilis are widely used either fresh or dried, particularly in the south, to give fire to sauces and pickles.

PARSLEY (Prezzemolo)

With its mild, agreeable grassy flavor, parsley is a ubiquitous Italian culinary herb. It is the foundation of many sauces and appears in a wide range of dishes. Use only the flavorful flat-leaf variety for cooking. The curly-leaved variety can be used for garnishing.

— Choose flat-leaf fresh parsley

SAGE (Salvia)

The musty, highly aromatic flavor of sage is well matched with white meats such as pork or veal. Sage is also used to flavor butter as a dressing for gnocchi or stuffed pasta. Fresh sage leaves, coated with a light batter and fried in olive oil, make a delicious antipasto.

BAY (Alloro)

Bay leaves should be used sparingly. One dried leaf is enough to lend a hint of its powerful aroma to a soup or stew. Bay should always be kept whole and removed after cooking. It is almost always dried, but can be used fresh.

Cinnamon sticks

MINT (Menta)

There are numerous varieties of mint used fresh in Italian cooking, including wild mint (mentucia) and catmint. Mint is added judiciously to stuffings, vegetable dishes, sauces, salads, and some fowl dishes.

ROSEMARY (Rosmarino)

Often found wild, rosemary is one of the most fragrant herbs. Its refreshing, pungent, pinelike aroma is retained even when dried. It is eminently suitable for flavoring roasted meats, particularly pork, lamb, and veal, but it also gives a zing to tomato sauces and stewed dishes.

Ground cinnamon

CINNAMON (Canella)

This spice comes from the dried inner bark of an evergreen tree from the laurel family. Except in Sicily, it is used primarily for desserts, in stick or powdered form.

SAFFRON (Zafferano)

Fiery-colored saffron comes from the stigmas of crocuses. As there are only three stigmas in each bloom, it is rare and costly.

CLOVES (Chiodi di garofano)

These nail-shaped cloves are the dried flower buds of an evergreen tree related to myrtle. They are used in baking and cooking.

FENNEL SEEDS (Semi di finocchio)

Sharp, aniseed-tasting fennel seeds are especially suited to pork. They are also used on roasts, in desserts, and in sausages.

ANISE SEEDS (Anice)

Anise has a flavor similar to fennel, but is sweeter with less bite. It is typically found in sweet breads, biscotti, and desserts.

NUTMEG (Noce moscata)

A small amount of this bitter, highly aromatic spice goes a long way, so it should be used conservatively. To experience its flavor fully, buy whole nutmegs and use them freshly grated.

THE PANTRY

Whether you are preparing a leisurely lunch or putting something together for a large family gathering or unexpected visitors, the foundation of the classic Italian kitchen is a well-stocked pantry that always contains high-quality, genuine products.

ADDITIONAL SUPPLIES
Bread crumbs, pickled gherkins, mostarda di frutta (candied fruit in mustard syrup), vegetable oil, unsalted butter, canned chestnuts, almonds, walnuts, brandy, rum.

The best tuna meat taken from the belly of the fish

DRIED PORCINI
These are the most tasty and sought-after wild mushrooms. In their dried form, the woodsy, intense flavor is even more concentrated. Select fleshy, pale pieces, not dark, brittle fragments. Soak them in warm water for 30 minutes, then rinse and squeeze dry before use. The flavorful soaking liquid should be strained and used.

CANNED TUNA IN OLIVE OIL
Italian canned tuna, characterized by its excellent sweet flavor and rosy color, is packed in olive oil, which imparts a fruity flavor to the meat.

ANCHOVIES IN OIL
Anchovies are preserved in olive oil or salt. The latter should be rinsed before use. They have a wide variety of uses, including as a flavoring for sauces and as a topping for pizza and focaccia.

OLIVES
There are many olive varieties, and they are usually named by their place of origin. All are green to begin with; the more they mature, the darker they become. Dry-cured olives have a wrinkled appearance and concentrated flavor.

PINE NUTS (Pinoli)
The kernels of stone pine cones, these nuts are used in cooking and baking. They turn rancid quickly, so should be refrigerated or frozen after purchase.

Black Gaeta olives

Salted capers

Olives marinated with herbs and olive oil

Pine nuts

CAPERS (Capperi)
These are the buds of a wild Mediterranean plant. They are picked before sunrise, and pickled or salted. Those preserved in salt must be rinsed.

Look for capers that are small and tightly closed

Dry-cured olives

Chianti vinegar

White wine vinegar

Olio santo

Extra-virgin olive oil

Balsamic vinegar

WINE (Vino)

Wine is a critical ingredient in many Italian dishes. Cook with the same good-quality red or white wine, or fortified wine such as vermouth, as you would drink. This sacred product is as much a part of the Italian meal as the food itself. It is the first thing to arrive, to calm the body, lift the spirit, arouse the appetite, and aid digestion.

VINEGAR (Aceto)

The most flavorful vinegars are made from fermented wine, and are aged. The percentage of acidity — from 5% to 7% — indicates tartness. Balsamic vinegar, a product of Modena, is made from the boiled-down must of white grapes, and is aged for at least ten years in a series of casks made of aromatic woods. It has a sweet, mellow, rich flavor.

OLIVE OIL (Olio d'oliva)

Highly aromatic, fruity, cold-pressed extra-virgin olive oil, derived from the first pressing, is essential. Its color varies from deep gold to grass green, and its flavor and aroma are affected by the olive variety, soil type, and climate. It is best used young. Standard olive oil is lower grade, good for deep-frying. Olio santo is seasoned with hot red peppers.

PISTACHIOS (Pistacchi)

Pistachios are used in stuffings and in baking, most notably in sweet yeast breads. They should be natural (not dyed red) and unsalted. Remove the shells and rub off the reddish membrane.

Canned peeled plum tomatoes

Sun-dried tomatoes

Tomato paste

TOMATO PRODUCTS

Whole canned tomatoes should not be too firm, and there should be a high proportion of tomatoes to liquid (or purée). Concentrated tomato paste should be used judiciously as a thickener, or for a touch of flavor or color. Sun-dried tomatoes may be packed in salt, formed into blocks, stored dry, or preserved in olive oil. Those not packed in oil should be rehydrated by soaking in warm water for 15–30 minutes, then strained, squeezed dry, and chopped. They are too leathery to eat whole, but can be added to sauces, stews, and stuffings.

SWEET FLAVORINGS & FRUIT

In contrast to the cooking traditions of many Arab and Asian countries, Italian cooking keeps sweet and savory ingredients apart, with sweet flavors generally reserved for the dessert course. Certain fruits and ingredients, such as lemon or fortified wine, span both tastes — for they are either somewhat neutral or versatile.

OTHER SWEET FLAVORINGS & FRUIT

Nectarines, raspberries, bilberries, cherries, plums, apples, melons, persimmons, loquats, pomegranates, quince, Vin Santo, brandy, rum, anisette, orange-flower water.

COFFEE (Caffè)

Italian coffee, espresso, is very dark, rich, and strongly flavored. In addition to its various beverage forms, it is used as an aromatic flavoring for granita *and* gelati *(ices and ice creams), and popular desserts such as* tiramisù.

CITRUS FRUIT

All fruits are consumed voraciously in Italy, no doubt because of their remarkable quality and flavor. Oranges, including blood and bitter varieties, tangerines, limes, lemons, citrons, and grapefruit are used as much in cooking as for table fruit. The zest and juice are indispensable in many savory dishes, breads, tarts, and marmalades. They are left to mature on the trees, and the fragrant zest is never treated or waxed.

Blood orange

MARSALA

A sweet, fortified wine from Sicily, Marsala adds a distinctive, mellow flavor and depth to chicken and veal dishes. It is also used in desserts.

PEACHES (Pesche)

Italy shares a place with America for the highest peach production in the world, but Italian peaches are especially sweet and luscious. There are white and red varieties, which are eaten fresh, or stuffed and baked, in pies, made into preserves, or dried. They have a higher mineral and vitamin content than many other fruit.

APRICOTS (Albicocche)

The Arabs brought the apricot to the Mediterranean, where it still flourishes. It is a good source of copper and potassium and is rich in vitamin A when ripe. Select only fully mature, unblemished fruit.

CACTUS FRUIT (Fichi d'India)

These fruit, also called prickly pears in Italy, are prevalent wherever the climate is torrid, especially in Sicily and Sardinia, where they grow wild. They must be fully ripe to eat. Cut the skin lengthwise and pull it away from the succulent pulp. The seeds may be eaten or discarded.

HONEY (Miele)

Italian honeys are fragrant and assertive, made by bees feeding on wild herbs and flowers. Look for Tuscan chestnut honey, Alpine wildflower honey, and orange blossom honey from Sicily.

AMARETTI

These are delightful crisp little cookies made from bitter almonds, egg whites, and sugar. They are made for eating as they are, but are also widely used in desserts and for fruit stuffings, such as Piedmontese stuffed peaches.

CHOCOLATE (Cioccolata)

Dark chocolate, high in cocoa solids, is widely used, primarily for desserts. There are a few savory dishes in which it appears in its unsweetened state, including Sicilian caponata and chocolate pasta, a legacy from the Renaissance kitchen.

GRAPES (Uva)

Different varieties of grapes are grown for wine and for the table, though all wine grapes are suitable for eating. Among the best table varieties are the white (green) and red muscatel, and miniature purple grapes called uva fragola. I have memories of walking down country lanes in Sardinia, Tuscany, and Lazio, and reaching up to pick grapes from the wild vines.

Unwaxed lemon

CANDIED FRUIT AND FLOWERS

All manner of fruit, even squash, is candied for use as a decoration on desserts and confections. This art is especially practiced by the Sicilians. Parma and Venice are famous for their candied violet petals; Liguria, for its candied rose petals.

Candied fruit and peel

Crystallized violets

DRIED FRUIT

Fruit is often dried for winter use at the end of the harvest. Typical are raisins, golden raisins, prunes, and figs, which may be stuffed with chocolate, candied peel, fennel, and almonds to make a wonderful sweet.

FIGS (Fichi)

The most common fig varieties are the black (purple) fig and the white (green) fig. These sugary-sweet fruits are delightful peeled and eaten as they are. Their natural sweetness is intensified when they are dried.

STRAWBERRIES (Fragoli)

Strawberries are eaten only in season, perhaps with a drop of balsamic vinegar or with sweet wine or mascarpone. Look for the tiny wild Italian species.

Dates

Raisins

NUTS

All kinds of nuts, particularly hazelnuts, almonds, chestnuts, and walnuts, are used in cooking, baking, and liqueur making. Chestnuts must be cooked; other nuts can be toasted to bring out their flavors.

Almonds

Chestnuts

PEARS (Pere)

Pears have existed in Italy since Roman times, though their varieties have increased manifold since then. They are an ingredient of mostarda di Cremona, a condiment of candied fruit and mustard.

VANILLA (Vaniglia)

Available in extract or the more aromatic bean form, vanilla is used to flavor confections, custards, and creams.

Vanilla pods

CLASSIC DISHES

This selection of dishes is designed to give you an impression of the flavors of classic Italian food. Selecting the recipes was not an easy task; there are so many dishes to choose from, both unusual and familiar. My decision was to draw from every part of the geographical boot — north, south, central, east, and west — to represent the taste of the sea, of the forests, of the mountains, and of the interior, and in so doing, to give a preview of Italy's enormously rich culinary tradition.

**All the dishes serve 4,
unless otherwise indicated.**

ANTIPASTI

In Italy, *antipasti* are not just perfunctory beginnings to dinner; rather, they can be among the most creative dishes in the Italian kitchen. Their variety is endless, the assortment delectable. Many antipasti are excellent served as main dishes, or as side dishes (*contorni*) or snacks.

CIPOLLINE IN AGRODOLCE

Sweet and sour onions

Italians are fond of pickling vegetables for antipasti. Unlike many pickles, these onions do not leave one's mouth puckered as the vinegar is tempered with sugar. They are excellent with cured meats, such as prosciutto, and the addition of cloves gives them a festive flavor, making them particularly suitable for serving with a ham, duck, goose, or turkey.

See page 63 for recipe.

ZUPPA DI MITILI ALLA PUGLIESE

Mussels in wine, Apulian style

This is not so much a soup as an appetite arouser. It is traditionally served over slices of bread that soak up the garlicky broth.

See page 65 for recipe.

POLPETTINE ALL' UMBRA

Little meatballs, Umbrian style

These savory little delicacies can be sautéed, or cooked in a wine or tomato sauce or broth.

See page 67 for recipe.

FUNGHI FRITTI ALLA SARDA

Crispy fried mushrooms, Sardinian style

In Sardinia, wild mushrooms called cisti are prized for their intensely meaty flavor. This starkly simple dish was first made for me by my Sardinian aunt and uncle, and uses wild mushrooms to excellent effect. The subtly crunchy semolina coating hides a moist interior. They are also good with roasted meats.

See page 63 for recipe.

FRITTATA AGLI ASPARAGI

Asparagus and mushroom frittata

Frittatas are made with a wide variety of fillings, such as spring vegetables or even leftover sauced pasta. This version has a filling of asparagus and mushrooms, which is a particularly harmonious combination. It can be made on the stove in a skillet, or it can be baked, whereupon it becomes a tortino.

See page 66 for recipe.

PEPERONI IMBOTTITI

Peppers stuffed with rice and Gorgonzola

Peppers are ideal for stuffing because their shape makes them perfect receptacles. Fillings can be bread- or rice-based, and often incorporate ham, sausages, cheeses, and mushrooms. Here, the pungent but still delicate flavor of Gorgonzola cheese is set off by the natural sweetness of the peppers.

See page 64 for recipe.

MINESTRONE INVERNALE

Winter minestrone

Winter *minestroni* typically contain fewer vegetables than the summer versions. Only water (no stock) is used in making this hearty soup, and it is often ladled steaming hot over slices of stale bread that have first been rubbed with garlic, toasted lightly and drizzled with the fruity olive oil from the winter oil pressing. The favorite way of eating a minestrone such as this is to make it up to three days in advance, then reheat it on the stove with slices of stale bread. In some regions, this is called *ribollita*, "reboiled," though the real ribollita of Tuscany is made with black cabbage and unsalted bread. Serves 6.

INGREDIENTS

⅓ cup (90ml) extra-virgin olive oil, plus extra for toast
1 large onion, chopped
2 large potatoes, peeled and finely diced
1 small savoy cabbage (cavolo verza), shredded
2 medium zucchini, finely diced
2 celery ribs with leaves, chopped
6oz (175g) string beans, trimmed and cut into pieces
1lb (500g) winter squash (such as butternut,
Hubbard, or acorn), peeled and diced
2 cups (500g) fresh or canned drained tomatoes,
peeled, seeded, and chopped
½ head cauliflower, broken up and cut into slices
1 cup (250g) dried haricot beans, soaked and cooked (see
page 161), or 1lb (500g) canned beans, rinsed and drained
8 cups (2 liters) bean cooking liquid (if used) or water
2 bay leaves
¼ cup (30g) chopped fresh rosemary, oregano,
and thyme, or 1 tsp each dried
1 tbsp salt and ½ tsp freshly ground black pepper
12 slices stale robust Italian or peasant bread
4 large garlic cloves, chopped into quarters

PREPARATION

1 Warm the oil in a large saucepan and add the onion and potato. Sauté over medium heat, stirring occasionally, until the onion is soft and the potato leaves a starchy film on the pan, about 8 minutes.
2 Add all the vegetables, the beans, cooking liquid or water, herbs, and seasoning. Simmer over medium-low heat, partially covered, until the cabbage is tender and the other vegetables cooked through, about 1½ hours. Check the seasoning.
3 Rub the bread on both sides with the garlic, then toast it lightly. Drizzle each slice with plenty of olive oil and place two slices in each soup plate. Pour the hot soup over the bread and serve.

KCal 570 P 22g C 82g S 1072mg SFA 3g UFA 14g (6)

Celery

Zucchini

Savoy cabbage

Potatoes

Onion

Olive oil

Italian bread

String beans

Winter squash

Tomatoes

Cauliflower

Beans and liquid

Bay leaves

Rosemary

Oregano

Thyme

Salt

Black pepper

Garlic

PIZZA AND FOCACCIA

B oth pizza and focaccia have become standard dishes of the *cucina povera* (poor kitchen), being fast, economical, and accessible. Their simplicity demands the use of only the highest-quality ingredients for the toppings.

PIZZETTA MARGHERITA

Small pizza with a tomato, mozzarella, and basil sauce

Little pizzas are excellent for snacks. One quantity of basic pizza dough (see page 170) will make eight of these little 6in (15cm) Neapolitan-style pizza bases. This classically simple topping uses sun-ripened tomatoes and aromatic fresh basil.

See page 68 for recipe.

PIZZETTA MARGHERITA

PIZZA CON SCAROLA
Pizza with wilted escarole and olives

PIZZA CON RICOTTA
Pizza with ricotta and fennel seeds

PIZZA

Authentic Neapolitan pizza is baked in wood-fired brick ovens, giving the pizza dough a unique aroma. This method is obviously not practical in home kitchens, but this recipe will produce an excellent crust in an ordinary home oven.

See page 68 for topping recipes.

PIZZA CON SALSICCIA
Pizza with sweet Italian sausage

CRISPELLE

Tiny fried pizzas

Pizza dough may be fried as well as baked. Crispelle are tiny fried pizza disks that are used to envelop salumi *(cured meats), cooked sautéed greens, soft cheeses, and other fillings, much like a sandwich.*

See page 69 for recipe.

Crispella stuffed with prosciutto

FOCACCIA ALLA SARDA
Focaccia with pancetta and sage

Crispella stuffed with scamorza cheese

Crispella stuffed with salami

FOCACCIA AL ROSMARINO
Focaccia with rosemary

FOCACCIA

Savory flat bread

Simple focaccie *can serve as the bread accompaniment in a meal, or be part of an antipasto. Those with more elaborate toppings make substantial snacks in their own right.*

See page 70 for topping recipes.

FOCACCIA ALLE OLIVE
Focaccia with sliced black olives

Linguine alle Vongole

Linguine with clam sauce

This is one of the few Italian dishes that varies little from region to region or cook to cook. No doubt this is because the flavors of olive oil, clams, garlic, parsley, and pepper are so adroitly matched that any other ingredient would simply be an imposition, although tomatoes may also be used, as here, to make the classic "red" clam sauce. Never add grated cheese to seafood sauces for pasta as the strong flavors are incompatible.

INGREDIENTS

4 dozen littleneck clams or 4lb (2kg) cockles, soaked (see page 163)
½ cup (125ml) extra-virgin olive oil
6 garlic cloves, finely chopped
6 tbsp chopped fresh flat-leaf parsley
1½ cups (375g) fresh or canned drained tomatoes, peeled, seeded, and chopped
½ cup (125ml) dry white wine
salt and freshly ground black pepper, to taste
1lb (500g) thin linguine or spaghetti

PREPARATION

1 Scrub the soaked clams with a stiff brush and rinse to remove any traces of grit (see page 163).
2 Combine the oil, garlic, and half the parsley in a wide, deep skillet large enough to hold the clams later. Turn the heat to medium-low and sauté gently until the garlic is soft but not colored.
3 Add the tomatoes to the pan. Simmer over medium-low heat, uncovered, until they form a fairly thick sauce, about 10 minutes.
4 Pour in the wine and continue to sauté until the alcohol is evaporated, about 3 minutes.
5 Add ½ teaspoon of salt and the clams and cover immediately. Increase the heat to medium and leave the lid on until the clams open, 4–10 minutes, depending on the variety of shellfish used. Discard any unopened clams or empty shells. Stir in plenty of black pepper. The sauce will be very brothy and thin, but full of flavor.
6 Meanwhile, bring 4 quarts (5 liters) of water to a boil. Add the linguine and 1½ tablespoons of salt and stir at once. Cook over high heat, stirring occasionally with a wooden or plastic fork, until the pasta is almost *al dente*, about 7 minutes.
7 Drain the pasta and add it to the pan with the clam sauce. Return the pan to the heat and toss the pasta and sauce together; the pasta will absorb some of the sauce, but plenty will remain. Serve immediately, sprinkled with the remaining parsley.

KCal 1015 P 73g C 102g S 1166mg SFA 5g UFA 27g (4)

Parsley

Garlic

Olive oil

Clams

Tomatoes

White wine

Salt

Black pepper

Linguine

RISOTTO ALLE VERDURE

Vegetable risotto

Here is a simple risotto that can be made year-round. Dried porcini or fresh wild mushrooms add a real boost of flavor, but cultivated mushrooms work well too. This dish should have a creamy, not mushy, consistency, and should be served with plenty of extra Parmesan cheese.

INGREDIENTS

½oz (15g) dried porcini mushrooms, or 4oz (125g)
fresh wild mushrooms or cultivated mushrooms, trimmed
4 cups (1 liter) Chicken Broth (see page 73) or
good vegetable stock
3 tbsp unsalted butter
3 tbsp extra-virgin olive oil
2 large garlic cloves, finely chopped
1 onion, chopped
1 large celery rib with leaves, chopped
1 small red or yellow pepper, or a combination,
cored, seeded, and chopped
2 cups (425g) Arborio rice
½ cup (125ml) dry white wine
1 cup (250g) fresh or canned drained tomatoes,
peeled, seeded, and chopped, or 3oz (90g) sun-dried
tomatoes, coarsely chopped
salt, to taste
¼ tsp saffron strands, or 1 envelope (130mg)
saffron powder
¼ cup (20g) freshly grated Parmesan, plus extra to serve

PREPARATION

1 If using dried mushrooms, soak them in hot water for 30 minutes. Lift them out of the liquid, rinse well, then chop coarsely. Alternatively, chop the fresh mushrooms and set aside.

2 Warm the broth in a saucepan over low heat.

3 Meanwhile, heat the butter and oil in a large skillet. Add the garlic, onion, celery with leaves, pepper, and mushrooms. Sauté just until softened. Transfer half the mixture to a plate and set aside.

4 Stir the rice into the vegetable mixture and sauté for 5 minutes. Make sure the grains are well coated.

5 Pour in the wine and, when it has been absorbed, stir in the tomato. Season, then add the saffron (if using strands, first crumble them into a little stock).

6 Add the hot broth to the rice a ladleful at a time, waiting until each addition is absorbed and stirring constantly. After 20–25 minutes all the broth should be absorbed and the rice should be tender.

7 Remove the pan from the heat, check for salt, then stir in the reserved vegetables and Parmesan. Serve immediately, offering additional cheese.

KCal 695 P 18g C 99g S 511mg SFA 10g UFA 15g (4)

Onion

Garlic

Olive oil

Butter

Chicken broth

Dried porcini

RISOTTO ALLE VERDURE

Celery
with leaves

Peppers

Arborio
rice

White wine

Tomatoes

Salt

Saffron

Parmesan

PESCE LESSO CON DUE SALSE

Poached fish with two sauces

The Italians often use a whole fish for this classically simple dish, which makes a very beautiful and dramatic presentation served with vibrant red and green sauces. Any fish, whole or filleted, can be cooked in this manner, although striped bass or salmon, whose flesh is more compact than sole and other such delicate fish, are better choices. White-fleshed fish is excellent with both a piquant Salsa Verde and a Salsetta Rossa Cruda made of sweet tomatoes, but the tomato sauce should not be served with salmon. Serves 6.

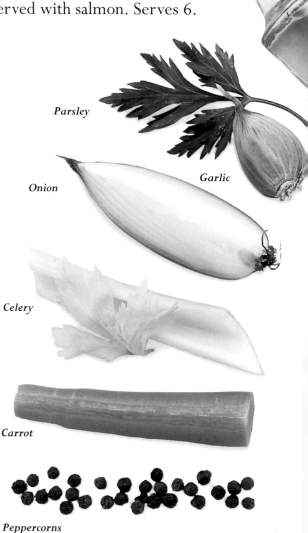

Parsley

Garlic

Onion

Celery

INGREDIENTS

1 tsp black peppercorns
1 large carrot, scraped
1 celery rib with leaves
1 onion, quartered
1 garlic clove, unpeeled
3–4 sprigs fresh flat-leaf parsley
1 cup (250ml) dry white wine
1 tbsp white wine vinegar
1½ tbsp coarse salt
1 whole striped sea bass, approximately 4lb (2kg), gutted and scaled, or 2 x 12oz (375g) fillets, skin attached
extra-virgin olive oil to brush fish
escarole or curly endive, to serve
Salsa Verde and Salsetta Rossa Cruda (see page 139), to serve

Carrot

Peppercorns

PREPARATION

1 Make the broth to poach the fish: Take a fish poacher or pot large enough to hold the fish without crowding and pour in 8 cups (2 liters) of water if using a whole fish, 6 cups (1.5 liters) if using fillets. Add the peppercorns, carrot, celery, onion, garlic, parsley, wine, and vinegar. Bring to a boil, then simmer over medium heat for 15 minutes.
2 Season the broth with salt, then lower in the fish, placing fillets skin side down. Poach at a gentle simmer until the flesh is opaque, about 10 minutes per 1in (2.5cm) of thickness (measure at the thickest part of the fish), or 9–10 minutes for fillets.
3 Using a large slotted metal spatula, transfer the fish to a platter and neatly remove the skin while still warm. Leave the head and tail intact if using a whole fish. Brush with olive oil to keep the flesh moist and imbue it with extra flavor.
4 Garnish a platter with escarole. Spoon half of each sauce over half the fish and pass the remainder at the table. Serve warm or at room temperature (the fish can be kept covered with plastic wrap at room temperature for up to 4 hours.)

KCal 480 P 26g C 9g S 531mg SFA 5g UFA 27g (6)

Sea bass

White wine

White wine
vinegar

Salt

Extra-virgin
olive oil

Escarole

Salsetta
Rossa
Cruda

Salsa Verde

GALLINELLE E POLENTA

Fricassee of game hen with polenta

Typical of the way wild game birds are cooked in Italy, this traditional dish is also wonderful made with game hens. Its flavors evoke the northern woodlands with the earthy presence of wild mushrooms and the pungent scent of rosemary. Creamy, soft polenta is a perfect match for the rich stew.

INGREDIENTS

1oz (30g) dried porcini mushrooms
6oz (175g) fresh mushrooms (preferably wild)
3 Rock Cornish game hens, each about
1¼lb (625g), quartered
3 tbsp unsalted butter
3 tbsp olive oil
¾ tsp salt, or to taste
freshly ground black pepper, to taste
1 tsp chopped fresh rosemary, or ½ tsp dried
¾ cup (175ml) dry white wine
½ cup (125g) fresh or canned drained tomatoes,
peeled, seeded, and chopped
1 quantity Polenta (see page 169)
2 tsp all-purpose flour, optional

PREPARATION

1 Soak the dried mushrooms in ¾ cup (175ml) of warm water for 30 minutes. Meanwhile, clean and slice the fresh mushrooms and set aside.
2 Drain the dried mushrooms. Strain the liquid through a sieve lined with paper towels, and reserve it. Rinse and coarsely chop the mushrooms.
3 Heat the butter and oil in a large deep pan, add the game hens, and sauté until browned all over.
4 Stir in the salt, pepper, rosemary, and wine. Bring the mixture to a boil and cook over medium heat for 5 minutes, to allow the alcohol to evaporate.
5 Add the dried and fresh mushrooms, the reserved soaking liquid, and the tomatoes to the pan. Cook over low heat, uncovered, for 30 minutes, turning the game hens occasionally.
6 Prepare the soft Polenta (see page 169).
7 When the game hens are ready, the sauce will be quite thin. If a thicker sauce is desired, transfer the game hens and mushrooms to a warm plate and set aside. Mix 3 tablespoons of sauce into the flour to make a paste, stir this back into the pan, and simmer until a smooth sauce forms. Return the hens and mushrooms to the pan and cook for 3 minutes.
8 Spread the polenta over a large warm platter, make a well in the center, and spoon in the game hens and sauce. Serve any extra sauce separately.

KCal 750g P 51g C 58g S 1877mg SFA 11g UFA 20g (4)

Mixed wild mushrooms

Dried porcini

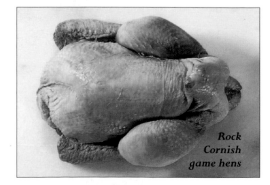

Rock Cornish game hens

Butter

Olive
oil

Salt

Black
pepper

Rosemary

White wine

Tomatoes

Polenta

OSSO BUCO ALLA MILANESE

Braised veal shanks, Milanese style

This is one of the most delicate of meat dishes. It is served with *gremolata*, a mixture of garlic, herbs, and lemon zest. To ensure tenderness, the veal pieces should be covered by the liquid in which they braise. The marrow, which is scooped out and eaten, is considered a great delicacy. Serve with Risotto alla Milanese (see page 92) or Purè di Patate (see page 129).

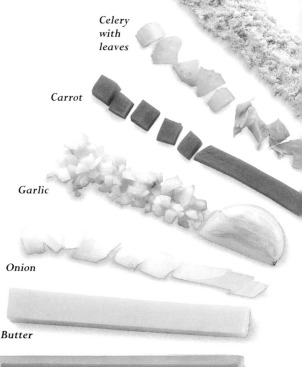

Celery with leaves

Carrot

Garlic

Onion

Butter

INGREDIENTS

4 tbsp olive oil
2 tbsp unsalted butter
1 small onion, finely chopped
1 large garlic clove, bruised
1 small carrot, finely chopped
1 celery rib with leaves, finely chopped
4 meaty veal hind shanks, sawed into 1½–2in
(3.5–5cm) lengths and tied (see page 164)
¼ cup (30g) flour for dredging
salt and freshly ground white or black pepper, to taste
½ cup (125ml) dry white wine
½ cup (125g) fresh or canned drained tomatoes,
peeled, seeded, and finely chopped
1 tbsp chopped fresh flat-leaf parsley
½ tsp chopped fresh thyme, or ¼ tsp dried
1 bay leaf
2in (5cm) strip lemon zest
1 cup (250ml) Meat Broth (see page 72), plus extra

Gremolata
1 tbsp finely chopped lemon zest
1 small garlic clove, finely chopped
2 tbsp chopped fresh flat-leaf parsley
½ tsp chopped fresh thyme, or ¼ tsp dried

Olive oil

PREPARATION

1 Preheat the oven to 350°F (180°C).
2 Heat half the oil with the butter in a casserole. Add the onion, garlic, carrot, and celery and sauté gently until softened, about 10 minutes.
3 Warm the remaining oil in a wide, heavy skillet over medium heat. Dredge the veal pieces in flour, place in the sizzling oil in a single layer, and brown for 15–20 minutes. Season with ½ teaspoon of salt and plenty of pepper, then place on top of the vegetables in the casserole.
4 Drain any oil from the pan and pour in the wine. Simmer for 3 minutes, until the alcohol evaporates. Add the tomatoes, herbs, lemon zest, and broth.
5 When the sauce is simmering, pour it into the casserole and bring to a boil. Cover, transfer to the oven, and cook for about 1¾ hours. Turn the meat regularly and add more broth if necessary.

Veal shanks

6 Transfer the veal to a warm platter. Discard the zest and check the sauce's seasoning.
7 Combine all the ingredients for the gremolata, stir the mixture into the casserole sauce, warm it through, and spoon it over the veal.

KCal 430 P 35g C 11g S 617mg SFA 8g UFA 17g (4)

Flour

Salt

Black pepper

White wine

Tomatoes

Parsley

Thyme

Bay leaf

Lemon zest

Meat broth

VEGETABLE DISHES

There is a universal Italian approach common to all regional styles. Ingredients should be exquisitely fresh and cooked in such a way as to preserve their natural flavors. Vegetable dishes in particular illustrate this ideal.

CONDIGGION

Summer vegetable salad

On the Italian table, foods are consumed when they are in season. Consequently, salads of fresh tomatoes and herbs are strictly summer fare. This is such a salad, made when tomatoes are in their luscious summer glory. The peppers are usually used raw, but I prefer to roast them first.
See page 133 for recipe.

PATATE AL FORNO

Scalloped potatoes baked in milk

Potatoes, which are essentially bland, are given a great boost by the rich, complex flavors of Parmesan cheese. This is a family recipe that never fails to delight.
See page 128 for recipe.

FAGIOLINI AL POMODORO

Green beans with tomato and garlic

Here is a dish that is as good — or better — at room temperature as it is hot. The beans should be young, buttery, and tender.
See page 129 for recipe.

FRIARELLI

Sautéed escarole with beans and ham

This dish of sautéed escarole with creamy cannellini beans and pancetta is the Campanian variation of a popular hearty northern Italian dish.

See page 130 for recipe.

ASPARAGI ALLA PARMIGIANA

Asparagus, Parma style

The glorious cheese of Parma is well matched with the unique flavors and buttery textures of cooked asparagus in this traditional recipe. Be sure to start with perfectly fresh, crisp asparagus and genuine parmigiano-reggiano cheese.

See page 131 for recipe.

FINOCCHI GRATINATI

Baked fennel

Fresh fennel is a very popular vegetable in Italy and is superb eaten cooked or raw. This dish is a splendid accompaniment to pork, chicken, and game dishes.

See page 130 for recipe.

TIRAMISÙ

Chocolate and mascarpone "pick me up"

There are many Italian recipes that transform leftover cake or biscuits, alcohol, and a cream filling into a puddinglike dessert. *Tiramisù*, literally "pick me up," is probably the most popular of these, having caught on in restaurant circuits in and outside of Italy. It is by its very nature an improvisational dessert and has many interpretations. However, to my mind, tiramisù is not tiramisù without the liqueur or without the Italian cream cheese, mascarpone. I prefer orange liqueur for soaking the cake, but others, such as amaretto, can be substituted. Serves 12.

INGREDIENTS

2 cups (500ml) strong espresso coffee, cooled
½ cup (125ml) dark rum
12oz (375g) ladyfingers or savoiardi biscuits
or stale sponge cake, cut into strips
6 eggs, separated
½ cup (125g) sugar
2lb (1kg) mascarpone
1 cup (250ml) orange or almond liqueur
4oz (125g) bittersweet chocolate, chopped
3 tbsp unsweetened cocoa powder

PREPARATION

1 Take a large serving dish, 3–4in (7–10cm) deep, that will accommodate half the biscuits or sponge cake in a single layer. Pour the coffee and rum into a shallow bowl and dip half of the biscuits or cake in the mixture, soaking both sides. Be careful not to let them disintegrate (firmer savoiardi biscuits will take a little longer to soak up enough liquid).
2 Cover the bottom of the dish with the soaked biscuits or cake. Set aside the coffee-rum mixture.
3 Place the egg yolks in a bowl and beat until pale yellow. Beat in all but 1 tablespoon of the sugar, the mascarpone, and liqueur until well blended.
4 In another bowl, whisk the egg whites until fluffy but not stiff. Add the remaining sugar and whisk until stiff but not dry (if egg whites are overbeaten, they will start to liquefy at the bottom of the bowl). Fold the whites into the egg-mascarpone mixture.
5 Pour half of the mascarpone mixture over the biscuit or cake layer. Top with the chopped chocolate. Soak the remaining biscuits or cake and place them on top of the chocolate.
6 Blend any leftover coffee-rum mixture with the remaining mascarpone mixture and spread it over the biscuits. Sprinkle the top with cocoa, cover, and refrigerate for 8 hours or overnight, or freeze for 2–3 hours before serving.

KCal 715 P 11g C 44g S 930mg SFA 30g UFA 17g (12)

Egg yolks

Ladyfingers

Dark rum

Espresso coffee

Orange liqueur

Egg white

Bittersweet
chocolate

Cocoa powder

Mascarpone

Sugar

RECIPES

The recipes in this chapter have survived decades and even centuries, and are still very much used in Italian cooking today. All reflect the rich history and regional traditions of Italy, as well as its culinary diversity. There is a fish soup from Gallipoli (which the locals claim dates back to 1000BC), duck with orange sauce (a creation of Caterina de' Medici's cooks in the fifteenth century), pasta dishes that are relative newcomers on the Italian scene, and delectable confections of modern popular fame.

**All the dishes serve 4,
unless otherwise indicated.**

ANTIPASTI

The *antipasto*, literally "before the meal" course, is composed of zesty little dishes offered individually or in assortment. Their variety is endless and this is as it should be, for what is the purpose of the starter but to create anticipation and excitement about the meal to follow? Many are excellent served as main dishes or as side dishes. An essential ingredient is often high quality extra-virgin olive oil. This aromatic, handmade oil imparts irresistible flavor and transforms even the simplest food into a finished dish.

SCARPASSA

Ligurian eggplant fritters

The flavor and creamy texture of eggplant is enhanced superbly by deep-frying, as these fritters show.

INGREDIENTS

1lb (500g) eggplant, peeled and cut into ⅜in (1cm) slices
salt
olive oil for brushing and frying
1 small egg, beaten
4 tbsp freshly grated Parmesan
6 tbsp fresh bread crumbs, lightly toasted,
plus extra for dredging
1 tsp chopped fresh marjoram, or ½ tsp dried

PREPARATION

1 Sprinkle the eggplant slices with salt and leave in a colander to drain for at least 40 minutes.
2 Preheat the oven to 450°F (230°C).
3 Line a baking sheet with foil. Wipe the eggplant slices with paper towels, then brush both sides with oil. Bake until tender, about 20 minutes. Remove from the oven and leave to cool slightly.
4 Finely chop the eggplant then combine it with the egg, Parmesan, 6 tablespoons of bread crumbs and the marjoram. The mixture will be fairly moist. Add a tablespoon of bread crumbs to firm up the texture if necessary. Shape the mixture into walnut-sized dumplings. Chill for at least 3 hours.
5 Pour oil to a depth of 1in (2.5cm) into a skillet and heat. Spread some bread crumbs on a plate.
6 When the oil is hot enough to make the mixture sizzle, dredge each fritter in the crumbs and then lower into the oil. Fry until golden, 45 seconds.
7 Transfer the fritters to a platter lined with paper towels and allow to drain. Serve hot.

KCal 385 P 11g C 14g S 641mg SFA 7g UFA 23g (4)

FRITTELLE DI ZUCCHINI

Zucchini fritters

A recipe from Udine in Friuli given to me by my friends Valerie and Elio Serra. These fritters can be served as an antipasto, or as a side dish. They are easy to make and utterly irresistible if made with young, tender zucchini.

INGREDIENTS

1lb (500g) fresh, young zucchini, no more than
6–8oz (175–250g) each
½ cup (60g) flour, plus 2 tbsp as necessary
½ cup (60g) freshly grated Parmesan
1 jumbo egg, beaten
pinch of freshly grated nutmeg
salt and freshly ground black or white pepper, to taste
olive oil for deep-frying

PREPARATION

1 Wash the zucchini and trim both ends. Slice them in half, and if they are very seedy, cut out and discard the seeds and stringy center.
2 Grate the zucchini on the large holes of a grater. Place the grated flesh in a bowl with the flour, Parmesan, egg, nutmeg, a small pinch of salt, and pepper. Stir all the ingredients thoroughly until a fairly thick batter is formed. If it seems thin, add up to 2 tablespoons of flour.
3 Pour olive oil into a skillet to a depth of ½in (1cm) and heat until hot enough to make the batter sizzle. Slip spoonfuls of the batter into the oil and push down lightly with the back of a spoon to flatten them slightly. Fry until golden brown, about 2 minutes on each side. Do not allow them to burn, but make sure the center is cooked.
4 Drain the fritters on paper towels, transfer to a warm plate, sprinkle with salt, if desired, and serve.

KCal 365 P 11g C 14g S 478mg SFA 7g UFA 21g (4)

FUNGHI FRITTI ALLA SARDA

Crispy fried mushrooms, Sardinian style

Illustrated on page 41.

INGREDIENTS

*12oz (375g) large fresh wild mushrooms such as porcini
or portobello, or large field mushrooms
1 cup (125g) finely ground semolina flour
olive oil for frying
freshly ground fine sea salt and black pepper, to taste
½ cup chopped fresh flat-leaf parsley, optional*

PREPARATION

1 Clean and trim the mushrooms (do not wash them). Cut the stems lengthwise into slices. If the caps are very large, slice them in half across.
2 Spread the semolina flour in a shallow dish. Pour oil to a depth of ¼in (5mm) into a skillet and heat.
3 When the oil is hot enough to make the mushrooms sizzle, dredge the first batch in the semolina, pressing down to coat them.
4 Slip the first batch of mushrooms into the oil and fry them over medium-high heat until crispy on both sides and cooked through, approximately 8 minutes. Drain them on paper towels, then dredge and fry the remaining caps and stems.
5 Sprinkle the mushrooms with salt and pepper. Scatter the parsley on top and serve hot.

KCal 280 P 6g C 30g S 302mg SFA 2g UFA 13g (4)

CIPOLLINE IN AGRODOLCE

Sweet and sour onions

Illustrated on page 40.

INGREDIENTS

*1½lb (750g) small (walnut-sized) white onions
2 tbsp olive oil
2 large garlic cloves, crushed
6 whole cloves
4 tbsp white wine vinegar
1 tbsp white sugar
¼ tsp salt
1 small dried hot red pepper (peperoncino), or
6 black peppercorns*

PREPARATION

1 Peel the onions and cook them in boiling water for 3 minutes. Drain and plunge them into cold water to stop the cooking.
2 Warm the oil in a heavy-bottomed pan. Add the onions and garlic and sauté gently for 5 minutes – do not allow them to color.

3 Meanwhile, combine 4 tablespoons of water, the cloves, vinegar, sugar, salt, and hot pepper in a bowl. Add this mixture to the onions and garlic.
4 Partially cover the saucepan and simmer the onions for 10 minutes, stirring occasionally.
5 Allow the onions to cool – they are best left for at least 24 hours before serving. They can be stored for up to 2 weeks in the refrigerator, and their flavor will strengthen as they keep.

KCal 150 P 2g C 19g S 105mg SFA 1g UFA 6g (4)

CASTELLANA DI PEPERONI

Stuffed roasted pepper "sandwiches"

*In this Piedmontese dish, roasted red peppers are peeled
and seeded, then given a simple stuffing of fontina cheese
and prosciutto. The resulting "sandwiches" are then briefly
returned to the oven in order to melt the cheese. The
result is exquisite. For extra flavor, try grilling the
peppers over charcoal. Serves 6.*

INGREDIENTS

*6 large red or yellow peppers
6 thin slices prosciutto
6 thin slices fontina
olive oil for brushing*

PREPARATION

1 Preheat the broiler or preheat the oven to 400°F (200°C).
2 Roast the whole peppers under the broiler or in the oven until the skins are charred and the insides tender (see page 160). Remove from the heat.
3 Preheat the oven to the above temperature if you have not yet done so, and line a baking sheet with foil. When the peppers are cool enough to handle, cut them in half vertically. Remove the stem and lift off the skin, then scrape out the seeds.
4 Place a slice each of prosciutto and fontina on the inside of one half of each pepper. Cover with the other half of the pepper. Brush with olive oil and place on a baking sheet in the middle of the oven. Cook until the cheese is melted and the peppers warmed through. Serve hot or warm.

KCal 195 P 11g C 14g S 399mg SFA 5g UFA 5g (6)

PEPERONI RIPIENI

Peppers stuffed with rice and Gorgonzola

*Illustrated on page 41. Serves 8 as a starter,
or 4 as a light lunch dish.*

INGREDIENTS

⅓ cup (90ml) olive oil
8 medium red or yellow peppers, or a mixture
1 onion, finely chopped
2 large garlic cloves, finely chopped
¾ cup (150g) long-grain white rice
1 tsp salt
2 sweet Italian pork sausages, about 8oz (250g),
casings removed and meat crumbled
4oz (125g) Gorgonzola, crumbled
2 tbsp freshly grated Parmesan
1 tsp fennel seeds
½ tsp freshly ground black pepper

PREPARATION

1 Preheat the oven to 400°F (200°C).
2 Warm the oil in a skillet over medium heat. Add the peppers and sauté until colored on all sides, but still firm to the touch, 5–7 minutes. Cook them in batches, if necessary.
3 Allow the peppers to cool, then slice off the tops and reserve them. Scoop out and discard the seeds and ribs, being careful not to pierce the flesh. Set the peppers aside.
4 Drain off and reserve all but 2 tablespoons of the oil in the pan and set over medium heat. Add the onion and garlic and cook until soft.
5 Stir in the rice and sauté until translucent, about 5 minutes. Add 1½ cups (350ml) of water and the salt and bring to a boil. Immediately reduce to a gentle simmer, cover and cook until all the liquid is absorbed, approximately 10 minutes. Taste for salt.
6 Pour a little of the reserved oil into a second skillet and cook the sausage just until it colors but does not harden, 4–5 minutes. Stir in the rice, cheeses, and fennel seeds. Check the mixture for salt and add the pepper. Remove from the heat and let cool slightly.
7 Stuff the peppers and replace their tops.
8 Select a large baking dish and arrange the peppers upright inside, adding 3 tablespoons of water to the dish. Cover tightly with a lid or with foil, arranging it dull side out.
9 Bake the peppers for about 30 minutes, until they are tender but still hold their shape. Check the rice – it should be tender, but not mushy. Allow the peppers to settle for 10–15 minutes. Serve hot or warm.

KCal 430 P 12g C 31g S 602mg SFA 10g UFA 18g (8)

MELANZANE RIPIENE

Stuffed eggplant, Ligurian style

So extraordinary is the Ligurian propensity for stuffing vegetables that one Genoese restaurant, now sadly gone, served nothing but stuffed vegetables. However, for some reason, eggplant grown outside of Italy are excessively seedy, particularly as they mature. This dish can be prepared a day in advance, up to the point of baking. Serves 6.

INGREDIENTS

3 medium or 4 small eggplant, no more than
12oz (375g) each
salt, to taste
8oz (250g) mushrooms, trimmed
2 tbsp olive oil
1 large onion, chopped
1 large garlic clove, finely chopped
4oz (125g) prosciutto, chopped
2 eggs, beaten
¼ tsp freshly ground black pepper
1 tbsp bread crumbs
2 tbsp freshly grated Parmesan or pecorino
1 tsp chopped fresh marjoram, or ½ tsp dried

PREPARATION

1 Cut the eggplant in half lengthwise and scoop out the pulp, leaving about ½in (1cm) intact. Chop the pulp coarsely, discarding excess seeds, sprinkle with salt, and weight down in a colander to drain.
2 Clean the mushrooms with a soft brush or cloth; do not wash them. Cut them in halves, or quarters if large, then slice.
3 Rinse the eggplant pulp, squeeze out the water and dry on paper towels.
4 Preheat the oven to 350°F (180°C).
5 Heat the oil in a large skillet, add the onion and garlic and sauté over medium-low heat until softened, about 5 minutes.
6 Add the mushrooms and prosciutto and continue to cook until the mushrooms are tender, about 2 minutes. Add the eggplant and toss for 1 minute. Let the mixture cool slightly.
7 Combine the eggs, ½ teaspoon of salt, pepper, and bread crumbs in a bowl. Add the eggplant and mushroom mixture, Parmesan, and marjoram. Mix well, then spoon the stuffing into the eggplant shells; the stuffing should not be heaped up.
8 Arrange the eggplant in a baking dish. Pour ½ cup (125ml) of water into the dish and cover with foil. Cook for 45 minutes, or until the eggplant shells are tender but not collapsed. Serve warm or at room temperature.

KCal 160 P 10g C 7g S 551mg SFA 3g UFA 6g (6)

ZUPPA DI MITILI ALLA PUGLIESE

Mussels in white wine, Apulian style

Serves 8 as a starter or 4 as a main course.

INGREDIENTS

6lb (3kg) mussels, scrubbed and debearded (see page 163)
4 tbsp olive oil
1 onion, chopped
3 large garlic cloves, chopped
3 tbsp chopped fresh flat-leaf parsley
2 tsp chopped fresh thyme, or 1 tsp dried
1 bay leaf, crumbled
1½ cups (350ml) good dry white wine
freshly ground black pepper, to taste

PREPARATION

1 Wash the mussels, then place them in a bowl of cold water and leave to soak for about 3 hours (see page 163). Discard any that have opened.
2 Rinse the mussels again. Take a large heavy casserole pot and heat the oil and onion until the onion softens. Scatter in the garlic and parsley and sauté for a few minutes until golden.
3 Stir the mussels into the onion and parsley mixture. Add the thyme, bay leaf, wine, and pepper, then cover and bring to a boil.
4 Turn the heat to low and simmer gently for 2–3 minutes, or until the mussels are open. Discard any mussels that remain closed.
5 Place the mussels in shallow bowls, ladle over some broth, and serve with fresh hot Italian bread.

KCal 205 P 20g C 3g S 242mg SFA 1g UFA 8g (8)

COZZE ARRACANATI
Baked mussels, Apulian style

Baked mussels are one of Apulia's specialties, as the region has abundant seafood and shellfish. In Pugliese cooking, arracanate, or arraganati, refers to anything baked with a bread crumb topping. I've often wondered if the popular American hybrid of this dish, "clams oreganata" isn't a mispronunciation of the name. The quantities here are for 2 people.

INGREDIENTS

*12 fresh large mussels or littleneck clams,
debearded and scrubbed (see page 163)
1 lemon, cut into wedges, to serve*
Topping
*3 tbsp extra-virgin olive oil, plus oil for drizzling
4 tbsp fresh white bread crumbs
pinch of hot red pepper flakes
1 tbsp chopped fresh flat-leaf parsley
½ tsp chopped fresh oregano, or ¼ tsp dried
1 garlic clove, finely chopped*

PREPARATION

1 Soak the mussels or clams (see page 163). Leave in the refrigerator for at least 3 hours to disgorge any grit or sand.

2 Scrub the mussels or clams and immerse them in hot water for 5–10 minutes to help open them. Working over a bowl to catch any juices, insert a small knife between the two halves of the shell and cut the shellfish in half, working toward the muscle on the base of the shell. Carefully detach the flesh, then place it in one of the shell halves, discarding the other half.

3 Preheat the broiler. Combine the topping ingredients and spoon some over each mussel or clam. Sprinkle with a little of the reserved juice to keep the flesh from burning, then drizzle with oil.

4 Place the mussels or clams in a dish and set it in the broiler as far from the heat source as possible. Broil for about 6 minutes, making sure that the topping doesn't burn. Baste with more juice if necessary. Serve hot with lemon wedges.

KCal 360 P 9g C 18g S 225mg SFA 4g UFA 23g (2)

FRITTATA AGLI ASPARAGI
Asparagus and mushroom frittata

Illustrated on page 41.

INGREDIENTS

*1lb (500g) asparagus, tough ends removed
salt, to taste
4oz (125g) small mushrooms, trimmed
1 tbsp butter
1 tbsp extra-virgin olive oil, plus oil for frying
6 scallions, including 1in (2.5cm) green tops, sliced
5 eggs
3 tbsp freshly grated Parmesan
pinch of freshly ground white or black pepper*

PREPARATION

1 Pare the thick skin at the base of each asparagus stalk to reveal the tender inside (see page 161). Steam or boil in salted water until just tender, 5–6 minutes. Plunge into cold water, drain, and cut diagonally into ¼in (5mm) slices.

2 Clean the mushrooms using a soft brush or cloth; do not wash them. Slice them across.

3 Heat the butter and 1 tablespoon of oil in a 10in (25cm) omelet pan. When hot, add the mushrooms and scallions and sauté for about 2 minutes, stirring frequently, until tender. Remove from the pan and set aside to cool.

4 Beat the eggs with the cheese, ½ teaspoon of salt, and the pepper. Add the asparagus, mushrooms, and onions, and combine thoroughly.

5 Heat a little oil in the omelet pan and when hot add the egg mixture. Cook over medium heat for 10 minutes, rotating the pan to allow the mixture to cook evenly. Preheat the broiler.

6 Place the frittata under the broiler and cook for 5–9 minutes, until lightly golden and set inside. Do not allow it to overcook. If the frittata is already browned but runny inside, finish cooking it on the top shelf of the oven at 450°F (230°C).

7 Let the frittata rest for 5–10 minutes, then turn out onto a serving dish and cut into wedges. Serve warm or at room temperature.

KCal 205 P 11g C 2g S 356mg SFA 5g UFA 10g (6)

POLPETTINE ALL' UMBRA

Little meatballs, Umbrian style, cooked four ways

*Outside Italy, meatballs are most often served atop a pile
of spaghetti, but in Italy, they are presented quite
differently. They make an excellent antipasto cooked in a
tomato or wine sauce, or coated in crunchy bread crumbs
and served plain. Alternatively, they can be poached in
broth for a primo, "first course." Illustrated on page 40.*

INGREDIENTS

2 slices stale white bread, crusts removed, cubed
½ cup (125ml) milk or stock for soaking bread
1½lb (750g) ground beef, or a mixture of beef and pork
2oz (60g) thinly sliced prosciutto, coarsely chopped
1 small onion, coarsely grated
2 tsp chopped fresh marjoram, or 1 tsp dried
zest of 1 lemon
2 tsp salt
freshly ground black pepper, to taste
1 egg, beaten

PREPARATION

1 Soak the bread in the milk or stock. When soft,
squeeze out and discard the liquid. Use your hands
to mix the bread with the remaining ingredients.
2 Take 2 teaspoons of the mixture at a time and
form it into little round balls (if serving them as a
main course, make the meatballs larger). Cook in
any of the following ways:

METHOD 1 *FRIED IN A CRISPY COATING*
1 Pour oil to a depth of 1in (2.5cm) into a skillet
and heat. Dredge the first batch of meatballs in flour,
then roll them in lightly toasted bread crumbs.
2 When the oil is hot enough to make the
meatballs sizzle, slip them into the pan one at a
time. Fry over medium heat until browned all
over, then drain on paper towels. Serve hot.

METHOD 2 *COOKED IN TOMATO SAUCE*
1 Dredge the meatballs in flour. Heat 4 tablespoons
of olive oil in a skillet over medium heat. When the
oil is hot, sauté the first batch until lightly browned
but still pinkish inside, about 10 minutes. Drain on
paper towels, and set aside.
2 Add 1 large grated carrot, 1 finely chopped
large celery rib with leaves, and 1 finely chopped
onion to the skillet with the meatball drippings.
Sauté over medium-low heat until the vegetables
are softened, about 7 minutes.
3 Stir in 5 cups (1.25kg) of fresh or canned and
drained plum tomatoes that have been peeled,
seeded, and chopped (see page 160). Season well,
then simmer for 10 minutes.
4 Transfer the browned meatballs to the sauce and
simmer over medium-low heat, uncovered, until

the sauce has thickened and the polpettine are
heated through, about 12 minutes. Serve hot.

METHOD 3 *COOKED IN WINE*
1 Heat 4 tablespoons of olive oil in a skillet.
Dredge the meatballs lightly in flour and when the
oil is hot enough to make them sizzle, sauté the
first batch over medium heat until lightly
browned. Drain on paper towels.
2 Add ½ cup (125ml) of dry white wine to the
drippings in the pan and stir with a wooden spoon.
Allow the alcohol to evaporate, about 2 minutes.
3 Reduce the heat to medium-low and return the
meatballs to the pan. Simmer for 8 minutes, until
the meatballs are heated through. Serve hot.

METHOD 4 *COOKED IN BROTH*
1 Bring 2 quarts (2.5 liters) of seasoned chicken
broth (see page 73) or meat broth (see page 72) to
a boil. Drop in a few meatballs at a time. They are
cooked when they float to the surface.
2 As the meatballs rise to the surface of the broth,
transfer them to a platter and keep them warm.
Serve in bowls with a little of the broth.

KCal 265 P 22g C 6g S 579mg SFA 7g UFA 9g (8: basic meatball mixture)

VARIATION

To make **Polpettine alla Toscana**, omit the marjoram
and lemon zest and replace with 1 tablespoon of
grated Parmesan and a pinch of nutmeg.

PIZZA NAPOLETANA

Pizza is fundamentally poor food. What makes Neapolitan pizza so good is the high-quality wheat used for the dough, the superb local tomatoes and olive oil, and also the aroma imparted by wood-fired ovens. Here is the classic Napoletana topping of olive oil, tomatoes, oregano, and garlic; Roman-style pizza adds mozzarella. For the basic Pizza Dough recipe and baking times, see page 170. Makes two 12in (30cm) bases. Serves 8–16.

INGREDIENTS

1 quantity Pizza Dough (see pages 170–71)
olive oil, for brushing
Napoletana topping
3 cups (750g) fresh or canned drained tomatoes, peeled, seeded, and chopped
3 large garlic cloves, chopped
2 tbsp chopped fresh oregano, or 1 tbsp dried
salt, to taste
4 tbsp extra-virgin olive oil
4oz (125g) mozzarella, shredded (for Roman-style)

PREPARATION

1 Preheat the oven to 400°F (200°C).
2 Meanwhile, make the pizza bases as shown on page 170. Brush with oil, then combine the tomato, garlic, oregano, and salt. Spread this mixture over the bases and drizzle with oil, adding more to taste.
3 Bake until golden (see chart on page 170). If using cheese, take the pizzas from the oven 5 minutes before the pizza is done and top with mozzarella. Return to the oven and bake just until the cheese is melted. Let cool slightly before serving.

KCal 380 P 12g C 50g S 470mg SFA 4g UFA 11g (8)

PIZZA TOPPINGS

Outside Italy, tomatoes have become associated with pizza almost exclusively. But in Italy, toppings include almost every conceivable food, including sautéed greens, seafood, local cheeses, chestnuts, olives, cured meats, and fresh herbs. The quantities given here are for two 14in (35cm) bases (see page 170 for recipe), but you can choose any other size of pizza base and adjust the amounts accordingly. Illustrated on page 44.

CON RICOTTA

2lb (1kg) ricotta (drained weight)
8oz (250g) provolone, shredded
1 tsp fennel seeds, crushed
salt and freshly ground black pepper, to taste
⅓ cup (30g) freshly grated pecorino

Combine all the ingredients except the pecorino and spread the mixture on the bases. Season to taste. Sprinkle with the pecorino. Bake until golden (see baking time chart on page 170).
KCal 555 P 29g C 50g S 1044mg SFA 16g UFA 8g (8)

MARGHERITA

3 cups (750g) fresh or canned drained tomatoes, peeled, seeded, and chopped
4 tbsp extra-virgin olive oil
4oz (125g) mozzarella, shredded
large handful of basil leaves, torn

Spread the tomatoes on the bases and drizzle with oil. Five minutes before the pizza is done, remove it from the oven and sprinkle with mozzarella and basil. Return to the oven and bake until the cheese is just melted (see baking time chart on page 170).
KCal 380 P 12g C 50g S 325mg SFA 4g UFA 11g (8)

CON SCAROLA

4 tbsp extra-virgin olive oil, plus more to taste
8 large garlic cloves, chopped
2lb (1kg) escarole, shredded
salt and freshly ground black pepper, to taste
2 tsp chopped fresh oregano, or 1 tsp dried
½ cup (90g) strongly flavored black olives, pitted and sliced

Pour the oil into a large skillet and sauté the garlic until softened. Add the escarole and cook until wilted, tossing it frequently. Season, add the oregano, and let cool. Spread the greens over the bases. Sprinkle with olives and more oil. Bake until golden (see baking time chart on page 170).
KCal 345 P 9g C 50g S 573mg SFA 2g UFA 11g

CON SALSICCIA

3 cups (750g) fresh or canned drained tomatoes, peeled, seeded, and chopped
2 large garlic cloves, chopped
1 tsp fennel seeds, crushed
salt, to taste
1lb (500g) sweet Italian pork sausage meat, crumbled
4 tbsp freshly grated pecorino or Parmesan
extra-virgin olive oil for drizzling

Mix the tomatoes with the garlic, fennel, and salt. Place the sausage meat in a cold skillet with 4 tablespoons of water. Sauté until the liquid has evaporated and the sausage is browned, then drain. Spread the tomato over the bases and top with sausage. Sprinkle with cheese and oil. Bake until golden (see baking time chart on page 170).
KCal 545 P 18g C 56g S 932mg SFA 10g UFA 18g (8)

CRISPELLE
Tiny fried pizzas

Illustrated on page 45. Serves 8.

INGREDIENTS

1 quantity Pizza Dough (see page 170)
olive oil, for frying
coarse sea salt, to taste
salami, prosciutto, or a soft or semisoft Italian cheese,
such as mozzarella, toma, taleggio, or stracchino, to serve

PREPARATION

1 Make the dough as directed on pages 170–71,
up to step 4. Divide the dough into pieces the size
of a small peach. Stretch each piece out to make a
thin 6in (15cm) disk.
2 Pour oil to a depth of 1in (2.5cm) into a skillet.
When the oil is hot enough to make the dough
sizzle, slip the disks into the pan and fry until
golden brown on both sides, about 5 minutes.
Remove and drain on paper towels.

3 Sprinkle the outside of the crispelle with a little
salt, then fold them around the chosen filling to
make a sandwich. Serve at once.

KCal 410 P 11g C 50g S 457mg SFA 4g UFA 15g (8: excluding fillings)

VARIATION

In Liguria, sage is added to the dough, which is
then formed into finger-shaped fritters called *scabei*.

Follow the basic Pizza Dough recipe (see pages
170–71), reducing the flour by 2 tablespoons.
Add 6 tablespoons of chopped fresh sage or
3 tablespoons of dried crumbled sage to the flour
and salt in step 2 of the recipe. If using a food
processor, work the dough for only 15 seconds.

Let the dough rise as for pizza, then punch it
down with your knuckles to expel the air and
divide it into 8 parts. Form each section into ½in
(1cm) ropes and cut each rope into 6in (15cm)
lengths. Cover with a damp dish towel and allow to
rise for 30 minutes. Fry the scabei in hot olive oil,
drain well on paper towels, and serve hot, lightly
sprinkled with sea salt.

FOCACCIA

The basic difference between focaccia and pizza is the thickness — focaccia is substantially thicker than pizza. Some are elaborate but many are just flat breads sprinkled with olive oil, herbs, or sea salt. The dough can be dimpled, which traps little pools of fragrant oil. Serves 6–8 as an accompaniment or as part of an antipasto. Makes one 14in x 18in (35cm x 45cm) base. Illustrated on page 45.

INGREDIENTS

1 quantity pizza dough (see page 170)
Alle Olive Topping
*½ cup (90g) pitted and sliced black olives,
such as Niçoise, Gaeta, or Ligurian
2 tsp chopped fresh marjoram, or 1 tsp dried
extra-virgin olive oil, for brushing*

PREPARATION

1 To form the focaccia, follow the steps for making pizza dough shown on page 171, up to step 3.
2 When the dough is elastic, use the palms of your hands to stretch it to a thickness of ⅓in (1cm) and form the dough into a circle or rectangle.
3 Transfer the focaccia to an oiled baking sheet, cover with a dish towel, and let rise for 30 minutes.
4 Mark the focaccia as shown on page 171, cover, and let rise until doubled in size, about 1 hour.
5 Preheat the oven to 400°F (200°C).
6 Push the olives into the dough. Brush the bottom with oil. Sprinkle the marjoram and oil on top.
7 Bake in the preheated oven until the edges are golden, 10–11 minutes. Let cool for 5 minutes before cutting. Serve hot or warm.

KCal 390 P 10g C 63g S 565mg SFA 2g UFA 10g (6)

FOCACCIA TOPPINGS

AGLIO E OLIO

*4 large garlic cloves, finely sliced or coarsely chopped
2½ tbsp extra-virgin olive oil*

Combine the garlic and olive oil and sprinkle over the focaccia base. Bake as described in main recipe.

DI GORGONZOLA

*12oz (375g) mild Gorgonzola, crumbled
2 large garlic cloves, roughly chopped
extra-virgin olive oil, for brushing*

Combine the Gorgonzola and garlic in a bowl. Scatter over the focaccia and drizzle with olive oil, then bake as described in main recipe.

AL ROSMARINO

*3 tbsp chopped fresh rosemary, or 1½ tbsp dried rosemary,
added to the flour in step 2 of the recipe
olive oil, for brushing
fresh sage leaves, to garnish, optional
coarse sea salt*

Add the rosemary to the flour in step 2 of the dough recipe on page 170. If using a food processor, work the dough for 15 seconds. Brush with oil, garnish with sage and salt, then bake as described in main recipe.

ALLA SARDA

*4oz (125g) pancetta or bacon, diced
4 tbsp fresh chopped sage, or 2 tbsp dried crumbled sage,
added to the flour and salt in step 2 of the recipe
olive oil, for brushing
coarse sea salt*

Sauté the pancetta, then drain and add to the dough mixture in step 2 of the dough recipe on page 170. If using a food processor, work the dough for 15 seconds. Brush with oil, sprinkle with salt, then bake as described in main recipe.

CROSTINI CON FEGATINI DI POLLO ALLA SALVIA

Sautéed chicken livers with sage on crostini toasts

One always comes across this lovely antipasto in Tuscany. Use only the immensely savory livers of free-range chickens.

INGREDIENTS

*½lb (250g) freshest plump chicken livers
2 tbsp unsalted butter
6 fresh sage leaves, or ½ tsp dried crumbled sage
12 thinly sliced rounds Italian or French bread, toasted
extra-virgin olive oil or butter, optional
2 tbsp dry white wine
salt and freshly ground black pepper, to taste*

PREPARATION

1 Trim any fat, connecting tissue, or discolored flesh from the livers, then quarter each one.
2 Heat the butter in a skillet and add the livers and sage. Sauté for 4–5 minutes, until browned on the outside but pinkish inside. Transfer to a plate.
3 Brush the bread with oil or butter if desired.
4 Add the wine to the juices left in the pan, stirring to incorporate any browned bits and add seasoning.
5 Return the livers to the pan for up to 1 minute, mashing them coarsely. Serve on the crostini.

KCal 320 P 16g C 25g S 602mg SFA 6g UFA 9g (4)

PANZEROTTI ALLA PUGLIESE

Apulian potato bread turnovers stuffed with pork

There are many names for this genre of breadlike turnovers – such as calzoni *and* pizzelle. *The name* panzerotti *derives from the Italian for "belly," which is what the crescent-shaped parcels look like when they swell up in the hot oil. Fillings can be as simple as a few anchovies, or a mixture of salami and mozzarella that melts into a pleasing ooziness. The dough is also used for pizza.*

INGREDIENTS

Dough
½lb (250g) whole boiling potatoes, unpeeled
½ cake (10g) fresh yeast, or 1 envelope active dry yeast
½ cup (125ml) warm water 100–110°F (38–43°C)
5¼ cups (650g) unbleached bread flour
2¼ tsp salt
1 cup (250ml) cold water
olive oil, for brushing

Filling
2 tbsp extra-virgin olive oil
1 onion, chopped
1½lb (750g) ground pork
5 slices (125g) stale bread, crusts removed
½ cup (125ml) stock
2 tbsp chopped fresh flat-leaf parsley
⅓ cup (30g) freshly grated pecorino
2 egg yolks
¾ tsp salt
freshly ground pepper, to taste
1 tbsp chopped fresh rosemary or sage, or ½ tsp dried

To finish
2 egg whites, lightly beaten
olive oil for frying
sea salt, to taste

PREPARATION

1 To make the dough, boil the potatoes until tender, about 20 minutes. Drain, let them cool enough to handle, then peel off the skins. Pass them through a potato ricer or mash while still warm.
2 In a small bowl, combine the yeast with 4 tablespoons of warm water. Let the mixture rest in a warm place for about 10 minutes, or until foamy.
3 In a large bowl, sift together 1 cup (125g) of the flour and the salt. Sprinkle over the potato and mix together lightly with your hands. Make a well in the center of the flour-potato mixture.
4 Add the remaining warm water and the cold water to the yeast mixture and pour into the well.
5 Gradually stir the flour-potato mixture into the liquid until absorbed. Work in another 2 cups (250g) of flour, sifting each addition. When the dough becomes stiff, use your hands to form it into a ball.
6 Lightly flour a pastry board. Knead the dough for 8–10 minutes while gradually sifting over as much of the remaining flour as is needed to form a dough that is silky and elastic.
7 Place the dough in a lightly oiled bowl and brush its surface with oil. Cover the bowl with a clean dish towel. Let rise at room temperature until doubled in size, 1–2 hours. (The longer the rising, the lighter the dough. If it rises too quickly, punch it down with your knuckles and let it rise again.)

FILLING

1 Meanwhile, make the filling. Heat the oil in a skillet, add the onion, and sauté over medium heat until soft, 3–4 minutes. Add the pork, reduce the heat, and sauté gently until the meat is browned but still rosy. Drain and transfer to a bowl.
2 Soak the bread in the stock until soft. Squeeze the bread dry and crumble it, discarding the stock. Add the bread to the pork mixture with the parsley, pecorino, egg yolks, seasoning, and herbs. Mix well.
3 Punch down the dough and divide it into 24 pieces. Sprinkle a pastry board with flour and roll out each piece to make a thin 4in (10cm) disk. Sprinkle one side with pepper.
4 Place a heaping tablespoon of filling in the center of each disk. Brush the edges of the disk with egg white. Fold over and press round the edges to seal. Transfer the turnovers to baking sheets lined with paper towels and cover with clean dish towels until ready to fry.
5 Pour olive oil to a depth of 1in (2.5cm) into a skillet. When the oil is hot enough to make the dough sizzle, slip the panzerotti into the pan and fry until golden on both sides, about 5 minutes. Remove and drain on paper towels.
6 Sprinkle with a little salt and eat hot.

KCal 240 P 11g C 25g S 255mg SFA 2g UFA 8g (per single turnover)

SOUPS

I am always amazed that many people will not go to the trouble of making soups at home, though they are among the most satisfying of dishes. Italian soups are especially appealing as they are so varied, being made from everything on hand, from beans to seafood or even bread. *Brodi* are clear broths in which soup pasta or *tortellini* may be cooked. *Minestre* are fairly light, while *minestroni*, "big soups," are packed with vegetables, beans, and perhaps pasta or rice. To complicate matters further, *minestrine* are light soups of puréed vegetables, and *zuppe* are thick, hearty soups of anything from vegetables to fish.

BRODO DI CARNE
Meat broth

A good meat broth can provide a starting point for more complex soups. It can also enrich sauces and stews. For maximum flavor, the meat and supporting vegetables should begin cooking in cold water. In this way, the meat juices are released into the broth rather than being sealed in by immediate intense heat. The best broth is made with a combination of meats and fowl. Serves 8.

INGREDIENTS

2lb (1kg) chicken backs or wings
2lb (1kg) beef chuck, shank, short ribs,
or other economy cut
1½lb (750g) mixed fresh uncooked veal and
beef shank and marrow bones
1 fresh or canned tomato
1 onion, unpeeled and quartered
1 large carrot, scraped and quartered
1 large celery rib with leaves
handful of flat-leaf parsley leaves and a bunch of stems
3 whole peppercorns
2–3 tsp salt

PREPARATION

1 Wash the chicken, removing any excess fat but keeping the skin on, and trim excess fat from the beef. Select a pot that will hold all the meat comfortably. Put in all the ingredients, except the salt. Add a maximum of 12 cups (3 liters) of cold water, to cover the meat by 2in (5cm). Cover the pot and bring to a boil.

2 Reduce the heat to low or medium-low and keep the broth at a gentle simmer. Leave the pot partially covered and skim the surface whenever scum forms. Cook at a steady, gentle simmer until the broth is full-bodied and tasty, about 3 hours. Check it occasionally, adjusting the flame so that it simmers gently and does not return to a boil.

3 Skim off any fat that has risen to the surface and remove the meat and bones. You can eat the meat separately: beef can be sliced, dressed with extra-virgin olive oil, lemon juice, and parsley, or with Salsa Verde (see page 139) and served as a salad.

4 Strain the broth through cheesecloth or a very fine sieve into a bowl. Add salt to taste only if using the broth immediately.

KCal 45 P 8g C neg S 196mg SFA neg UFA neg (8)

PASTINA IN BRODO DI POLLO
Chicken broth with pastina

In the Italian version of this proverbial soup, a richly flavored broth is served clear except for a little pastina (soup pasta). The chicken is served as a second course with some of the sauces described in pages 138–39 or Maionese Verde (see page 140). Although the vegetables are strained out, it is essential to use flavorful parsley and celery leaves. Follow this recipe, omitting pastina, to make a chicken broth for use in other recipes. Serves 6.

INGREDIENTS

1 free-range chicken, about 3½lb (1.75kg), including
neck, heart, and giblets, washed and trimmed
1 bay leaf
1 onion, unpeeled and quartered
1 carrot, scraped and roughly chopped
1 large celery rib with leaves
1 fresh or canned tomato
1 small bunch flat-leaf parsley
2 tsp salt, or to taste
¼ tsp whole black or white peppercorns
1 cup (175g) pastina, such as stelline, "little stars,"
orzo, "barley," or acini di pepe, "peppercorns"
freshly grated Parmesan, to serve

PREPARATION

1 Place the bird in a pot in which it just fits comfortably (the aim is to cover the chicken without diluting the broth with too much water). Put in all the ingredients, except the pastina and Parmesan, reserving a little parsley for a garnish. Add up to 8 cups (2 liters) of cold water, to cover the chicken by about 1in (2.5cm). Cover and bring to a boil.
2 Reduce the heat and cook the broth at a gentle simmer. Leave the pot partially covered and check the broth occasionally, skimming the surface whenever scum forms. Cook until the chicken meat is tender but not falling from the bones, about 1 hour. Do not allow it to return to a boil.
3 Skim off any fat and take the pot from the heat. Transfer the chicken to a serving dish and cover.
4 Strain the broth through cheesecloth or a fine sieve. Check the seasoning, return to a pot, and bring the broth to a boil. Stir in the pastina. Cook over medium heat until the pastina is tender, about 5 minutes, according to shape.
5 Garnish each serving with a pinch of chopped parsley and a tablespoon of grated Parmesan.

KCal 215 P 18g C 22g S 479mg SFA 4g UFA 3g (6)

MINESTRA DI MANZO E VERDURA CON ORZO
Beef soup with barley and vegetables

This exuberant minestra is one of the standbys of the home kitchen. With its collection of cold-weather vegetables and barley, it is an unbeatable first course in winter, and fortifying enough to be a one-pot meal for lunch or light supper. Various cuts of beef can be used, including rump and hind shank, but I find short ribs from the corner of the breast particularly succulent and meaty. Part of the joy of eating this comforting soup is to gnaw on the rib bones, so don't remove them before serving. Serves 6.

INGREDIENTS

3lb (1.5kg) beef short ribs
2 bay leaves
1 onion, unpeeled and cut in half
1 large celery rib with leaves
½ cup (100g) barley
1 tbsp plus ½ tsp salt
¾lb (375g) cabbage, finely shredded
1 large potato, peeled and diced
2 small carrots, finely diced
½ lb (250g) rutabaga, finely diced
½ tsp freshly ground black pepper
freshly grated pecorino or Parmesan, to serve

PREPARATION

1 In a large pan, combine the meat, 10 cups (2.5 liters) of water, the bay leaves, onion, and celery. Bring to a boil, then reduce to a steady simmer. Cook until the meat is tender, about 1½ hours. Check occasionally and skim off any scum that forms on the surface.
2 Meanwhile, bring 3 cups (750ml) of water to a boil in a saucepan, and add the barley and ½ teaspoon of salt. Cook over medium heat until tender, about 30 minutes. Drain and set aside.
3 After the meat has been cooking for about 1 hour, add the cabbage, potato, carrots, rutabaga, and 1 tablespoon of salt.
4 Five minutes before the end of cooking, add the cooked barley and pepper.
5 When the soup is cooked, remove the onion and bay leaves. Transfer the beef ribs to a cutting board, trim off any excess fat, and divide the ribs into servings. Return them to the soup and check the seasoning. Serve hot, passing the cheese at the table.

KCal 290 P 29g C 30g S 876mg SFA 3g UFA 4g (6)

MINESTRA DI GAMBERETTI E BIETOLA

Swiss chard and shrimp soup with rice

Here is a variation of a recipe I learned from Lidia Bastianich, the chef-owner of Felidia, one of New York City's best Italian restaurants. While on a trip to Apulia, Lidia and I toured the local markets. I couldn't resist the beautiful scampi at the Gallipoli fish markets and brought some back to our hotel. Lidia charmed our way into the hotel's kitchen, where she cooked them up into a lovely soup. Serves 8.

INGREDIENTS

1lb (500g) medium raw shrimp
2lb (1kg) fish bones, including 1 or 2 fish heads
(gills removed) from lean white fish such as cod, haddock,
halibut, red snapper, bass, and whiting
2 small onions, 1 unpeeled
2 large carrots, 1 cut in half and 1 coarsely grated
1 celery rib
3 whole white peppercorns
1½ tbsp salt
4 tbsp extra-virgin olive oil
½lb (250g) boiling or baking potatoes, peeled and diced
2 tsp tomato paste
½ cup (100g) Arborio rice
2lb (1kg) Swiss chard tops, finely shredded, then chopped
freshly ground black pepper, to taste

PREPARATION

1 Shell and devein the shrimp (see page 163), reserving the shells for the stock. Chop each shrimp into four pieces, halving them lengthwise, then cutting them across. Cover and refrigerate.
2 Put the fish bones in a large stockpot with the shrimp shells and 12 cups (3 liters) of water. Halve the unpeeled onion and add with the halved carrot, celery, peppercorns, and salt. Cover loosely so steam can escape, and bring to a boil. Reduce the heat and simmer for 30 minutes. Let cool, then strain the stock through a fine sieve; discard the solids.
3 In a large pan, warm the olive oil and sauté the potatoes over medium heat until they begin to color. Finely chop the remaining onion and add to the pan. Add the grated carrot and cook until soft.
4 Stir in the tomato paste, then add the fish stock. Bring to a boil and add the rice. Simmer, partially covered, until the rice is three-quarters cooked, about 10 minutes.
5 Add the Swiss chard and cook until tender, about 10 minutes more. Remove the soup from the heat and stir in the shrimp. Add pepper, adjust the seasoning, and serve hot.

KCal 195 P 9g C 22g S 1091mg SFA 1g UFA 7g (8)

White peppercorns

Celery

Carrots

Onions

Fish stock

Shrimp

Salt

Olive oil

Potatoes

Tomato
paste

Arborio
rice

Swiss
chard

Black pepper

KNÖDL ALLA TIROLESE IN BROD
Bread dumplings in broth

Stale bread is never thrown away in Italian kitchens, and bread dumplings are a Tyrolean specialty. Use sturdy, sugar-free peasant-style bread. Serves 6–8.

INGREDIENTS

1 quantity Meat Broth or Chicken Broth (see pages 72–3)
Dumplings
½lb (250g) stale bread, crusts removed, sliced
4 tbsp unsalted butter
1 large onion, coarsely grated
4 tbsp chopped fresh flat-leaf parsley
2 extra-large eggs, beaten lightly
1 tsp salt
¼ tsp freshly ground white or black pepper
½ cup (125ml) milk
½ tsp baking powder
¼ cup (30g) flour

PREPARATION

1 Shred the bread into tiny pieces and set aside.
2 Melt the butter in a skillet and add the onion and parsley. Sauté gently until the onion is soft, then add the bread and toss everything together. Sauté for about 7 minutes, tossing occasionally.
3 Meanwhile, mix together the eggs, salt, pepper, and milk. Sift in the baking powder and flour and mix well. Allow the bread mixture to cool slightly, then add it to the egg mixture. Mix the ingredients by hand, cover, and let rest for 1–3 hours.
4 Bring the broth to a boil in a large pot. Shape the bread mixture into dumplings the size of large olives and drop into the broth, making sure they do not touch as they cook. Cover the pot and simmer very gently for 5 minutes. Serve hot.

KCal 290 P 19g C 28g S 801mg SFA 7g UFA 4g (6)

ZUPPA DI SCAROLA
Escarole soup

Either escarole or curly endive may be used for this light, appealing soup. I grew up with this dish. The aroma of croutons frying in fruity olive oil, and their beguiling sizzle as my mother transferred them into our bowls of steaming soup, still lingers when I think of it. Serves 6.

INGREDIENTS

1 quantity Chicken Broth (see page 73)
1lb (500g) escarole or curly endive, washed thoroughly
½lb (250g) stale peasant bread, crusts removed, cubed
⅓ cup (90ml) extra-virgin olive oil, for frying bread
freshly grated Parmesan, to serve

PREPARATION

1 Warm the chicken broth in a large pot.
2 Cut the escarole across into very fine shreds, then cut the shreds into 2in (5cm) pieces.
3 Bring the broth to a boil. Stir in the greens, cover partially, and allow to cook for about 8 minutes, until tender but not disintegrated.
4 Meanwhile, warm the oil in a skillet. Add the bread cubes and fry until golden, about 5 minutes. Drain on paper towels. Pour the soup into bowls, toss in the hot croutons, and serve with Parmesan.

KCal 275 P 16g C 18g S 496mg SFA 2g UFA 13g (6)

MINESTRINA DI ZUCCHINE
Zucchini soup

One of the many soup fantasias from my mother's kitchen. The natural sweetness of zucchini is intensified in this soup, where it is combined with onion, butter, and milk. It is perfect as a first course when fish is on the menu.

INGREDIENTS

2lb (1kg) small zucchini, topped and tailed
4 tbsp unsalted butter
1 tbsp sunflower oil
1 onion, chopped
1 large celery rib with leaves, chopped
2 bay leaves
1 tsp chopped fresh marjoram, or ½ tsp dried
2 tbsp flour
1 cup (250ml) scalded (hot) milk
3 cups (750ml) Chicken Broth (see page 73) or stock
1 tsp salt
¼ tsp freshly ground black pepper

PREPARATION

1 Finely chop or coarsely grate the zucchini.
2 Heat half the butter with the oil in a large pan. Add the onion and sauté until soft, about 4 minutes. Add the celery and leaves, zucchini, bay leaves, and marjoram and sweat over medium-low heat for 7–8 minutes, stirring to coat them in the oil.
3 Cover the pan and continue to cook over low heat until completely softened, about 15 minutes.
4 Meanwhile, make a béchamel sauce. Melt the remaining butter and gradually stir in the flour until absorbed. Add the milk a little at a time, stirring constantly. Stir in the broth. Remove the bay leaves from the vegetable mixture.
5 Pour the béchamel-broth mixture into a blender with the vegetables and liquefy. Return the soup to the pan and heat through; do not allow it to boil. Season and serve hot or at room temperature.

KCal 295 P 13g C 17g S 565mg SFA 10g UFA 8g (4)

Minestra di Zucca

Pumpkin soup

Zucca, a type of pumpkin whose flesh is very like butternut squash in its color, compact texture, and sweetness, is used very imaginatively in the Italian kitchen. It finds its way into gnocchi, pasta stuffings, risotto, all manner of vegetable dishes, fritters, and desserts. This pumpkin soup recipe, however, is as much a testimony to my mother's resourcefulness and imagination as it is to the Italian way with squash. Serve it hot or at room temperature.

INGREDIENTS

2lb (1kg) small pumpkins or butternut squash
3 tbsp unsalted butter
1 small onion, grated or finely chopped
2 cups (500ml) Chicken Broth (see page 73)
½ cup (125ml) milk
good pinch of freshly grated nutmeg
zest of half an orange
1 tsp salt
pinch of white pepper

PREPARATION

1 Preheat the oven to 400°F (200°C).
2 Cut the pumpkins in half lengthwise and place them flesh side down on baking sheets. Bake until tender, about 40 minutes. When cool enough to handle, remove the seeds and rind. Reserve about ½lb (250g) of the flesh and dice the rest.
3 Melt the butter in a pot. Add the onion and sauté gently until softened. Stir in the pumpkin and sauté for 5 minutes to marry the flavors.
4 Add the broth, milk, nutmeg, orange zest, and salt, and simmer for 2 minutes. Remove the pot from the heat and let cool slightly.
5 Purée the mixture in a blender, then return it to the pot to heat through. Cut the reserved pumpkin into bite-sized slices and add to the soup with the pepper. Serve hot or warm.

KCal 150 P 6g C 7g S 490mg SFA 7g UFA 3g (4)

VARIATION

Add two chopped fennel stalks and 2 tablespoons of fennel fronds to the pot with the onion. Sprinkle finely chopped fronds over the soup before serving.

PASTA

This chapter includes delectable recipes for both fresh, homemade pasta and myriad types of dried, factory-produced pasta. In the first category fall light potato *gnocchi, crespelle* (akin to French crepes), noodles, and little pasta parcels with savory fillings. Most of the 350 or more varieties of dried pasta are made solely from durum wheat and water. They range from tiny *pastine* for soups to large pasta for stuffing. All these shapes and sizes actually vary in taste. They also absorb and combine with sauces differently. Dried pasta requires different cooking and saucing considerations than does delicate fresh pasta.

GNOCCHI DI PATATE

Potato gnocchi with tomato sauce and cheese

Gnocchi are simple to make and can be the most satisfying of pasta dishes. It is impossible to give an exact recipe as the amount of flour needed depends on the moisture content of the potatoes. Gnocchi are best made with floury-textured, older potatoes that have a lower water content. The less flour used, the lighter the gnocchi. If possible, use a potato ricer (see page 161) to mash the potatoes; a hand masher is the next best option. Makes enough for 6 as a main course or 8 as a first course. Illustrated on page 83.

INGREDIENTS

2lb (1kg) white, floury boiling or baking potatoes of uniform size, washed and dried
1⅓ cups (180g) all-purpose flour, plus more as needed
1 tsp coarse sea salt
¼ tsp freshly ground white pepper
Sauce
1 quantity Sugo di Pomodoro (see page 138) or Pesto (see page 141)
⅓ cup (40g) shredded soft cheese such as scamorza or mozzarella
freshly grated Parmesan, optional

PREPARATION

1 Preheat the oven to 400°F (200°C).
2 Bake the potatoes until tender, about 1 hour, depending on their size. Meanwhile, line three baking sheets with paper towels. Pour the flour onto a work surface and make a well in its center.
3 Smear a large shallow serving dish with a little of the sauce and keep warm.
4 When the potatoes are just cool enough to handle, peel off their skins (they must be warm when mixed with the flour). Pass them through a potato ricer into the center of the flour well (see page 161), or mash them and add to the well. Sprinkle with salt and pepper.
5 Incorporate the flour into the potatoes with a spoon, drawing it in to form a uniform, tender dough. It should be very soft without being sticky.
6 Knead the dough lightly for 5 minutes. Cut it into quarters and work with one piece at a time. Keep the remainder refrigerated until ready to use (it can be refrigerated for up to 30 minutes).
7 Using your hands, roll the dough into a rope ¾in (1.5cm) thick. Cut this into ¾in (1.5cm) pieces. Take each piece and drag it along the side of a cheese grater to make a concave dumpling (see page 161). If the dough becomes a little sticky,

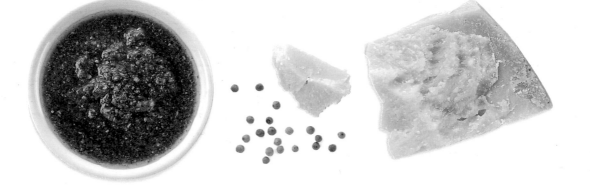

sprinkle it and the grater with flour; if the dough becomes very sticky, knead in more flour.

8 Transfer the gnocchi to the baking sheets, placing them in a single layer so they are not touching. Meanwhile, bring a large pot of water to a boil.

9 Slide the first batch of gnocchi into the water. Add 2 tablespoons of salt and stir with a wooden spoon. As soon as the gnocchi float to the surface, scoop them out and transfer to a colander. Repeat with the remaining gnocchi, then place them in the serving dish. Spoon on the sauce and scatter with the soft cheese, if using. Bake in an oven preheated to 425°F (220°C) for 5 minutes, or until the cheese melts. Serve immediately with Parmesan.

KCal 400 P 10g C 59g S 517mg SFA 3g UFA 11g (6)

VARIATION

- Make a Gorgonzola sauce. Melt 4 tablespoons of unsalted butter in a pan. Crumble in 6oz (175g) of Gorgonzola and stir until melted. Pour in 1 cup (250ml) of heavy cream and heat through. Remove from the heat, stir in freshly ground white pepper and 2 tablespoons of freshly grated Parmesan.

- Make a sage butter sauce. Melt 6 tablespoons of unsalted butter in a pan. Add a handful of fresh sage leaves and sauté them for 3 minutes, pressing down on them with a wooden spoon. Pour the sage butter over the gnocchi and sprinkle with Parmesan.

GNOCCHI ALLA FONTINA VALDOSTANA

Baked potato gnocchi with fontina

Fontina from the Valle d'Aosta is one of Italy's great cheeses. Its sweet creaminess combines with butter and Parmesan to make an appealing topping for gnocchi. Serves 6.

INGREDIENTS

1 quantity Gnocchi di Patate (see page 78)
4 tbsp unsalted butter, melted, plus butter to grease
pinch of freshly grated nutmeg
½ cup (60g) shredded fontina
2 tbsp freshly grated Parmesan

PREPARATION

1 Make the gnocchi dumplings as directed. Grease a shallow baking dish with butter and arrange the drained gnocchi in a single layer.

2 Preheat the oven to 450°F (230°C).

3 Drizzle the butter over the gnocchi, sprinkle with nutmeg, then scatter over the fontina and Parmesan. Bake at the top of the oven until the fontina has melted, about 5 minutes. Serve at once.

KCal 355 P 11g C 51g S 372mg SFA 9g UFA 4g (6)

RAVIOLI ALLA POTENTINA

Ravioli with ricotta, prosciutto, and pecorino

In this particular recipe from Potentina in the southern region of Basilicata, prosciutto is added to the traditional local filling of creamy ricotta and sharp pecorino. The result is an appealingly tangy mixture. The classic northern Emilian filling of ricotta, Parmesan, Swiss chard or spinach, and nutmeg is also delicious. Serve with Sugo di Pomodoro (see page 138) and a sprinkling of ricotta salata, or simply with butter and grated pecorino cheese. Makes about 90 ravioli, enough for 4–6 as a main course.

INGREDIENTS

1 quantity Pasta Fresca (see page 166), made with an equal mixture of semolina flour and plain flour
1 egg white
Sugo di Pomodoro (see page 138) and/or freshly grated ricotta salata or pecorino, to serve
Filling
2lb (1kg) ricotta
2 egg yolks
¾ cup (90g) freshly grated pecorino
2oz (60g) thinly sliced prosciutto, finely chopped
½ tsp salt
¼ tsp freshly ground white pepper
2 tbsp finely chopped fresh flat-leaf parsley

PREPARATION

1 To make the filling, place the ricotta in a sieve or cheesecloth and let drain over a bowl in the refrigerator for 3–4 hours, until firm. Mix it thoroughly with the remaining ingredients.

2 Roll out the pasta (see page 168). Work with only two strips of dough at a time; keep the rest covered until ready to use. Set the strips side by side, as described for Making Ravioli, step 1.

3 Distribute the filling and paint crisscross lines of egg white between the mounds of filling, as described in step 2.

4 Place the second strip of pasta over the filled one, then seal and cut into squares, as described in step 3.

5 Place the ravioli, without overlapping them, on trays lined with dish towels dusted with cornmeal. Let dry for up to 4 hours, turning occasionally.

6 Bring a large pan of salted water to a boil. Add the ravioli, cover until the water boils again, then cook gently for 3–5 minutes, uncovered, stirring occasionally. Transfer them to a warm serving bowl.

7 Spoon the sauce over the ravioli, if desired, and pass the grated ricotta or pecorino at the table.

KCal 880 P 50g C 64g S 1309mg SFA 25g UFA 18g (4)

CAPPELLETTI

Little pasta dumplings with meat and cheese

Pasta dumplings are a specialty of Emilia-Romagna. The dough is always made purely of white flour and eggs, but the fillings vary considerably throughout the region. This is the recipe for the traditional stuffing of Bologna and Modena – a fragrant, subtly seasoned mixture of pork, cured meats, turkey breast, and Parmesan. Cappelletti are usually cooked in broth, as here; they can also be served with a cream sauce, or simply with butter and fresh Parmesan. Makes enough for 10–12 as a soup course or 4–5 as a sauced pasta dish.

INGREDIENTS

Pasta

1 quantity Pasta Fresca (see page 166), made with 2¼ cups (300g) flour and 3 large eggs (no oil and salt) milk or beaten egg to seal dumplings, optional flour, to dust

Filling

2 tbsp unsalted butter
¼lb (125g) boneless turkey or chicken breast, diced
¼lb (125g) boneless pork loin, finely diced
2oz (60g) prosciutto, thinly sliced
3oz (90g) mortadella or high-quality salami, such as soppressata (see page 27), thinly sliced
⅓ cup (30g) freshly grated Parmesan
¼ tsp freshly grated nutmeg
½ tsp salt
freshly ground white pepper, to taste
1 egg

For cooking in broth (in brodo)

1 quantity Meat Broth (see page 72) or Chicken Broth (see page 73)

PREPARATION

1 To make the filling, melt the butter in a skillet over medium heat. Add the turkey and sauté for no more than 2 minutes over medium-low heat until it loses its pinkness – do not allow it to brown and get hard. Transfer the turkey to a bowl.

2 Reduce the heat slightly, add the pork to the butter in the pan and sauté for 2–3 minutes. Mix the pork with the turkey and chill until cooled, about 10 minutes.

3 Combine the prosciutto and mortadella on a board and chop them fine. Alternatively, cut them into dice and then work them in a food processor for no more than a few seconds at a time, taking care not to grind the meat to a paste.

4 When the turkey and pork have cooled, chop them very fine, as described above. Thoroughly combine the meats, cheese, nutmeg, salt, pepper, and egg with a wooden spoon, but do not beat them. Set the mixture aside.

TO FORM THE CAPPELLETTI

1 Roll the dough out as thin as possible, either by hand or with a pasta machine (see page 167). Work with a quarter of the dough at a time. Keep the strips covered with a slightly damp dish towel until ready to use.

2 Using a pastry wheel or knife, cut each strip of pasta into 2in (5cm) strips, then cut each of these into 2in (5cm) squares. Stuff and shape the cappelletti as shown opposite.

3 Line a baking sheet with a dish towel sprinkled with flour and let the cappelletti dry. Do not overlap the cappelletti, and turn them occasionally so they dry evenly. Let dry for up to 4 hours before cooking, refrigerating, or freezing them.

TO COOK THE CAPPELLETTI

1 Bring the broth to a boil in a large pot.

2 Slide the cappelletti into the broth. Stir, then cover the pot and bring back to a boil. Simmer gently to prevent the cappelletti from breaking. After 3–5 minutes, taste the pasta for doneness. Remove from the heat and serve immediately.

KCal 560 P 32g C 40g S 702mg SFA 17g UFA 12g (6)

VARIATIONS

• For cappelletti with butter and cheese, bring a large pot of water to a boil. Slide the cappelletti into the water. Stir, then cover and bring back to a boil. Simmer for 3–5 minutes, then taste for doneness. Transfer the cappelletti to a warm serving bowl and scatter with 6–8 tablespoons of unsalted butter and ½ cup (60g) of Parmesan. Serve at once with extra Parmesan.

• For cappelletti in a cream sauce *(alla panna)*, melt 4 tablespoons of butter in a skillet. Add ¾ cup (175ml) of heavy cream and simmer gently until the sauce thickens, about 10 minutes. Meanwhile, cook the cappelletti as described above. Remove the sauce from the heat, drain the cappelletti, and add to the pan with ½ cup (60g) of freshly grated Parmesan. Check the seasoning and serve.

MAKING CAPPELLETTI

1 Spoon ¼ teaspoonful of mixture onto the center of each square of pasta. Dip a pastry brush or your finger into a little water, milk, or beaten egg and run it along the inside edges.

2 Fold the square in half to make a triangle, bringing up the edges of one side to just below the other. Press together. The dumpling should resemble a small stuffed kerchief.

3 Wrap the dumpling around your finger, holding the peaked end up, with the stuffed side away from you. Overlap the two bottom corners of the triangle and pinch together.

**TAGLIATELLE CON
SALSA BOLOGNESE**
*Tagliatelle with
bolognese sauce*
(page 88)

GNOCCHI DI PATATE
*Potato gnocchi with tomato
sauce and cheese
(page 78)*

CONCHIGLIE ALLA PUTTANESCA
*Pasta shells with harlot's sauce,
Tuscan style
(page 85)*

LASAGNE IMBOTTITE
Stuffed lasagne in the style of Naples

This elaborate festive dish is usually reserved for giovedì grasso, "fat Thursday," at the end of Carnival. Meatballs and sausages are typically included, and sometimes sliced hard-boiled eggs. Omit the meatballs for a quicker version. Serves 8 as a main course.

INGREDIENTS

½ quantity Polpettine meatballs (see page 67), optional
olive oil for frying
1lb (500g) dried lasagne or other wide noodles
Sauce
2¾ cups (875g) canned tomatoes in juice
⅓ cup (75ml) extra-virgin olive oil
2oz (60g) pancetta or prosciutto, sliced paper thin,
finely chopped
2 tbsp chopped fresh flat-leaf parsley
1 carrot, finely chopped
1 celery rib with leaves, finely chopped
2 large garlic cloves, finely chopped
1 small onion, finely chopped
1lb (500g) sweet Italian sausages
¾lb (375g) ground lean beef or pork, or a mixture
1¼ tsp salt
4 tbsp tomato paste
¾ cup (175ml) good-quality dry red wine
freshly ground black pepper, to taste
1½lb (750g) ricotta
1¼ cups (155g) freshly grated pecorino or Parmesan
1¼lb (625g) mozzarella, shredded

PREPARATION

1 Sauté the meatballs in oil, if using, then set aside.
2 Drain the tomatoes, reserving their juice. Strain the juice and seed the tomatoes. Chop the tomatoes and set aside with their juice.
3 Warm the oil in a pan. Add the pancetta and sauté until golden. Stir in the parsley, carrot, celery, garlic, and onion, and sauté until softened, 10–12 minutes.
4 Remove the casings of three sausages and mix the meat with the ground beef. Add to the vegetables in the pan and sprinkle with salt. Sauté until the meat is lightly colored, about 8 minutes.
5 Stir in the tomato paste and wine. Simmer for 3 minutes, then add the tomatoes and juice. Cover partially and simmer until a thick sauce forms, about 1 hour. Check the seasoning and set aside.
6 Meanwhile, cook the remaining sausages until lightly browned (see page 164). Cover and refrigerate until ready to use.
7 Bring 4 quarts (5 liters) of salted water to a boil. Add the lasagne and cook until almost done, about 9 minutes, stirring occasionally. Drain, reserving

⅓ cup (90ml) of cooking water. Rinse the lasagne under cold water, then lay it out on wax paper.
8 Blend the ricotta, reserved pasta water, and half the pecorino in a bowl. Cut the cooked sausages into long thin slices. Halve the meatballs, if using.
9 Preheat the oven to 425°F (220°C).
TO ASSEMBLE
1 Spread a little meat sauce over the bottom of a 10 x 14in (25 x 35cm) baking dish. Cover with a layer of lasagne noodles. Spread some of the ricotta mixture over the pasta, then sprinkle with pecorino.
2 Follow with a layer of sauce, some of the sliced sausages and meatballs, then a layer of mozzarella.
3 Repeat the process, layering all the ingredients in the same order until they are used up. You should have three layers of pasta. Top the final layer with meat sauce, and scatter with sliced sausages, meatballs, mozzarella, and pecorino.
4 Bake the lasagne at the top of the oven until it is bubbly and golden, about 25 minutes. Let rest for 15 minutes before serving.

KCal 1215 P 71g C 65g S 2130mg SFA 34g UFA 35g (8)

ORECCHIETTE CON SALSICCIA E CIME DI RAPA
Orecchiette with sausage and broccoli rape

Cime di rapa is the authentic green to use in this Apulian dish, but kale makes a good substitute. Serves 6.

INGREDIENTS

⅓ cup (75ml) extra-virgin olive oil
12oz (375g) sweet Italian sausages, casings removed
4 garlic cloves, finely chopped
¼ tsp red pepper flakes, or to taste
2lb (1kg) cime di rapa (broccoli rape) or kale, stems
peeled and trimmed, chopped into 1in (2.5cm) pieces
salt, to taste
1lb (500g) orecchiette

PREPARATION

1 Warm 2 tablespoons of oil in a deep skillet. Add the sausage meat and brown over medium-low heat for 10 minutes. Stir in the garlic and pepper flakes and cook until softened, about 3 minutes.
2 Add the broccoli rape and ½ cup (125ml) of water to the sausage. Toss thoroughly, then cook, covered, over medium-low heat, until the greens are tender, about 10 minutes, stirring occasionally.
3 Meanwhile, bring 4 quarts (5 liters) of salted water to a boil, add the pasta, and cook until *al dente*. Drain the pasta, toss with the sauce and remaining oil, and season well before serving.

KCal 685 P 22g C 73g S 770mg SFA 10g UFA 23g (6)

BUCATINI ALL' AMATRICIANA
Bucatini with tomato and bacon sauce

INGREDIENTS

*3 cups (750g) canned tomatoes in juice, or 2½ lb
(1.25kg) fresh tomatoes, peeled, seeded, and chopped
2 tbsp unsalted butter, or 2 tbsp olive oil
1 small onion, chopped
2 large garlic cloves, bruised
2oz (60g) slab pancetta or 2oz (60g) thickly sliced lean
bacon strips, blanched in boiling water for 1 minute
pinch of red pepper flakes
salt, to taste
1lb (500g) bucatini or spaghetti
freshly grated Parmesan or pecorino, or a mixture, to serve*

PREPARATION

1 If using canned tomatoes, drain them, reserving
the juice. Remove any seeds, chop the flesh, and
set aside. If using fresh chopped tomatoes, place
them in a colander to drain for 5 minutes.
2 Warm the butter or oil in a pan. Add the onion
and garlic and sauté until golden, 6 minutes. Chop
the pancetta into julienne and sauté for 5 minutes.
3 Stir in the pepper flakes, tomatoes and juice, and
½ teaspoon of salt. Simmer until thickened, about
35 minutes, stirring occasionally. Discard the garlic.
4 Meanwhile, bring 4 quarts (5 liters) of salted
water to a boil, add the pasta and stir. Cook over
high heat, stirring occasionally, until *al dente*.
5 Drain the pasta and toss it with the sauce. Serve
hot, with plenty of grated cheese.
KCal 610 P 26g C 100g S 911mg SFA 8g UFA 5g (4)

CONCHIGLIE ALLA PUTTANESCA
Pasta with harlot's sauce, Tuscan style

While the Neapolitans serve this dish hot, the puttanesca
*sauce I've had in the homes of Tuscan friends has almost
always been uncooked and chilled. Try it when good, sun-
ripened tomatoes are available. Illustrated on page 82.*

INGREDIENTS

*1¼ lb (625g) fresh tomatoes, peeled, seeded, and chopped
½ cup (125ml) extra-virgin olive oil
2 large garlic cloves, chopped
8 large fresh basil leaves, torn into small pieces
1 tbsp chopped fresh flat-leaf parsley
¼ cup (45g) black olives, such as Gaeta or Niçoise, sliced
1 tbsp small capers, rinsed and drained
¼ tsp crushed red pepper flakes, or to taste
½ tsp salt, or to taste
1lb (500g) conchiglie or spaghetti*

PREPARATION

1 Mix the sauce ingredients together. Marinate
for at least 1 hour at room temperature.
2 Cook the pasta as described in step 4, left. Drain
and add it to the bowl with the sauce, tossing
everything together. Serve at room temperature.
KCal 775 P 18g C 103g S 481mg SFA 5g UFA 28g (4)

SPAGHETTI ALLA CARBONARA
Spaghetti with eggs and bacon

*Although this popular spaghetti dish is fairly modern,
it has become so widespread that it deserves a place
among the classics. Part of its success depends upon
using some of the pasta's cooking water to moisten
the egg-based sauce. Serves 4–6.*

INGREDIENTS

*5oz (150g) slab pancetta or bacon, blanched in boiling
water for 1 minute, cut into very thin slices then diced
3 tbsp extra-virgin olive oil
5 large garlic cloves, bruised
⅓ cup (90ml) dry white wine
4 extra-large eggs, beaten
2 tbsp light cream, optional
¼ cup (20g) freshly grated Parmesan
2 tbsp freshly grated pecorino
salt, to taste
1lb (500g) spaghetti
plenty of freshly ground pepper*

PREPARATION

1 Put the pancetta and 3 tablespoons of water in a
large nonstick skillet over medium heat. When the
water has evaporated and the pancetta starts to
color, drain off all but 1 tablespoon of fat.
2 Add the oil and garlic to the skillet. Sauté over
medium-low heat until the pancetta is browned
and the garlic is golden, about 4 minutes.
3 Deglaze the pan by stirring in the wine. Discard
the garlic and take the pan off the heat.
4 Beat the eggs with the cream (if using), cheese,
and ½ teaspoon of salt in a separate bowl.
5 Bring 4 quarts (5 liters) of salted water to a boil
and add the pasta. Stir quickly, then cook over high
heat, stirring occasionally, until *al dente*.
6 Drain the pasta, reserving 1 cup (250ml) of the
cooking water. While the pasta is still wet and
piping hot, toss it thoroughly with the pancetta.
7 Quickly add the egg mixture to the skillet,
tossing it thoroughly. Add enough cooking water
to create an abundant, creamy sauce. Sprinkle with
pepper and serve at once.
KCal 740 P 34g C 93g S 1326mg SFA 7g UFA 18g (4)

CICERI E TRIA
Salentine fettuccine with chickpeas and onions

The Salento region extends to the very tip of the heel of the Italian boot. Many of its unique dishes are based on vegetables, beans, and seafood, and are almost spartan in their simplicity. My variation of this robust dish is a pleasing combination of soft and crispy textures.

INGREDIENTS

½ cup (125ml) extra-virgin olive oil
1 onion, chopped
1 large celery rib with leaves, chopped
1 carrot, coarsely grated
3 large garlic cloves, finely chopped
1½ cups (200g) dried chickpeas, soaked and cooked (see page 161), plus 1¾ cups (400ml) of their cooking liquid, or 3 cups (475g) canned chickpeas, drained
1½ tsp chopped fresh rosemary, or ¾ tsp dried
salt, to taste
½ quantity Pasta Fresca (see page 166), made with 2 cups (250g) semolina flour, 2 eggs and ½ tsp salt, cut into fettuccine, or 12oz (375g) dried fettuccine or tagliatelle
2 tbsp chopped fresh flat-leaf parsley
freshly ground black pepper, to taste

PREPARATION

1 Heat ⅓ cup (90ml) of the oil in a large skillet. Add the onion, celery, carrot, and garlic, and sauté gently until softened, about 10 minutes.
2 Add the chickpeas, rosemary, and ¾ teaspoon of salt to the skillet. Crush most of the chickpeas with a potato masher or fork, leaving a handful whole.
3 Stir in the reserved chickpea cooking liquid, if using rehydrated chickpeas, or 1¾ cups (400ml) of fresh water. Simmer until the flavors blend and a sauce is formed, about 8 minutes.
4 Meanwhile, bring 4 quarts (5 liters) of salted water to a boil for the pasta. Add 8oz (250g) of the pasta and set the rest aside. Bring to a boil again and cook over high heat until tender, about 2 minutes from the second boil for fresh pasta and 6–8 minutes for dried. Drain, reserving 1 cup (250ml) of cooking water. While still dripping wet, transfer the pasta to the pan with the chickpeas.
5 Add the parsley to the skillet and toss thoroughly. If necessary, moisten the sauce with some of the reserved cooking water. Check the seasoning.
6 Heat the remaining oil in a skillet. When it is hot, toss in the reserved uncooked noodles. When they are browned, add them with their oil to the other noodles, scattering them on top. Sprinkle with plenty of pepper and serve.

KCal 600 P 16g C 52g S 885mg SFA 6g UFA 30g (4)

Garlic

Carrots

Celery

Onion

Olive oil

Chickpeas

Rosemary

Salt

Fettuccine

Flat-leaf
parsley

Black
pepper

TAGLIATELLE CON SALSA BOLOGNESE

Tagliatelle with bolognese sauce

Outside Italy, bolognese sauce has become synonymous with a nondescript meat and tomato mixture, but the authentic version is complex and fragrant. A variety of meats, and sometimes cured meats, are simmered with celery, tomatoes, and onion, and a little milk and white wine, to form a delicate, creamy sauce. I include ground pork for its rich flavor and sweetness, and mortadella for its subtle spiciness. Serves 6–8. Illustrated on page 82.

INGREDIENTS

1 cup (250g) fresh or canned drained tomatoes, peeled, seeded, and chopped, with juice reserved
2 tbsp unsalted butter
½ tbsp extra-virgin olive oil
1oz (30g) slab pancetta, finely chopped
1 small onion, finely chopped
1 small celery rib with leaves, finely chopped
1 small carrot, finely chopped
1 tbsp chopped fresh flat-leaf parsley
6oz (175g) lean ground beef
3oz (90g) ground pork
1oz (30g) mortadella, finely chopped, optional
salt, to taste
⅓ cup (90ml) good-quality dry white wine
⅓ cup (90ml) milk
good pinch of freshly grated nutmeg
2 tbsp tomato paste
⅔ cup (175ml) Meat Broth (see page 72), or good stock
1 quantity Pasta Fresca (see page 166), cut into tagliatelle, or 1½lb (750g) dried pasta, such as fusilli or orecchiette
freshly ground white or black pepper, to taste
freshly grated Parmesan, to serve

PREPARATION

1 Strain the tomato juice and discard the seeds. Set aside the chopped tomatoes and their juice.
2 In a large heavy-bottomed pan or deep skillet, melt 1½ tablespoons of butter with the oil. Stir in the pancetta and sauté until lightly colored.
3 Add the onion, celery, carrot, and parsley, and sauté until softened but not browned, about 12 minutes. Keeping the heat very low, add the ground meat, mortadella (if using), and the salt. Allow the meat to color lightly, about 2 minutes, and use a wooden spoon to break up the chunks.
4 Pour in the wine. Simmer very gently until the alcohol evaporates and the liquid begins to be absorbed, about 3 minutes.
5 Add the milk and nutmeg and simmer for 10 minutes. Stir in the tomato paste dissolved in ¼ cup (60ml) of broth. Add the tomatoes and

juice. As soon as the sauce begins to simmer, turn the heat down as low as possible. Cover partially and cook for at least 4 hours, stirring occasionally. Add the remaining broth as the sauce cooks.
6 When the sauce is thick, creamy, and fragrant, remove it from the heat and stir in the remaining butter and the pepper. Check the seasoning.
7 Bring 4 quarts (5 liters) of salted water to a rapid boil. Cover the pot, and as soon as the water returns to a boil, remove the lid and stir again. Cook the fresh pasta for 10 seconds after the water has returned to the boil, then drain immediately, or cook the dried pasta until *al dente,* then drain.
8 Transfer the tagliatelle to a warm serving bowl, toss with the sauce, and sprinkle with Parmesan.
KCal 445 P 25g C 43g S 600mg SFA 8g UFA 10g (6)

MACCHERONI ALLA BARESE CON CAVOLFIORE

Penne with cauliflower and onions, Bari style

Apulian cuisine is known for its many imaginative vegetable dishes. I learned this flavor-packed and nutritious recipe from Anna Amendolara Nurse, whose parents emigrated to New York from Bari. Serves 4–6.

INGREDIENTS

1 large cauliflower, about 2½–3lb (1.25–1.5kg), trimmed and cut into small florets
salt, to taste
½ cup (125ml) extra-virgin olive oil
2 onions, cut lengthwise into thick slices
1lb (500g) penne rigate or other ridged tubular pasta
1 tbsp chopped fresh flat-leaf parsley
pinch of crushed red pepper flakes
freshly ground black pepper, to taste

PREPARATION

1 Bring 6 quarts (7.5 liters) of water to a boil. Add the cauliflower and 2 tablespoons of salt, and boil until almost tender, 4–5 minutes. Transfer the florets to a bowl; do not discard the cooking water.
2 Gently heat the oil in a heavy pan. Add the onion and cook until golden.
3 Return the cauliflower water to a boil. Add the pasta and cook until almost *al dente,* about 7 minutes. Add the cauliflower and cook until heated through, about 1 minute longer. Drain off all but 1 cup (250ml) of the cooking water. Transfer the cauliflower, pasta, and water to a warm bowl.
4 Quickly reheat the oil and onion and add to the penne. Season with the parsley, pepper flakes, salt, and black pepper, and serve at once.
KCal 840 P 27g C 107g S 424mg SFA 5g UFA 28g (4)

CRESPELLE
Crepes

Crespelle are little pancakes that appear throughout the Italian regions, and have different names wherever they are found: in Tuscany, they are fazzoletti, "handkerchiefs," in Calabria, manicotti, "little muffs." They may be filled with meat, seafood, vegetables, or cheese, then rolled up, covered with tomato or béchamel sauce, and baked. For light, delicate crepes, the batter must be very thin, almost watery. Don't worry if the first one or two in the batch are imperfect; you'll soon get the hang of it and the rest will no doubt be flawless. Makes 20 crepes.

INGREDIENTS

4 large eggs
2½ cups (600ml) milk, or more if necessary
pinch of sugar
½ tsp salt
1½ cups (175g) unbleached white flour
sunflower oil for frying

PREPARATION

1 Whisk together the eggs, milk, sugar, and salt. Add the flour, sifting it in while beating with the whisk. The batter should be extremely thin – almost watery. Cover and let rest for 30 minutes.
2 Over medium-high heat, warm ½ teaspoon of oil in a cold, nonstick 8in (20cm) crepe pan (or shallow frying pan with curved sides), rotating it to coat the entire base of the pan. Test the heat of the oil by pouring in a teaspoon of batter. It should sizzle.
3 Cook the crespelle one at a time, pouring about 3 tablespoons of batter into the hot pan for each one. The batter should spread until it makes a large, thin pancake, completely covering the pan. Tilt and rotate the pan to spread the mixture evenly.
4 When tiny holes begin to form in the crepe, after about 1 minute, flip it over and cook lightly on the reverse side for about 30 seconds.
5 Transfer the crespelle to a platter and cover with plastic wrap until ready to use. Repeat with the remaining batter, adding more oil when needed.

KCal 85 P 3g C 8g S 68mg SFA 1g UFA 3g (per crepe)

MANICOTTI
Crepes stuffed with ricotta, Calabrian style

Manicotti are crepes stuffed with ricotta and baked in a tomato sauce. This particular version is traditionally served at the Calabrian cenone, the meatless meal eaten on Christmas Eve, or on Sundays or holidays. Serves 6.

INGREDIENTS

1 quantity Crespelle (see left)
¼ quantity Sugo di Pomodoro (see page 138)
Filling
1lb (500g) ricotta, drained in a strainer for 2 hours
2½ tbsp freshly grated pecorino or Parmesan
1 egg
1 tbsp chopped fresh flat-leaf parsley
¼ tsp salt
pinch of freshly ground white or black pepper
4oz (125g) mozzarella, cut into strips about 2in (5cm) long and ¼in (5mm) wide

PREPARATION

1 Make the crespelle as described on left.
2 Combine the ricotta with two-thirds of the grated cheese, the egg, parsley, salt, and pepper. Taste and adjust the seasoning if necessary.
3 Preheat the oven to 400°F (200°C).
4 Spread a thin layer of tomato sauce on the bottom of two baking dishes. Place a tablespoon of filling at one end of each crepe. Lay a strip of mozzarella on the filling and roll the crepe up tightly.
5 Take a little of the filling on your finger and run it along the inside edge of the crepe, then press down the edges to seal. Place the manicotti in the baking dish, leaving space around each one.
6 Spoon 3–4 tablespoons of the tomato sauce on top of the manicotti to moisten them; do not drench them. Sprinkle with the remaining grated cheese. If there is any mozzarella left, cut it into small dice and sprinkle over the top.
7 Bake the dish in the top of the oven until bubbly and golden, 10–15 minutes. Allow to cool for 10 minutes before serving.

KCal 425 P 19g C 29g S 705mg SFA 9g UFA 15g (6)

BEANS, RICE, AND POLENTA

Corn and beans, introduced to Europe from the New World, have become staples in the Italian diet. In its simplest guise polenta, made from ground corn, is served "loose" as a sort of porridge, but, as befits its versatility, it may appear in many other forms. Beans are used fresh and dried and include lentils, chickpeas, cannellini and borlotti. Risotto is impossible without Italian rice, which is uniquely suited to slow cooking in a small amount of liquid. Rice is always served as a first course, except for Risotto alla Milanese, the traditional accompaniment to Osso Buco (see page 54).

FAGIOLI IN STUFA

Beans stewed with garlic and herbs

The Tuscans are inordinately fond of eating beans and consequently they have many recipes for bean dishes. This aromatic stew of beans and herbs is typical of the region's cooking, being effectively simple. Serves 4–6.

INGREDIENTS

2 cups (375g) dried cannellini or Great Northern beans, or 4 cups (1.5kg) drained canned beans
2 bay leaves
salt, to taste
4 tbsp extra-virgin olive oil
2 large garlic cloves, chopped
2 tbsp chopped fresh flat-leaf parsley
1½ tsp chopped fresh marjoram, or ¾ tsp dried
freshly ground white pepper, to taste

PREPARATION

1 If using dried beans, rehydrate and cook them as described on page 161, adding 2 bay leaves to the cooking pot. Season the cooked beans with salt and let steep in their liquid until the salt is absorbed, at least 15 minutes. Drain, reserving 3 tablespoons of the cooking liquid.
2 Warm the oil and garlic together until the garlic is soft but not colored, about 3 minutes. Stir in the parsley and marjoram, then add the beans and the reserved liquid or 3 tablespoons of fresh water.
3 Cover the pan and simmer for 10–15 minutes. Check the seasoning, add pepper, and serve hot.

KCal 480 P 26g C 60g S 443mg SFA 3g UFA 13g (4)

VARIATION

Add ½ cup (125g) of peeled, seeded, and chopped tomatoes to the beans with the herbs.

LENTICCHIE ALLA CASALINGA

Lentils with butter and parsley

While this dish is traditionally served alongside pork and game, it can satisfy as a vegetarian meal if accompanied by a salad or other side dish. The cooked lentils are also good served cold with a dressing of lemon juice, extra-virgin olive oil, parsley, and chopped onion.

INGREDIENTS

½lb (250g) brown lentils, rinsed and drained
2 tsp coarse salt
1 large bay leaf
small bunch of parsley stems, tied together
3 large garlic cloves, cut in half
3 tbsp unsalted butter, at room temperature
juice of ½ lemon, plus 1½ lemons, cut into wedges, to serve
2 tbsp finely chopped fresh flat-leaf parsley
freshly ground black pepper, to taste

PREPARATION

1 Place the lentils in a pan with 4 cups (1 liter) of water, the salt, bay leaf, parsley, and garlic. Bring to a boil, then simmer over medium-low heat until the lentils are tender but not falling apart, about 25 minutes.
2 Drain the lentils, discarding the parsley stems, bay leaf, and garlic.
3 Meanwhile, beat the butter in a small bowl until it is creamy. Blend the lemon juice into the butter, then beat in 1 tablespoon of chopped parsley. Mix the parsley butter into the hot lentils, tossing them gently. Check the seasoning.
4 Sprinkle the remaining tablespoon of parsley over the lentils and grind some pepper over them. Serve the lentils hot or warm with lemon wedges.

KCal 280 P 16g C 32g S 256mg SFA 6g UFA 3g (4)

CASSERUOLA DI LENTICCHIE CON SALSICCE

Lentil stew with sausages

Pork and lentils have a natural affinity for each other. My mother always served this hearty, fortifying stew in winter. It takes little effort to make and can be prepared hours or even days in advance. Serves 6.

INGREDIENTS

1lb (500g) brown lentils, rinsed and drained
2 bay leaves
2 small celery ribs with leaves,
1 whole and 1 finely chopped
1 tbsp salt
2 tbsp olive oil, plus extra if necessary
8 meaty pork sausages, preferably Italian
1 carrot, chopped
1 small onion, finely chopped
2 large garlic cloves, finely chopped
3 tbsp tomato paste

PREPARATION

1 Place the lentils in a pan with 8 cups (2 liters) of water, the bay leaf, whole celery rib, and salt. Bring to a boil, then simmer gently until the lentils are *al dente*, about 25 minutes. Drain, reserving 3 cups (750ml) of the cooking liquid. Discard the bay leaf and celery.

2 Warm the oil in a large pan or casserole over medium-low heat. Add the sausages and pierce them with a fork to release some of the fat. Sauté until browned all over, about 12 minutes. Remove from the pan and drain off all but 2 tablespoons of the fat (if there is not enough fat, add more oil).

3 Add the chopped celery and leaves, the carrot, onion, and garlic and sauté gently until softened, about 8 minutes. Stir in the tomato paste and the lentil cooking liquid and slowly bring to a boil.

4 Return the lentils and sausages to the pan, cover, and simmer until the sausages are cooked through, about 10 minutes. Check the seasoning and serve.

KCal 615 P 30g C 52g S 1647mg SFA 11g UFA 20g (6)

RISOTTO ALLA MILANESE

Saffron risotto, Milanese style

Risotto is a simple dish to make if the following things are remembered: use authentic Italian Arborio, Carnaroli, or Vialone nano rice; make sure the broth is kept hot (cold liquid will bring down the temperature), and, as always in Italian cooking, use the best and purest ingredients available. Serves 6.

INGREDIENTS

*6 cups (1.5 liters) Meat Broth (see page 72) or
Chicken Broth (see page 73)
6 tbsp (90g) unsalted butter
2 tbsp beef marrow, chopped or 2 tbsp additional butter,
or 2oz (60g) finely chopped pancetta
1 onion, finely chopped
2 cups (475g) Arborio, Carnaroli, or Vialone nano rice
½ cup (125ml) dry white wine
generous ½ tsp saffron strands
½ cup (45g) freshly grated Parmesan,
plus extra for serving
freshly ground white pepper, to taste*

PREPARATION

1 Gently heat the broth and keep it warm over a low flame.

2 Heat half the butter with the beef marrow or additional butter or pancetta in a pan. When the marrow is melted, add the onion and sauté over low heat until softened, about 5 minutes.

3 Add the rice and sauté for 3–4 minutes, stirring constantly to coat the grains. Pour in the wine and reduce the heat slightly. When all the wine has been absorbed, add a ladleful of broth and stir again.

4 Once the broth has been almost completely absorbed, add another ladleful. Continue stirring and adding the broth, a ladleful at a time, until the rice is half-cooked, about 15 minutes. At this point, dissolve the saffron in a ladleful of hot broth and pour into the pan. Add the remainder of the broth, waiting for each ladleful to be absorbed before adding the next.

5 When the rice is tender but still slightly chewy, remove it from the heat; it should be creamy but not mushy. Stir in the remaining butter and the Parmesan. Check the seasoning and serve.

KCal 535 P 16g C 70g S 262mg SFA 13g UFA 7g (6)

RISOTTO ALLA MARINARA

Seafood risotto

There are infinite variations on the theme of seafood risotto throughout the northern coastal regions. Most versions contain squid and shrimp. Fish, clams, and mussels may also be included. The finished texture of a risotto should be what the Venetians call al onda, "with a wave"— that is, very moist, almost wet. Parmesan is never served with seafood dishes. Serves 4–6.

INGREDIENTS

*1lb (500g) whole white-fleshed fish, such as porgy,
snapper, mullet, or bass, scaled and gutted
1½lb (750g) small tender squid
½lb (250g) unpeeled raw small or medium shrimp
1 onion, unpeeled and quartered, plus 1 onion, chopped
2 carrots, 1 whole and 1 chopped
2 celery ribs with leaves, 1 whole and 1 chopped
4 sprigs fresh flat-leaf parsley
1 whole fennel stalk, plus 3 tbsp chopped tender
fennel fronds, if available, or 2 bay leaves
¼ tsp black or white peppercorns
salt
4 tbsp unsalted butter
1 tbsp extra-virgin olive oil
1 large garlic clove, bruised
2 cups (475g) Arborio, Carnaroli, or Vialone nano rice
½ cup (125ml) good dry white wine
2 envelopes (260mg) saffron powder, or ¼ tsp saffron strands
freshly ground black pepper, to taste*

PREPARATION

1 Fillet the fish, reserving the head, tail, and bones for stock. Cut the fish fillets into 1in (2.5cm) dice. Cover until ready to use.

2 Clean the squid (see page 99). Cut the body into ¼in (5mm) rings and quarter or halve the tentacles. Rinse and dry all the squid pieces.

3 Peel and devein the shrimp (see page 163), reserving the shells. Rinse the shrimp, pat dry, then cut in half lengthwise. Cover until ready to use.

4 Make a stock. Place the shrimp shells and fish trimmings in a pot with the whole onion and carrot, the whole celery rib, parsley sprigs, whole piece of fennel, and peppercorns. Add 7 cups (1.75 liters) of cold water and 1 tablespoon of salt. Bring to a boil, then simmer over medium-low heat for 35 minutes, skimming the foam off the top. Strain the stock into a pan and keep warm.

5 Heat 1 tablespoon of butter in a nonstick skillet. Add the shrimp and diced fish and sauté until lightly colored, 4–5 minutes. Set aside.

6 Heat the remaining butter with the olive oil in a wide, deep skillet. Add the garlic, chopped onion, carrot, and celery. Sauté gently until the vegetables soften, about 8 minutes, stirring occasionally. Add the squid, raise the heat to high, and sauté until nicely colored all over, about 6 minutes. Reduce the heat to medium-high and remove the garlic.

7 Stir in the rice and sauté for 3–4 minutes, stirring constantly to coat the grains in the oil. Pour in the wine and reduce the heat slightly. When the wine has been fully absorbed, add a ladleful of hot fish stock, stirring well.

8 Once the stock has been almost completely absorbed, add another ladleful. Continue adding the stock, a ladleful at a time, until the rice is half-done, approximately 15 minutes. At this point,

dissolve the saffron in a little stock and stir into the rice. Add all but a tablespoon of the remaining stock a ladleful at a time, waiting for each addition to be absorbed before adding the next. Stir in the fish and shrimp just before adding the last ladleful.

9 Stir the final tablespoon of stock into the fish skillet to deglaze it, then pour these pan juices into the risotto pan. When the rice is tender but still slightly chewy, remove the pan from the heat. The finished consistency of the rice should be creamy but not mushy. Check for salt, add pepper to taste, and stir in the chopped fennel fronds, if using. Serve immediately.

KCal 905 P 57g C 112g S 879mg SFA 10g UFA 9g (4)

RISOTTO CON POMODORO E BASILICO
Risotto with tomato and basil

Here is a good risotto to make in the summer when sweet, vine-ripened tomatoes and fresh basil are available.

INGREDIENTS

3–3½ cups (750–900ml) Meat Broth (see page 72)
4 tbsp unsalted butter
2 large garlic cloves, bruised
1 onion, chopped
1½ cups (300g) fresh or canned drained tomatoes,
peeled, seeded, and chopped
1½ cups (325g) Arborio, Carnaroli, or Vialone nano rice
4 tbsp freshly grated Parmesan,
plus extra for serving
10 large fresh basil leaves, torn into very small pieces
salt and freshly ground black pepper, to taste

PREPARATION

1 Gently heat the broth and keep it warm over a low heat.
2 Meanwhile, melt half the butter in a saucepan, add the garlic and onion, and sauté gently until softened, 4–5 minutes. Discard the garlic.
3 Stir in the tomatoes and simmer over medium-low heat until the sauce is thickened and aromatic, about 20 minutes, stirring occasionally.
4 In a large skillet over medium heat, melt the remaining butter and add the rice. Sauté for 3–4 minutes, stirring constantly to coat the grains.
5 Heat the tomato sauce through and stir it into the rice. Reduce the heat to medium and simmer until the sauce is absorbed, stirring constantly.
6 Add a ladleful of the hot broth and stir frequently. When it has been almost completely absorbed, add another ladleful of hot broth and stir well. Continue adding the broth, a ladleful at a time, until the rice is tender but still slightly chewy, 20–25 minutes. It should be creamy but not mushy.
7 Remove the pan from the heat. Stir in the grated Parmesan and the basil. Taste for salt and add pepper. Serve the finished risotto piping hot, passing additional Parmesan at the table.

KCal 495 P 15g C 75g S 572mg SFA 10g UFA 6g (4)

VARIATION

Just before serving, stir in 1 cup (125g) of diced mozzarella and allow it to melt slightly.

RISO IN PEVERADA
Rice with chicken livers in the style of the Veneto

The description peverada *indicates that a dish includes* pepitella, *a peppery herb in the mint family used to flavor Venetian game and risotto dishes. Mint can be substituted for pepitella in this pleasant risotto, which successfully brings together several distinctive ingredients. Serves 6.*

INGREDIENTS

½lb (250g) chicken livers
6¼ cups (1.5 liters) Meat Broth (see page 72)
2 tbsp unsalted butter
2 tbsp olive oil
2 tbsp beef marrow, chopped, or 2 tbsp additional butter,
or 2oz (60g) finely chopped pancetta
1 onion, chopped
2in (5cm) strip of lemon zest, blanched
2 tbsp chopped fresh mint or flat-leaf parsley
2 cups (475g) Arborio, Carnaroli, or Vialone nano rice
½ cup (125ml) dry white wine
salt, to taste
⅓ cup (30g) freshly grated Parmesan, plus extra to serve

PREPARATION

1 Wash the livers and trim off any connective tissue, fat, or discolored parts. Dice the livers.
2 Gently heat the broth and keep it warm over a low flame.
3 Meanwhile, combine half the butter, the oil, and the beef marrow in a pan over medium-low heat. When the butter is melted, add the onion, lemon zest, and half the mint. Sauté gently until softened but not colored, about 5 minutes.
4 Add the livers and sauté them with the onion mixture until they are browned on all sides, about 2 minutes. Add the rice and sauté for 3–4 minutes, stirring constantly to coat the grains. Pour in the wine and reduce the heat slightly.
5 Add a ladleful of hot broth and stir thoroughly. When it has been almost completely absorbed, add another ladleful of hot broth and stir well. Continue adding the broth, a ladleful at a time, until the rice is tender but still slightly chewy, 20–25 minutes. It should be creamy but not mushy. Taste for salt.
6 Remove the pan from the heat, then stir in the remaining butter and mint and the grated Parmesan cheese. Serve piping hot, passing additional Parmesan at the table.

KCal 555 P 23g C 70g S 270mg SFA 9g UFA 10g (6)

RISO ARROSTO

Roasted rice with sausage and artichokes

Unlike a risotto, this Ligurian rice dish can be made well
in advance. Veal sweetbreads or other economical meat
cuts are typically included. Italian rice produces excellent
results, but other rice varieties can be used. Serves 6.

INGREDIENTS

4 artichokes, 6–8oz (175–250g) each
salt, to taste
1 tbsp vegetable oil
1lb (500g) crumbled pork sausage meat
3 tbsp unsalted butter
1 onion, chopped
2 tbsp chopped fresh flat-leaf parsley
1½ cups (325g) Arborio, Carnaroli, or Vialone nano rice
⅓ cup (30g) freshly grated Parmesan
1½ cups (350ml) Meat Broth (see page 72), or good stock

PREPARATION

1 Prepare the artichokes. Cut off and trim the
stems, then halve them lengthwise. Using a paring
knife, tear off the artichoke's outer leaves, leaving
the tender inner leaves. Slice across the top of the
artichoke with a serrated knife, leaving 1⅛in (3.5cm)
of the base. Trim off any tough parts, cut each base
into quarters lengthwise, and cut out the choke.
Place in water acidulated with lemon juice.
2 Bring enough salted water to cover the
artichokes to a boil and drop them in. Cook until
half-done, 3–6 minutes. Drain and set aside.
3 Heat the oil in a skillet and add the sausage.
Brown for about 7 minutes, stirring occasionally.
Drain off any excess oil and set aside.
4 Preheat the oven to 400°F (200°C).
5 Heat 2 tablespoons of butter in another skillet.
Add the onion and parsley and sauté until the
onion is translucent, about 3 minutes. Add the
parboiled artichokes and the rice and sauté for
1–2 minutes, stirring constantly. Remove from the
heat. Combine the sausage meat, the artichoke,
and rice mixture, and all but 2 tablespoons of the
Parmesan. Transfer the mixture to a baking dish.
6 Stir ½ teaspoon of salt into the broth and stir the
broth into the rice mixture. Cover the dish with
foil and bake in the oven until the broth is absorbed
and the rice tender, 20–25 minutes. Remove from
the oven and preheat the broiler.
7 Uncover the dish and dot the rice with the
remaining butter and Parmesan. Set the dish about
6in (15cm) below the broiler heat source and let
broil until a golden crust forms, 2–4 minutes. Let
rest for 10 minutes before serving hot or warm.

KCal 655 P 21g C 60g S 998mg SFA 16g UFA 21g (6)

POLENTA MARITATA

Baked polenta casserole

Maritata means "married," signifying that the
components of this pasticcio (literally a "mess" or
"muddle," but meaning any kind of baked dish) are well
suited to one another. Of the various types of polenta
pasticcio found in Italian cooking, many of which include
a meat sauce, this is the simplest and lightest. It is an
excellent dish in the summer months. Serves 8.

INGREDIENTS

1 quantity Polenta (see page 169)
1½ tbsp chopped fresh basil
10oz (300g) mozzarella, shredded
Sauce
3 tbsp extra-virgin olive oil
4 large garlic cloves, bruised
2½lb (1.25kg) fresh or canned drained tomatoes,
peeled, seeded, and chopped
3 tbsp chopped fresh basil
salt and freshly ground black pepper, to taste

PREPARATION

1 To make the sauce, warm the oil in a pan over
medium heat. Add the garlic and sauté until
golden, about 4 minutes.
2 Add the tomatoes and basil and stir. Bring to
a simmer and continue to cook for 25 minutes.
3 Remove the sauce from the heat and allow it to
cool slightly, then pass it through a food mill or
strainer, pushing through as much pulp as possible.
Add salt and pepper to taste and set aside.
4 Preheat the oven to 400°F (200°C).
5 Make the polenta crostini as described on page
169, cutting the hardened polenta into 3in (7cm)
squares (do not fry or grill them).
6 Layer half the polenta squares on the bottom of
a prepared dish. Pour on half the sauce and scatter
over half the basil and mozzarella.
7 Place the remaining polenta squares on top,
then spoon over the remainder of the sauce.
Sprinkle with the rest of the basil and cheese.
8 Bake in the middle of the oven until the cheese
is melted and golden on top and the pasticcio is
bubbling, 20–25 minutes. Remove from the oven
and let it rest for 10 minutes before cutting it into
squares. Serve hot.

KCal 320 P 140g C 32g S 924mg SFA 6g UFA 9g (8)

FEGATINI DI POLLO CON FUNGHI E POLENTA

Chicken livers and mushrooms with polenta

This dish of chicken livers, with its earthy sauce of shallots, mushrooms, sage, and red wine, is a perfect dish with which to serve polenta. The polenta can take any form – fried, grilled, or loose. The only chicken livers that will do are springy plump ones.

INGREDIENTS

½ quantity Polenta (see page 169), prepared according to taste
Sauce
1lb (500g) very fresh chicken livers
5oz (150g) wild or cultivated mushrooms
2 tbsp extra-virgin olive oil
2 tbsp unsalted butter
2 tbsp finely chopped shallots or scallions
½ tsp crushed dried green peppercorns, or freshly ground black or white pepper, to taste
¼ tsp salt, or to taste
4 tbsp good red wine
1 tsp all-purpose flour
⅓ cup (90ml) Meat Broth (see page 72)
1 tbsp chopped fresh flat-leaf parsley

PREPARATION

1 If serving fried or grilled polenta crostini, make the polenta and let it set, as described on page 169. If serving loose polenta, prepare the chicken livers before making the polenta.
2 Wash the livers and trim any connective tissue, fat, or discolored areas. Separate any pairs, but leave each liver whole.
3 Clean and trim the mushrooms; do not wash them. Slice them and set aside.
4 Heat half the oil with the butter in a skillet. Add the shallots or scallions and cook gently until softened, 4–5 minutes. Add the mushrooms and sauté, tossing occasionally, until lightly golden, 1–2 minutes. Remove the shallots and mushrooms from the pan and set aside.
5 Warm the second tablespoon of olive oil in the pan and, when it is hot enough to make the livers sizzle, add them. Sear over medium heat until golden all over, about 3 minutes. Do not allow the livers to overcook.
6 Return the shallots and mushrooms to the pan and add the crushed peppercorns and salt.
7 Pour in the wine and allow it to evaporate, 2–3 minutes, turning the livers in the wine occasionally. Transfer the livers, shallots, and mushrooms to a plate and set aside while you finish the sauce.

8 Stir the flour into 2–3 tablespoons of broth to form a smooth paste. Add the paste to the juices in the pan with the remaining broth. Simmer over medium heat until the sauce thickens, about 4 minutes. Return the livers to the pan and stir in the parsley. Set aside until ready to serve (it will take 1–2 minutes to heat through).
9 Serve the sauce with loose polenta dotted with 2 tablespoons of unsalted butter or the grilled or fried polenta crostini.

KCal 590 P 33g C 58g S 1086mg SFA 8g UFA 14g (4)

POLENTA PASTICCIATA DI MIA NONNA

My grandmother's baked polenta

There are many versions of polenta pasticciata – polenta baked in a casserole with sauce and, usually, cheese. I am particularly fond of this one, inherited from my maternal Sardinian grandmother, Giulia Esu. Typically a northern dish, polenta was probably introduced to Sardinia in the 19th century by Piedmontese travelers. Serves 8.

INGREDIENTS

1 quantity Polenta crostini (see page 169)
Sauce
¼oz (5g) dried porcini mushrooms
2 tbsp olive oil
2 tbsp unsalted butter
1 small onion, chopped
1 carrot, chopped
1 celery rib, chopped
2 tbsp chopped fresh flat-leaf parsley
¾lb (375g) lean ground beef or a mixture of beef and pork
2 tbsp tomato paste
½ cup (125ml) red wine
2½ cups (625g) canned tomatoes in purée or juice, seeded and chopped but purée or juice retained
½ tsp salt, or more to taste
freshly ground black pepper, to taste
½lb (250g) semisoft pecorino, coarsely grated

PREPARATION

1 Make the polenta crostini as described on page 169, cutting the hardened polenta into 3in (7cm) squares (do nor fry or grill them).

2 To make the sauce, soak the dried mushrooms in 4 tablespoons of warm water for about 30 minutes, then drain, reserving the liquid. Rinse the mushrooms under cold water then coarsely chop.

3 Heat the oil and butter together, then add the onion, carrot, celery, and parsley. Sauté gently until softened, approximately 10 minutes.

4 Add the meat and cook over low heat until it is just colored but still slightly pink inside, 5 minutes. Do not overcook the meat or it will harden.

5 Stir in the mushrooms, tomato paste, mushroom liquid, and wine. Simmer for 3 minutes to evaporate the alcohol. Add the tomatoes and purée or juice, salt, and pepper. Simmer gently, partially covered, for 30 minutes, stirring occasionally.

6 Preheat the oven to 450°F (230°C).

7 Layer the polenta squares in the baking dish. Spoon a layer of sauce over the polenta. Scatter over a layer of cheese. Repeat the procedure, ending with a layer of cheese on top. You may have a little sauce left over that you can use in another dish.

8 Place the dish on the upper rack of the oven and bake for 15–20 minutes, or until the casserole is bubbling and the cheese is golden on top. Let rest for 10–15 minutes before serving.

KCal 405 P 23g C 32g S 1446mg SFA 9g UFA 6g (8)

VARIATION

If semsoft pecorino is unavailable, use Spanish Manchego cheese (a sheep's cheese), or caciocavallo.

FISH AND SEAFOOD

The one characteristic that marks Italian seafood is its astonishing flavor; the very essence of the sea seems to be found in every bite. In general, Italians prefer to cook fish whole as a great deal of flavor permeates the fish from the head, bones, and skin. Most seafood dishes are quite simple, except perhaps for the celebrated *zuppa di pesce*, "fish soup," which typically contains all manner of local fish from the daily catch. *Baccalà*, "salt cod," is in a category all its own, enjoying immense popularity from north to south.

ZUPPA DI PESCE ALLA GALLIPOLINA

Seafood "soup" in the style of Gallipoli

In Italy there are seemingly endless versions of zuppa di pesce. *The Tuscans, for example, make their famous* cacciucco; *in Venice, there is* brodetto; *in Genoa,* burrida. *Some are brothy soups; some are chowders thick with shellfish. All are poured over slices of sturdy bread rubbed with garlic and sprinkled with fruity olive oil. Gallipoli, an ancient seaport on the west coast of Apulia, is renowned for its fish soup, which the locals claim dates back to 1000 BC. The Gallipoli version is made largely of crustaceans cooked in their shells and locally caught fish, but this recipe, my own adaptation, is based on more readily available fish and shellfish. Serves 6.*

INGREDIENTS

1lb (500g) littleneck clams or cockles, well scrubbed
12 small mussels, debearded and scrubbed (see page 163)
1lb (500g) young, tender squid
½lb (250g) medium shrimp in their shells
⅔ cup (175ml) extra-virgin olive oil
1 large onion, chopped
3 large garlic cloves, 2 finely chopped and 1 halved
6 tbsp chopped fresh flat-leaf parsley
pinch of crushed red pepper flakes
½ cup (125ml) dry white wine
3 cups (750g) fresh or canned drained tomatoes, peeled, seeded, and chopped
3 tbsp tomato paste
1 tsp sea salt
1lb (500g) whole white-fleshed fish such as sea bream, whiting, snapper or hake, scaled, gutted, and cut into pieces, or ½lb (250g) fillets from any of the above or grouper, cod, or bass
12 slices, about ½in (1cm) thick, coarse peasant-style bread, to serve

PREPARATION

1 Place the clams and mussels in a bowl of water to soak (see page 163). Partially cover and refrigerate for several hours, or up to 2 days (if refrigerating longer than overnight, change the water). Drain and scrub them well.
2 Clean the squid (see opposite). Cut the body into ¼in (5mm) rings and cut the tentacles into halves or quarters, depending upon their size.
3 Slit the shrimp down the back through the shell to remove the dark intestinal vein. Rinse them in cold water, but leave the shells attached on the underside (they will add flavor to the broth).
4 Warm ¼ cup (60ml) of oil in a large deep skillet over medium heat. Add the onion and the chopped garlic and sauté until softened, about 4 minutes. Add all but 2 tablespoons of parsley and the crushed red pepper and sauté for another minute.
5 Stir in the wine and continue to cook until the alcohol evaporates, about 3 minutes. Add the tomatoes and tomato paste, the salt, and 2 cups (500ml) of water. Cover partially and continue to cook at a steady simmer until the sauce thickens, about 15 minutes, stirring occasionally.
6 Add the clams, mussels, and squid. Stir, cover, and cook for 3–4 minutes. Stir in the shrimp and fish, cover, and cook over medium heat for 6–7 minutes, removing the cover once or twice to turn the seafood so that it cooks evenly. Taste the broth for seasoning and add the remaining parsley to the pan. Remove the *zuppa* from the heat.
7 Meanwhile, use the remaining halved garlic clove to rub the slices of bread. Sauté the bread in the remaining olive oil, then drain it on paper towels. Place two slices of fried bread in each soup plate and ladle over hot broth. The seafood may be served on top or as a separate course.

KCal 705 P 43g C 57g S 1189mg SFA 5g UFA 25g (6)

CLEANING SQUID

  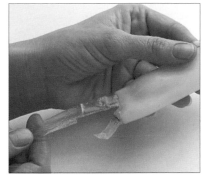

1 Separate the head and tentacles from the body by grasping the head below the eyes and pulling this top section away from the body cavity. Remove and discard the ink sac from the head.

2 Cut the head from the tentacles at the "waist" above the eyes. Remove the hard "beak" from the base of the tentacles. Under cold running water, peel off the speckled skin.

3 Remove the cellophane-like "spine" from the body and clean out any insides remaining in the cavity. Rinse well. Cut the body and tentacles as described, then rinse and dry the pieces.

FRITTO MISTO DI MARE
Mixed fish fry

This is a dish that appears on tourist menus all along the Italian coastline. An Italian fish fry is exquisite when made with the freshest seafood. In the simplest method, the seafood is dredged in flour and then deep-fried in olive oil. I prefer to use a pastella, "batter," and I add wine to the batter to produce a particularly crispy coating. Deep-fried foods absorb less oil than sautéed foods, if made properly. It is essential that the fish be absolutely fresh (frozen fish becomes waterlogged), and the seafood must be dried thoroughly after washing to allow the batter to adhere. It may seem extravagant to use olive oil for deep-frying, but its fruity flavor is irreplaceable. Serves 4–6.

INGREDIENTS

3lb (1.5kg) fresh mixed seafood, including large shrimp, small squid, and fish fillets such as hake, whiting, snapper, grouper, sole, flounder, haddock, or cod
1 tbsp coarse sea salt
olive oil for deep-frying
fine sea salt and 2 lemons, cut into wedges, to serve
Batter
¾ cup (100g) all-purpose flour
½ tsp finely ground sea salt
3 tbsp dry white wine
½ cup (125ml) water
1½ tbsp olive oil
1 egg, separated

PREPARATION

1 Peel and devein the shrimp (see page 163). Clean the squid (see page 99). Cut the body into ¼in (5mm) rings and chop the tentacles in half.
2 To make the batter, sift together the flour and salt in a bowl. Mix the wine and water and then add it to the flour, combining it thoroughly. Stir in the oil, then the egg yolk. Cover the bowl and let stand at room temperature for 2 hours.
3 Meanwhile, cover the seafood with cold water and add the tablespoon of coarse sea salt. Cover and chill for approximately 1 hour. Drain, then dry thoroughly with paper towels or clean dish towels.
4 Beat the egg white until it stands up in peaks, then fold it into the batter.
5 Pour enough olive oil into a deep-fryer or deep skillet to reach 2in (5cm) up the sides of the pan. Heat to 375°F (190°C), or until a drop of batter sputters when dropped into the oil – it must be hot enough to produce a crispy coating. It is advisable to use a splatter shield over the pot because the squid tentacles cause the hot oil to spit.
6 When you are ready to fry, drop the first batch of seafood into the batter, saving the squid for the last batch. Turn it so that it is evenly coated. Carefully slip the first batch into the oil – do not crowd the pan as this causes the oil temperature to drop, making the fish absorb too much oil.
7 Fry the seafood until golden on all sides, about 4 minutes. Remove it with a slotted spoon and drain on paper towels. Repeat with the remaining seafood. Serve immediately with finely ground sea salt and lemon wedges. (The olive oil can be filtered after frying and reused.)

KCal 750 P 64g C 20g S 1166mg SFA 6g UFA 35g (4)

SCAMPI ALLA GRIGLIA CON SALVIA
Grilled shrimp with sage

Scampi, or gamberoni, are large, succulent shrimp that make a terrific antipasto or main course when cooked on an open fire. Serves 2.

INGREDIENTS

1lb (500g) large shrimp, peeled
2 tsp finely ground sea salt, plus salt to serve
½ cup (125ml) extra-virgin olive oil
3 large garlic cloves, finely chopped
2 tsp finely chopped fresh sage, or
¾ tsp dried crumbled sage
freshly ground white or black pepper, to taste

PREPARATION

1 Peel and devein the shrimp (see page 163), but do not cut so deeply as to butterfly them. Rinse them well under cold running water.
2 Place the shrimp in a bowl of ice water. Add 2 tablespoons of sea salt and let stand for 15 minutes to bring out some of the shrimp's briny flavor. Drain, then dry with paper towels.
3 In a bowl, combine the shrimp with the oil, garlic, and sage. Cover and let marinate in the refrigerator for up to 3 hours.
4 Meanwhile, prepare a charcoal grill or preheat an indoor grill. Position the rack close to the heat source so that it heats through.
5 Thread the shrimp securely onto metal skewers and brush with the marinade.
6 Transfer the skewers to the grill, and cook about 2in (5cm) from the heat source for 1½ minutes on the first side and 1 minute on the second, brushing them with any remaining marinade. The outside of each shrimp should be crispy and charred, the inside moist and tender. Sprinkle to taste with sea salt and pepper, and serve immediately.

KCal 660 P 22g C neg S 1792mg SFA 10g UFA 52g (2)

SCAMPI AL FORNO

Baked shrimp with garlic and parsley

This way of cooking shrimp is so obvious that I almost left it out. But it occurred to me that as there are various methods for cooking this classic dish, I should include the recipe here. In this method, the shrimp are baked rather than cooked on top of the stove. Serve with plenty of crusty bread to mop up the deliciously garlicky juices. Serves 2. Illustrated on page 105.

INGREDIENTS

1lb (500g) large shrimp
1 tsp sea salt
½ cup (125ml) extra-virgin olive oil
4 large garlic cloves, finely chopped
pinch of crushed red pepper flakes, or 1–2 whole
dried small hot red peppers (peperoncini)
2 tbsp chopped fresh flat-leaf parsley
4 tbsp (60ml) freshly squeezed lemon juice

PREPARATION

1 Preheat the oven to 400°F (200°C).
2 Peel, devein, and butterfly the shrimp
(see page 163). Soak in ice salt water and allow to stand for 15 minutes to bring out their briny flavor (removing their shells robs the shrimp of some of their natural flavor). Drain, then dry the shrimp thoroughly with paper towels.
3 In a baking dish, combine the olive oil, garlic, pepper flakes, half the parsley, half the lemon juice, and the shrimp.
4 Slide the dish onto the middle rack of the oven and bake until the shrimp turn pink, about 10 minutes. Remove from the oven immediately.
5 Sprinkle with the remaining parsley and lemon juice, and serve immediately.

KCal 670 P 22g C 2g S 1020mg SFA 8g UFA 52g (2)

VARIATION

To make a delightfully crispy coating for the shrimp, toss 2 tablespoons of toasted fresh bread crumbs with the shrimp just before baking.

CALAMARI IN ZIMINO ALLA LIVORNESE

Stewed squid with spinach, Leghorn style

Throughout Italy, squid is commonly paired with tomatoes when it is stewed, and it is very good indeed done in this style, but I like this uniquely Tuscan way of cooking squid with Swiss chard or spinach. Serves 4–6.

INGREDIENTS

1½lb (750g) Swiss chard, trimmed, or
1lb (500g) fresh spinach, stems removed
1½lb (750g) squid
3 tbsp extra-virgin olive oil
1 large garlic clove, chopped
1 small onion, chopped
1 small carrot, chopped
1 small celery rib with leaves, chopped
2 tbsp chopped fresh flat-leaf parsley
⅓ cup (90ml) dry white wine
½ tsp salt
1 tbsp tomato paste
2 tsp chopped fresh rosemary, or ½ tsp dried
pinch of crushed red pepper flakes

PREPARATION

1 Place the washed Swiss chard or spinach in a pan with drops of water still clinging to the leaves. Cover and cook over medium heat until the leaves wilt and become tender, about 3 minutes. Remove from the heat and let cool. Squeeze out as much water as you can. Chop the leaves and set aside.
2 Clean the squid (see page 99). Cut the body into rings ¼in (5mm) wide and cut the tentacles into halves or quarters, depending upon their size. Rinse and dry the squid pieces thoroughly.
3 Pour the oil into a large skillet and warm over medium heat. Add the garlic, onion, carrot, celery, and parsley. Sauté until the vegetables soften, about 7 minutes, stirring occasionally.
4 Add the squid pieces and immediately raise the heat to high. Sauté for 5 minutes, making sure the flesh is seared evenly.
5 Add the wine and continue to sauté, still over high heat, until the alcohol is evaporated, about 3 minutes. Reduce the heat to medium and then stir in the salt, tomato paste, 2 tablespoons of water, and the rosemary.
6 Partially cover the pan and simmer for an additional 20 minutes, stirring occasionally to cook evenly. Add the wilted Swiss chard or spinach and the pepper flakes. Cook until the greens are warmed through, about 5 minutes more, then check for salt and pepper. Serve immediately.

KCal 300 P 29g C 10g S 960mg SFA 2g UFA 10g (4)

Sogliole al Cartoccio

Sole in parchment

Cooking in parchment is an ancient practice, but the simplicity of the method is well suited to the needs of the modern cook. Parchment or foil, used dull side out, are suitable. All the flavors and moisture are sealed in, making this method ideal for delicate foods. Keeping the fish whole allows the most savory parts to flavor the flesh, but fillets can be cooked this way (see variation). It is best to use fresh herbs; their aroma penetrates the delicate flesh without overpowering it. If rosemary and sage are not available, use parsley, basil, or fennel fronds. Serve with Salsetta Rossa alla Ligure (see page 138), or simply with slices of lemon.

INGREDIENTS

*4 whole sole or other white-fleshed fish such as flounder,
red snapper, pompano, or sea bream,
about ¾lb (375g) each, gutted and scaled
extra-virgin olive oil
fine sea salt and freshly ground white pepper
4 garlic cloves, thinly sliced
4 sprigs fresh rosemary
4 leaves fresh sage
1 quantity Salsa Rossa alla Ligure (see page 138)*

PREPARATION

1 Preheat the oven to 425°F (220°C).
2 Wash the fish well inside and out, then pat dry inside and out with paper towels.
3 Cut four pieces of parchment paper or foil, each large enough to wrap the fish completely.
4 Rub the inside and the exterior of the fish with oil and sprinkle with salt and pepper. Stuff the cavity of each fish with the garlic and herbs.
5 Place each fish in the center of the parchment or foil, folding the edges in to seal well (use paper clips to secure the parchment). Place the packets in a baking dish and cook for 20 minutes.
6 If using parchment, each person can be served a fish packet at the table. If using foil, open the packet and transfer the fish to a serving dish, or to individual plates. Pass the sauce at the table.

KCal 500 P 50g C 6g S 1382mg SFA 3g UFA 18g (4)

VARIATION

Replace the whole fish with four fillets, each about 10oz (300g). Preheat the oven to 400°F (200°C). Cut four pieces of parchment or foil. Finely slice one onion and divide it among the packets. Drizzle the fillets with the oil then season. Scatter the herbs and garlic over the fish. Seal and cook as above.

PAGRO ALLA GRIGLIA
Grilled porgy with garlic

Porgies are in the sea bream family. They are often not thought of as good eating fish, but they should be as they are very tasty in comparison to other white-fleshed fish.

INGREDIENTS

*8 whole porgies, each about ½lb (250g), scaled and gutted
fine sea salt and freshly ground pepper, to taste
6 garlic cloves, thinly sliced lengthwise
4 sprigs fresh rosemary
½ cup (60g) flour for dredging
olive oil, to baste
2 fresh lemons, cut into wedges, to serve*

PREPARATION

1 Preheat the broiler and oil the broiler pan.
2 Rinse the porgies and dry thoroughly with paper towels. Sprinkle the insides of the fish with salt and pepper. Make two slits on each side of the fish and insert a sliver of garlic in each. Stuff the remaining garlic slices and the rosemary into the cavities.
3 Dredge the fish in flour and sprinkle both sides with plenty of oil. Place them side by side on the preheated broiler pan. There should be some space around each of them.
4 Place the pan 6–7in (15–18cm) from the broiler flame and leave until the fish is cooked thoroughly and golden brown on the surface, about 4 minutes. Turn the fish, sprinkle with a little more oil, and broil for an additional 3 minutes.
5 Serve immediately with lemon wedges.

KCal 480 P 46g C 14g S 667mg SFA 5g UFA 25g (4)

SOGLIOLE ALL'ABRUZZESE
Sole with garlic, lemon, and olives, Abruzzi style

Small Adriatic sole are cooked this way in the Abruzzian province of Teramo. Flounder may be used, but they need longer cooking. Illustrated on page 104. Serves 2.

INGREDIENTS

*2 whole sole, ¾lb–1lb (375–500g) each, scaled and gutted, or 4 fillets, each about ¼lb (125g)
approximately ⅓ cup (45g) flour for dredging
3–4 tbsp extra-virgin olive oil (only 3 tbsp for fillets)
2 large garlic cloves, bruised
2 tbsp freshly squeezed lemon juice
10 sharply flavored black olives, pitted and chopped
small pinch crushed red pepper flakes
¼ tsp salt, or to taste
2 tbsp chopped fresh flat-leaf parsley*

PREPARATION

1 Rinse the fish, then dry them on paper towels.
2 Spread the flour on a plate. Warm the oil and garlic in a large nonstick skillet. Sauté gently until the garlic is golden, then discard it.
3 Dust the fish with flour, then raise the heat and slip them into the hot oil. Sauté until golden, about 4 minutes on each side for whole fish and 1 minute on each side for fillets, according to thickness. Transfer to a warm plate and reduce the heat.
4 Stir the lemon juice and 2 tablespoons of water into the pan. When the liquid begins to bubble, add the olives, pepper flakes, salt, and parsley. Heat through briefly, then pour over the fish and serve.

KCal 560 P 48g C 24g S 1014mg SFA 4g UFA 20g (2)

TONNO ALLA STEMPERATA
Tuna with onion, olives, and capers, Sicilian style

This popular way of cooking tuna and swordfish produces a pleasantly tart sauce. The fillets shouldn't be too thick as tuna tends to become dry if cooked too long.

INGREDIENTS

*4 x ½in (1cm) thick tuna fillets, each about 5oz (150g), skinned and trimmed
3 tbsp flour, for dusting
5 tbsp (75ml) extra-virgin olive oil
1 large onion, finely sliced then roughly chopped
4 tbsp white wine vinegar
pinch of salt
½ cup (90g) pitted and sliced black olives
3 tbsp small capers, drained
freshly ground black pepper, to taste*

PREPARATION

1 Rinse the fillets, then dry them on paper towels.
2 Spread the flour on a plate. Warm the oil in a large, preferably nonstick skillet.
3 Dust the fillets in flour, then slip them into the hot oil all at once. Brown them lightly on each side for 45 seconds–1 minute, then turn them quickly and brown on the other side for no more than 45 seconds. Transfer them to a warm plate.
4 Add the onion to the skillet, reduce the heat slightly, and cook until soft and lightly colored, about 6 minutes. Stir in the vinegar, salt, olives, and capers, then pour in ⅓ cup (90ml) of water. Cook, stirring occasionally, for about 2 minutes.
5 Return the tuna steaks to the pan, placing them on top of the onion. Cover and cook for another 45 seconds. Serve with plenty of pepper.

KCal 455 P 38g C 13g S 971mg SFA 5g UFA 21g (4)

BACCALÀ AL FORNO
Baked salt cod with
potatoes and tomatoes
(page 109)

SOGLIOLE ALL'ABRUZZESE
Sòle with garlic, lemon, and
olives, Abruzzi style
(page 103)

SCAMPI AL FORNO
Baked shrimp with
garlic and parsley
(page 101)

PESCE SPADA AL SALMORIGLIO
Swordfish with lemon sauce

In Sicily and Calabria, swordfish is typically grilled on the open fire and served with lemon sauce, which purists say should contain a splash of sea water. The quality of the oil used is very important, because it and the lemon juice are the dominating flavors. Fresh tuna can be substituted for swordfish with equally good results. It is delicious served with Patate Fritte, as here.

INGREDIENTS

*2lb (1kg) swordfish or tuna steaks,
about 1in (2.5cm) thick, skinned
freshly ground black pepper, to taste*
Marinade
*4 tbsp olive oil
⅓ cup (90ml) dry white wine
2 large garlic cloves, cut lengthwise into thin slivers
1 onion, halved and thinly sliced
1 bay leaf*
Salmoriglio sauce
*2 tbsp freshly squeezed lemon juice
¼ cup (60ml) extra-virgin olive oil
1 small garlic clove, finely chopped
¼ tsp chopped fresh oregano, or a pinch of dried
1 tsp chopped fresh flat-leaf parsley
pinch of sea salt*

PREPARATION

1 Prepare a charcoal grill or preheat an indoor grill. If broiling, line a broiler pan with foil and preheat the broiler and the pan.

2 Combine the ingredients for the marinade. Place the fish in the marinade. Cover and chill for 30 minutes–1 hour, turning the pieces once.

3 To make the sauce, put the lemon juice in a bowl. Add the oil in a slow, steady stream, using a whisk or electric beater to emulsify it thoroughly. Add the garlic, continuing to beat, then stir in the oregano, parsley, and salt.

4 Remove the fish from the marinade, reserving the liquid. If making kebabs, cut the fish into chunks and thread onto skewers, leaving space between each piece. Alternatively, cut the steaks in half.

5 Brush the fish with marinade. Place the kebabs or pieces on the broiler pan or oiled barbecue rack and position 2in (5cm) away from the heat; leave the door open if using an electric oven. Grill until the fish colors, about 2 minutes. Turn and baste with marinade, then cook for 2 minutes longer.

6 Transfer the fish to a serving dish. Sprinkle with pepper, drizzle with the lemon sauce, and serve immediately with Patate Fritte (see page 127).

KCal 565 P 45g C 1g S 521mg SFA 7g UFA 31g (4: excl. fried potatoes)

Garlic

Dry white wine

Olive oil

Swordfish

Bay leaf

Lemon juice

Oregano

Flat-leaf parsley

Sea salt

Black pepper

Onion

MERLUZZO ALLE ERBE
Poached hake fillets with fresh herbs

Here is a light, simple way to cook fish fillets. They are best served at room temperature and can be cooked up to 2 hours in advance of serving. Our family often cooked hake or cod this way, but any white-fleshed fish fillets can be used. Cooking time should be somewhat less for very delicate fish fillets such as flounder or sole. Serves 2–3.

INGREDIENTS
*1 bay leaf
1 small scallion, including green tops, trimmed, sliced lengthwise and cut into three pieces
2 sprigs fresh flat-leaf parsley
½ tsp sea salt
1½lb (750g) hake or cod fillets*
Topping
*1 small scallion, including 2in (5cm) of green top, trimmed and very thinly sliced
1½ tbsp chopped fresh flat-leaf parsley
2 tsp chopped fresh thyme, or ½ tsp dried
roughly grated zest of ½ lemon
juice of 1 large lemon
4 tbsp extra-virgin olive oil
freshly ground white or black pepper, to taste*

PREPARATION
1 Pour 4 cups (1 liter) of cold water into a large skillet wide enough to accommodate the fillets without crowding. Add the bay leaf, scallion, and parsley sprigs. Bring to a boil and add the salt.
2 Slip the fillets into the skillet, cover completely, and lower the heat to medium so that the water boils gently. Cook for 5–7 minutes, depending on the thickness of the fillets. Use a wide spatula to transfer the fillets, one by one, to a serving plate without breaking them. Reserve 1 tablespoon of the cooking water.
3 In a small bowl, combine the topping ingredients and stir in the reserved tablespoon of cooking water. Spoon the topping over the fish, cover, and allow to come to room temperature before serving.

KCal 375 P 44g C 1g S 455mg SFA 3g UFA 17g (3)

TAIEDDA
Baked fish fillets with vegetables, potatoes, and white wine

Taiedda, also called tiella, *is an Apulian dish with a Spanish history. Its name is thought to have derived from the Spanish* paella *and, in common with* paella, *it is a one-pot dish. But the similarities stop there. Taiedda is a layered baked dish composed largely of vegetables (sometimes vegetables alone), with fish, shellfish, or salt cod often added. Purists insist that the true version must include potatoes (of which the locals are inordinately fond) and grated cheese, but it is often made with rice instead. Like most Italian food, the dish has peasant roots. It was prepared before the family left for their day's work in the fields and left to cook slowly in the ashes of the hearth until they were reunited for dinner. Serves 6.*

INGREDIENTS
*1½lb (750g) potatoes, cooked, peeled and thinly sliced
1 onion, quartered and very thinly sliced
2 large carrots, finely shredded or grated
2lb (1kg) white fish fillets such as flounder, sole, or haddock
½ tsp salt
freshly ground white pepper, to taste
3 tbsp unsalted butter, melted, plus butter to grease
½ cup (125ml) dry white wine
2 tbsp bread crumbs*

PREPARATION
1 Preheat the oven to 375°F (190°C).
2 Grease a baking dish approximately 9 x 12in (23 x 30cm). Place half of the potatoes in the dish; then follow with half the onion, half the carrot, and half the fish. Sprinkle with half of the salt and dust lightly with pepper. Drizzle over half of the butter.
3 Make a second layer with the remaining potatoes, onion, carrots, fish, and salt. Sprinkle lightly with additional pepper. Pour the wine over the top; when it has seeped through to the bottom of the dish, sprinkle the top with the crumbs and drizzle over the remaining butter.
4 Cover the dish with foil and bake it in the center of the oven for 20–30 minutes (cooking time will be affected by the size of the dish), or until the fish is tender but not overcooked. Remove the foil during the last 5 minutes of baking.
5 If the dish contains an excessive amount of pan juices, pour them into a small saucepan. Simmer over medium heat for 5–10 minutes, until reduced, and then pour the juices over the dish just before serving. Serve hot.

KCal 295 P 31g C 24g S 373mg SFA 4g UFA 2g (6)

BACCALÀ STUFATO CON OLIVE E PATATE

Salt cod stewed with olives and potatoes

Baccalà, "salt cod," has been prominent in the cuisines
of Mediterranean seafaring peoples since ancient times,
when dried foodstuffs were important staples. The
Italians are especially fond of it, and use it in many
imaginative ways. Once rehydrated and cooked, salt cod is
enormously versatile, and is used in salads, croquettes
and fritters, soups, and stews. See page 163 for advice on
choosing and preparing salt cod. Serves 6.

INGREDIENTS

1½lb (750g) baccalà (salt cod),
preferably skinned and boned
3 tbsp olive oil
1 onion, chopped
2 garlic cloves, finely chopped
2 tbsp chopped fresh flat-leaf parsley
12 sharply flavored green olives
1 tbsp small capers, drained
1 tbsp freshly squeezed lemon juice
4 boiling potatoes, peeled and halved
freshly ground black or white pepper, to taste

PREPARATION

1 To rehydrate the salt cod, soak it in cold water
(see page 163), keeping it covered in the
refrigerator. Drain and rinse in fresh water, remove
any skin and bones that remain, and cut the flesh
into 2in (5cm) chunks.
2 Place the oil, onion, and garlic in a large skillet
and sauté until softened but not browned. Stir in
the parsley, keeping the pan over low heat. Add
the salt cod and gently sauté on both sides for
about 5 minutes.
3 Add the olives and capers, ¾ cup (175ml) of
water, and the lemon juice. Cover and leave to
simmer until tender, about 18–20 minutes.
4 Meanwhile, cut the potatoes into ¼in (5mm)
slices. Place them in a pan and cover with cold
water. Boil until half-cooked, about 10 minutes,
then drain. Add them to the skillet 15 minutes
before the salt cod has finished cooking. Cover
and cook gently. Serve hot.

KCal 340 P 36g C 28g S 1238mg SFA 2g UFA 7g (6)

VARIATION

For a tomato version, replace the lemon juice with
1 tablespoon of wine vinegar blended with
2 tablespoons of tomato paste and increase the
amount of water to 1 cup (250ml).

BACCALÀ AL FORNO

Baked salt cod with potatoes and tomatoes

Anna Amendolara Nurse, a well-known teacher of
Italian cooking, gave me this recipe for her favorite
baccalà dish. Illustrated on page 104.

INGREDIENTS

1½lb (750g) baccalà (salt cod),
preferably skinned and boned
2½ cups (625g) fresh or canned drained tomatoes,
peeled, seeded, and coarsely chopped
4 boiling potatoes, peeled and cut into sixths lengthwise
1 large onion, cut into sixths lengthwise
2 garlic cloves, halved
½ cup (90g) oil-packed black olives, drained
½ cup (30g) chopped fresh flat-leaf parsley
salt and freshly ground black pepper, to taste
¾ cup (60g) dry bread crumbs
½ cup (125ml) extra-virgin olive oil

PREPARATION

1 To rehydrate the salt cod, soak it in cold water
(see page 163), keeping it covered in the
refrigerator. Drain and rinse in fresh water, remove
any skin and bones that remain, and cut the flesh
into 2in (5cm) chunks.
2 Preheat the oven to 375°F (190°C).
3 Place half of the tomatoes in a 10 x 14in (25 x
35cm) baking dish. Place the salt cod, potatoes, and
onion in a single layer over the tomatoes. Arrange
the remaining tomatoes, garlic, and olives on top.
4 Sprinkle over the parsley, salt, and pepper, then
cover with bread crumbs. Drizzle the top with the
oil, distributing it evenly over the dish. Pour over
1 cup (250ml) of water, being careful not to
disturb the bread crumbs.
5 Bake the dish in the preheated oven until the
potatoes are tender and the bread crumbs are
golden brown, about 1½ hours.

KCal 770 P 56g C 55g S 2536mg SFA 5g UFA 29g (4)

MEAT DISHES

The meat course is not the focus of an Italian meal. Having been preceded by the substantial *primo*, meat usually follows in relatively small portions. The flavor of Italian meat is excellent because farmed animals are still raised naturally. Italians are also inordinately fond of game of any kind. Cooking methods are often simple. Wood-fired grills are used outdoors and in restaurants, while pot-roasting and boiling are the most common techniques in the home, producing succulent dishes with rich, concentrated sauces.

MANZO LESSO CON SALSE VARIE

Boiled beef with various sauces

Meat cooked in water has exceptional sweetness, for it remains juicy and succulent as it bathes in its own luscious broth. This is a splendid dish if the selected cut is well marbled and carves easily. Compatible sauces include Salsetta Rossa Cruda, Salsa Verde, in any of its variations, (see page 139), and Maionese Verde (see page 140).

INGREDIENTS

3lb (1.5kg) beef rump roast, brisket, or tied chuck roast
1 carrot, scraped and quartered
1 celery rib with leaves, halved
1 onion, unpeeled and quartered
1 small tomato, peeled, seeded, and quartered
handful of parsley sprigs
1 bay leaf
2 tbsp salt, or to taste
½ tsp whole black or white peppercorns
Salsa Verde and/or Salsetta Rossa Cruda (see page 139)
or Maionese Verde (see page 140), to serve

PREPARATION

1 Place the beef, vegetables, herbs, salt, and peppercorns in a large pot, with 2in (5cm) of water to cover, and bring to a boil. Lower the heat and simmer gently, partially covered, for 3½ hours, turning the meat halfway through cooking. If necessary, add more water to keep the meat covered and skim off any foam as it forms.
2 Check the broth for salt. Transfer the meat to a cutting board. Strain the broth and set it aside, then slice the meat thin. Arrange it on a platter, spooning over a little broth. Serve with the chosen sauces, reserving the remaining broth for use as a soup.

KCal 695 P 74g C 5g S 954mg SFA 15g UFA 23g (4: excluding sauces)

POLPETTONE FARCITO

Meat loaf stuffed with ham and frittatine

Do not confuse this lovely, moist meat loaf with the spongy, gray, gravy-covered "square meal" variety. The Italian version is made with several kinds of meat, giving it a complex, delicate flavor. There is often an omelette or hard-boiled eggs in the middle, which looks very pretty when the loaf is sliced. In this recipe, ham and frittatine, "omelettes," speckled with parsley, are rolled into the middle of the loaf, producing a pink, yellow, and green helix in the center of every slice. It may be served hot or cold, with the fortified pan juices or Salsetta Rossa Cruda. Serves 10–15. Illustrated on page 121.

INGREDIENTS

Polpettone mixture
4oz (125g) stale white bread, crusts removed
½ large beef bouillon cube, or 1 small one, dissolved in 1½ cups (350ml) hot water
3lb (1.5kg) mixed lean ground beef and pork, or 3lb (1.5kg) lean ground beef
1 onion, grated
⅓ cup (90g) sun-dried tomatoes, chopped
1½ tsp salt
¾ tsp freshly ground black pepper
2 eggs, beaten
1 tsp chopped fresh marjoram, or ½ tsp dried
2 tbsp freshly grated Parmesan
1 tbsp lightly toasted bread crumbs
4 tbsp red wine, for basting the meat loaf
Filling
1 egg
2 tsp chopped fresh flat-leaf parsley
pinch of salt
freshly ground black pepper, to taste
½ tsp butter or olive oil
4 slices boiled ham

PREPARATION

1 Preheat the oven to 350°F (180°C).
2 Soak the bread in the stock, then squeeze it dry, reserving the liquid. Shred the dampened bread and combine it with the remaining polpettone ingredients, except for the toasted bread crumbs and wine. Use your hands to mix it well.
3 Make the frittatine. Beat the egg with the parsley, salt, and pepper. Heat the butter or oil in a 9in (23cm) omelet pan. Add half of the egg mixture, tilting the pan so that it spreads evenly. When the egg is set, about 30 seconds, turn it and allow it to set on the reverse side, about 15 seconds. Set aside and make the second omelet. Let cool.
4 Meanwhile, scatter the bread crumbs on a dry work surface. Spread the meat mixture over the crumbs, using your hands to form a 12 x 18in (30 x 45cm) rectangle about ½in (1cm) thick.
5 Cover the rectangle with ham slices, then with the frittatine, laying them side by side to cover the whole surface of the meat mixture. Working from the long edge, roll the polpettone into a long, narrow, sausagelike loaf (see page 164).
6 Place the loaf in an ungreased baking dish and pour half of the reserved stock into the dish. Bake in the center of the oven for 15 minutes, then add the remaining stock. Cook for 20 minutes longer, basting from time to time with the pan juices. Add a tablespoon or two of water if necessary – there should be sufficient juice for basting and for serving.
7 Add the wine to the dish and return the meat loaf to the oven for 15 minutes. Allow it to settle for 15 minutes before slicing. Serve with the pan juices or Salsetta Rossa Cruda (see page 139).

KCal 225 P 25g C 6g S 505mg SFA 4g UFA 7g (15)

BISTECCA ALLA FIORENTINA

Chargrilled steak in the style of Florence

This is one of the best meat dishes Italy has to offer. Ideally, the steak should be chargrilled over the white embers of a hardwood (oak or olive) fire, which produces little smoke. If this is impractical, cook it over coals.

INGREDIENTS

*4 x 8oz (250g) beef rib steaks on the bone, cut 1½–2in (3.5–5cm) thick, excess fat trimmed
sea salt and freshly ground black pepper, to taste
highest quality cold pressed extra-virgin olive oil
4–8 rosemary sprigs, optional*

PREPARATION

1 Prepare a barbecue using dry hardwood such as oak, if possible, or charcoal; do not use chemical starter fuels. When the embers or coals are white and glowing, position a grill rack approximately 2in (5cm) above them and allow it to preheat.
2 Place the steaks on the sizzling-hot grill rack. Cook them until they are well charred on one side, 2–3 minutes for medium to medium-rare. Turn the steaks and cook them on the reverse side for 2–3 minutes. Transfer them to warm plates.
3 Sprinkle each steak with salt and pepper and drizzle with a little olive oil. Garnish with the rosemary and serve immediately.

KCal 595 P 30g C 0g S 480mg SFA 21g UFA 29g (4)

SCHMORBRATEN

Sour pan-roasted beef in the style of Alto Adige

I have always been fond of beef cooked this way. We never had a name for it when I was growing up, but years later, when my travels took me to the Tyrol, I realized that it was actually Schmorbraten, a signature dish of Alto Adige. The cooking traditions of that region are more Austrian than Italian, as this dish demonstrates. It is best made 2 or 3 days in advance. Serves 6.

INGREDIENTS

*1 piece of bottom round beef, about 3lb (1.5kg)
3 large carrots, cut diagonally into ½in (1cm) slices
2 large onions, halved and thinly sliced
3 tbsp olive oil
¾ cup (175ml) full-bodied dry red wine or beer
1 tsp salt*
Marinade
*1 cup (250ml) red wine vinegar
2½ cups (600ml) water
4 bay leaves*

PREPARATION

1 Combine the meat, vegetables, and marinade in a large bowl. Place a plate over the meat, and on top of this put a weight of at least 4lb (2kg). Refrigerate for 48 hours, turning the meat occasionally.
2 Discard the marinade. Pat dry the meat and rinse the vegetables under cold water.
3 Heat the oil in a heavy-bottomed pot. Add the meat and sauté on all sides for 10 minutes to seal in the juices (the meat will not actually brown).
4 Add the wine or beer and allow it to evaporate. Stir in the vegetables, 1 cup (250ml) of water, and the salt. Cover partially and cook over medium-low heat until tender, about 2 hours, stirring the vegetables and turning the meat occasionally.
5 Cut the meat into very thin slices and serve hot with the vegetables.

KCal 800 P 43g C 8g S 398mg SFA 25g UFA 36g (6)

PEPERONATA CON CARNE DI MAIALE

Pork and peppers in the style of Basilicata

Here is a good, simple dish that can be served with Purè di Patate (see page 129), or tossed with short pasta – 1lb (500g) pasta is sufficient for this amount.

INGREDIENTS

3lb (1.5kg) pork tenderloin or pork cutlets from the leg, cut into ¼in (5mm) thick slices and trimmed of fat
½ cup (125ml) corn oil
2 onions, halved and very thinly sliced
2 large garlic cloves, finely chopped
2 tbsp red wine vinegar
2 tbsp chopped fresh rosemary, or 1 tsp dried
1 tsp salt
large pinch of freshly ground black pepper
2 red and 2 yellow peppers, cored, seeded, and cut into 1in (2.5cm) squares

PREPARATION

1 Cut the pork into strips approximately ½in (1cm) wide and 2in (5cm) long.
2 Warm half the oil in a deep skillet and add the onion and garlic. Sauté gently until the onion is translucent, about 4 minutes. Add the pork and increase the heat to high. Sauté quickly until excess liquid evaporates from the meat, about 5 minutes.
3 Reduce the heat to medium and add the vinegar. Sauté until the vinegar evaporates, about 2 minutes. Add the rosemary and 1 cup (250ml) of water.
4 Cover the pan and simmer until the meat is tender, stirring occasionally and adding more water, if necessary, to prevent the meat from drying out. Tenderloin and high-quality leg cutlets will cook in 15–20 minutes. Tougher meat will require lengthier cooking – up to 45 minutes. Add salt and pepper.
5 Meanwhile, heat the remaining oil in a separate skillet. Add the peppers and cook, partially covered, until tender, about 15 minutes.
6 Transfer the peppers to the pan with the pork, toss well, and serve immediately.

KCal 810 P 65g C 18g S 628mg SFA 12g UFA 38g (4)

ARISTA FIORENTINA CON PATATE

Florentine loin of pork with pan-roasted potatoes

In Tuscany, roast pork is part of the landscape. It is a common sight to see street stalls selling luscious porchetta, spit-roasted suckling pig sliced and sandwiched between two thick slices of bread. Arista, a tender cut from the loin end, is another specialty. In and around Florence, the flavorings are invariably rosemary and garlic; in Umbria, fennel is used. Buy only the tender center loin, and ask the butcher to give you the bones. The traditional accompaniment is boiled cannellini beans dressed with olive oil, but roasted potatoes are also good. Serves 6.

INGREDIENTS

1 boneless center loin-end pork roast, about 4lb (2kg), or 1 unboned center cut loin roast, about 6lb (3kg)
6 large garlic cloves, cut into slivers
8 rosemary sprigs
20–25 small potatoes, peeled and parboiled for 5 minutes, optional
sea salt, to taste
Rub
2 tbsp extra-virgin olive oil
coarsely ground black pepper, to taste
2 tbsp finely chopped fresh rosemary, or 3 tsp crushed dried rosemary

PREPARATION

1 Bring the meat to room temperature. Combine the rub ingredients and use to massage the meat. Make ⅓in (1cm) deep incisions all over the roast with a small sharp knife. Slip the garlic slivers into the cuts. If desired, the pork can now be covered, refrigerated, and left to marinate overnight.
2 Preheat the oven to 350°F (180°C).
3 Set the roast fat side up on a rack in a large roasting pan, arranging the detached bones underneath. Slip the rosemary sprigs in between the bones. Roast the pork for about 30 minutes, then baste it with the pan juices.
4 Continue to cook the pork for 25 minutes, then, if using potatoes, place them around the roast and cook for 45 minutes longer, or until the meat's internal temperature reads 150°F (65°C). Baste every 20 minutes or so. Turn the potatoes halfway through cooking.
5 Remove the pan from the oven and sprinkle the roast and the potatoes with salt, then cover with foil. Let the roast rest for 15 minutes – the meat will continue to cook as it rests.
6 Skim the fat from the pan juices and serve them hot with the meat.

KCal 1045 P 58g C 23g S 465mg SFA 28g UFA 46g (6)

AGNELLO ALLA SARDA

Roast leg of lamb, my mother's way

Nothing reminds me more of my childhood, and of Sardinian cuisine, than lamb roasted over the embers of a hardwood fire. The method is simple and the results are utterly delicious. An indoor wood-burning oven is not a feature of the average modern kitchen, but an outdoor barbecue can be substituted. It is essential to start the fire with kindling rather than chemical starter fuels, which affect the flavor and aroma of the meat. Serves 8.

INGREDIENTS

1 leg of lamb, about 6lb (3kg), trimmed
Rub
3 large garlic cloves, finely chopped
2 tsp finely chopped fresh rosemary, or ½ tsp crushed dried rosemary
⅓ cup (20g) chopped fresh flat-leaf parsley
⅓ cup (90ml) extra-virgin olive oil
½ tsp coarse freshly ground black pepper
sea salt, to taste

PREPARATION

1 Bring the lamb to room temperature. Combine the ingredients for the rub. With a small sharp knife, make shallow, evenly spaced incisions on all sides of the leg, then work in the rub mixture (see page 164). Transfer the lamb to a roasting pan and let it stand at room temperature for 2 hours.
2 Preheat the oven to 400°F (200°C) or prepare a barbecue, using dry hardwood such as oak, if possible, or charcoal.
3 If using a barbecue, check that the embers or coals are white and glowing. Arrange most of the fuel around the edges of the grill to produce indirect heat, leaving a few coals in the center. Transfer the lamb to the grill and cover, turning occasionally, until the internal temperature of the thickest part of the leg registers 130°F (54°C) for medium rare, 45–60 minutes. If roasting in an oven, reduce the oven temperature to 350°F (180°C) and roast the lamb until the thickest part of the leg reaches a temperature of 130°F (54°C), or until cooked to taste, about 1 hour.
4 Transfer the lamb to a serving platter and let rest for 10 minutes. Skim the fat from the pan juices. Sprinkle the lamb with sea salt, carve, and serve immediately with the pan juices.

KCal 825 P 54g C neg S 352mg SFA 30g UFA 34g (8)

COSTOLETTE D'AGNELLO IMPANATE
Pan-fried breaded lamb chops

Veal chops are often breaded and fried, but in Liguria, tender young lamb rib chops are preferred. The rosemary-scented coating in this recipe is especially delicious.

INGREDIENTS
olive oil for frying
½ cup (60g) plain flour for dredging
freshly ground black pepper, to taste
1 heaping tsp crushed dried rosemary
3 eggs
½ cup (45g) bread crumbs
12 small lamb rib chops, trimmed
salt, to taste
1 lemon, cut into wedges, to serve

PREPARATION

1 Pour as much olive oil as necessary to reach halfway up the sides of the chops in a heavy skillet. Warm the oil over medium-high heat until hot enough to make the meat sizzle upon contact with it, without burning the coating.
2 Place the flour, pepper, and rosemary on a plate. Beat the eggs lightly in a shallow bowl. Sprinkle the bread crumbs on a separate plate.
3 Just before you are ready to cook, dredge the chops in the flour, shaking off excess. Dip each chop into the egg mixture, and then in the crumbs. Slip the chops into the oil immediately. Do not crowd the pan because the chops will not cook properly. Cook until golden on both sides but still pink in the middle, about 5 minutes total.
4 Drain the chops on paper towels, sprinkle with salt, and serve immediately with lemon wedges.
KCal 315 P 30g C 20g S 222mg SFA 6g UFA 6g (4)

VARIATION

Costolette di Vitello alla Salsa di Pomodoro Crudo e Rucola (Veal chops with fresh tomato and arugula sauce). Coat 1lb (500g) of veal chops in the above bread crumb mixture, omitting rosemary. To make the sauce, combine 1lb (500g) of seeded and chopped ripe tomatoes with 4 tablespoons of extra-virgin olive oil, 1 minced garlic clove, ¼ teaspoon of salt and plenty of freshly ground black pepper. Chop ⅓ cup (60g) of washed and dried arugula leaves, then toss with the other ingredients. Let stand at room temperature for 30 minutes to allow the flavors to blend. Fry the chops until golden and cooked through but still tender, about 4–5 minutes on each side. Spoon over a little sauce, passing the remainder at the table. Serves 2.

SPEZZATINO DI VITELLO IN UMIDO CON LIMONE E PINOLI
Braised veal with wine, lemon, and pine nuts

Lemon is often used in cooking veal because its sharpness provides a counterpoint of flavor without overwhelming the delicate character of the meat. This dish is designed for an economy cut of veal that will stand up to lengthy cooking. Slow braising produces enough gravy for 8oz (250g) of short pasta, such as farfalle. Purè di Patate (see page 129) also makes an excellent side dish.

INGREDIENTS
2½lb (1.25kg) veal shoulder steaks,
½–1in (1–2.5cm) thick
4 tbsp flour, for dredging
2 tbsp unsalted butter
2 tbsp sunflower or corn oil
½ cup (125ml) dry white wine
1 sprig fresh thyme, or ¼ tsp dried
2 cups (500ml) chicken stock
2 x 2in (5cm) strips lemon zest
½ tsp salt
1 tbsp pine nuts, coarsely chopped
¼ tsp freshly ground white or black pepper

PREPARATION

1 Cut each steak in half and remove any excess fat. If there is bone, include it in the dish as it will add flavor. (The marrow can be eaten like a miniature *osso buco*.) Spread the flour on a large plate.
2 Heat the butter and oil together in a deep skillet. Meanwhile, dredge the veal in flour, and when the butter and oil are hot, add the steaks to the pan. Brown them on both sides for about 8 minutes.
3 Stir in the wine and thyme. Allow the wine to evaporate, about 3 minutes, then pour in about ⅓ cup (90ml) of stock. Adjust the heat to medium-low, cover the pan and simmer gently. Continue to add stock, about 4 tablespoons at a time, every 10 minutes or so, or as needed. Stir occasionally.
4 Cook the veal for 1–1½ hours, depending on the toughness of the meat. Halfway through, add the lemon zest. Sprinkle the salt and pine nuts into the pan juices 15 minutes before the end of cooking. Remove from the heat, stir in the pepper, and serve.
KCal 535 P 64g C 12g S 586mg SFA 8g UFA 15g (4)

UCCELLETTI SCAPPATI

Veal rolls stuffed with prosciutto and fontina

Literally "little birds," these bundles of tender veal stuffed with cheese and sage are typical of Roman cooking. It is very important to use thin, high-quality veal slices cut from the leg. There is plenty of delicious gravy, which can be served with 4oz (125g) of fresh tagliatelle (see page 166), or dried egg noodles. Alternatively, Purè di Patate (see page 129) is an ideal accompaniment.

INGREDIENTS

8 veal scaloppine slices, about 1½lb (750g), cut
from the leg, each ⅜in (1cm) thick
8 fresh sage leaves, or ½ tsp dried crumbled sage
8 slices prosciutto crudo or ham
⅓ cup (90g) fontina or provolone, shredded
2 tbsp unsalted butter
2 tbsp olive oil
½ cup (60g) all-purpose flour for dredging
½ cup (125ml) dry white wine
salt and freshly ground black pepper, to taste

PREPARATION

1 Lightly pound the veal (see page 164).
2 Put a fresh sage leaf or a tiny sprinkling of dried sage on each piece of veal. Cover each piece of meat with a slice of prosciutto or ham, trimming the edges if necessary. Sprinkle about 1 teaspoon of cheese evenly over each slice of ham.
3 Starting at one of the short ends, roll up each veal slice tightly and secure with two toothpicks.
4 Heat the butter and oil in a large skillet.
5 Just before you are ready to cook the rolls, dust them with flour. When the butter and oil are hot, slip the rolls into the pan. Sauté gently until browned all over, 8–10 minutes.
6 Stir in the wine, salt, and pepper. Use a wooden spoon to dislodge any bits of meat stuck to the bottom of the pan. Allow the wine to evaporate, about 3 minutes. Stir in ½ cup (125ml) of water and reduce the heat to low. Cover and simmer until the meat is tender, about 40 minutes. If necessary, add a little more water. Check the seasoning and serve.

KCal 585 P 60g C 11g S 1699mg SFA 13g UFA 16g (4)

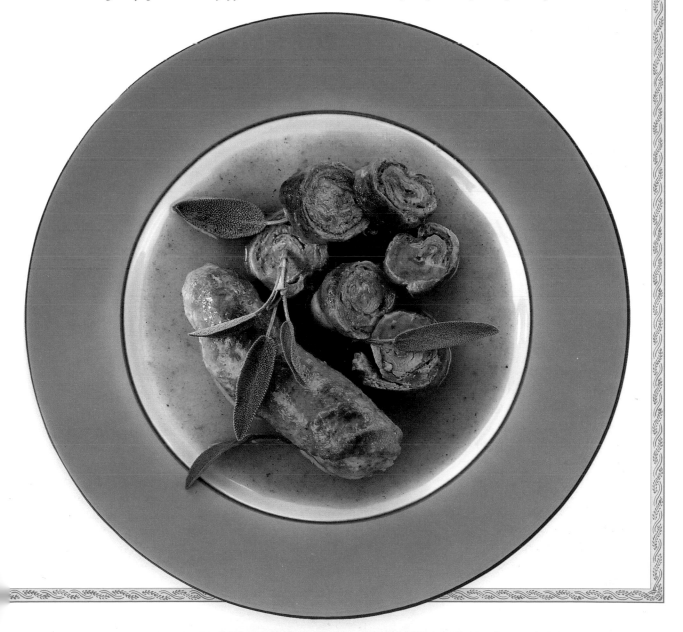

POLLO ALLA CACCIATORA
Chicken hunter style

The term alla cacciatora, *"hunter style," describes a dish based on game, lamb, or chicken cooked slowly in a tomato-based sauce. This is my mother's recipe. Its rich sauce contains giblets and livers, making it particularly appealing, and wine vinegar adds a lovely piquancy. Serve with Polenta (see page 169) or toasted bread. Serves 4–6.*

INGREDIENTS

3½lb (1.75kg) chicken, cut up, including giblets
6 chicken livers
5oz (150g) wild or 8oz (250g) cultivated mushrooms
7 tbsp extra-virgin olive oil
approximately ⅔ cup (90g) all-purpose flour
2 large garlic cloves, bruised
1 onion, chopped
1 large carrot, chopped
1 large celery rib with leaves, chopped
1 tbsp chopped fresh flat-leaf parsley
3 tsp chopped fresh rosemary, or ½ tsp dried
2½ tbsp wine vinegar
1lb (500g) fresh or canned tomatoes, peeled, seeded, and chopped, plus ⅓ cup (90ml) juice or water
salt and freshly ground black pepper, to taste

PREPARATION

1 Remove excess fat from the chicken. Trim any fat or membranes from the giblets and livers and finely dice. Wash and dry the chicken pieces.
2 Clean the mushrooms with a soft brush or cloth; do not wash them. Trim their stems, discarding any that are woody. Cut the caps into quarters, if large, then slice them across.
3 Heat 4 tablespoons of oil in a skillet. Spread the flour on a plate. When the oil is hot, dredge the chicken pieces in flour and slip them immediately into the oil. Do not crowd the pan. When all the pieces are golden brown, about 15 minutes, transfer them to a platter and set aside. Wash and dry the pan.
4 Warm the remaining oil in the pan with the garlic, pressing down on the cloves to release their juices. When the garlic begins to color, add the onion, carrot, celery, and parsley. Increase the heat slightly and cook for 5 minutes, stirring occasionally.
5 Add the rosemary, giblets, and livers, and brown them for 2–3 minutes. Add the mushrooms, cook for 4 minutes, then stir in the vinegar, the tomatoes, the tomato juice or water, and salt to taste.
6 Transfer the chicken to the sauce, stirring to coat the pieces thoroughly. Cover partially and cook gently until the chicken is tender and juicy, about 25 minutes. Sprinkle with pepper and serve.

KCal 570 P 73g C 28g S 705mg SFA 6g UFA 10g (4)

Garlic

Flour

Extra-virgin olive oil

Wild mushrooms

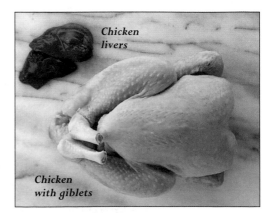

Chicken livers

Chicken with giblets

Flat-leaf parsley

Rosemary

Wine vinegar

Tomatoes and juice

Salt

Black pepper

Celery with leaves

Carrot

Onion

POLLO IN TEGAME
Pan-roasted chicken with rosemary and garlic

My mother usually made this simple but succulent pan-roasted chicken for Saturday or Sunday supper and served it with homemade egg noodles. Because the chicken is cooked in a covered pan over slow, steady heat, plenty of richly flavored gravy is produced — enough for 8oz (250g) of noodles. It is also good served with Purè di Patate (see page 129) or loose Polenta (see page 169).

INGREDIENTS

1 roasting chicken, about 3½lb (1.75kg)
2 tbsp extra-virgin olive oil
2 tbsp red or white wine vinegar, or cider vinegar
½ tsp salt, or to taste
Inside rub
1 sprig fresh rosemary, or ½ tsp crushed dried rosemary
2 large garlic cloves, bruised
freshly ground black pepper, to taste
Outside rub
2 tbsp extra-virgin olive oil
1 large garlic clove, finely chopped
1 tsp fresh finely chopped rosemary, or
½ tsp crushed dried rosemary
plenty of freshly ground black pepper
½ tsp sweet paprika

PREPARATION

1 Wash the chicken well. Dry it inside and out with paper towels. Combine the ingredients for the inside rub and spread it around the cavity. Make the outside rub and work it into the chicken skin.
2 Select a deep, heavy-bottomed pan wide enough to accommodate the chicken. Warm the oil over medium heat and when it is hot enough to make the chicken sizzle, add the bird to the pan. Immediately lower the heat to medium-low to prevent the rub from burning, and brown the chicken lightly on all sides, 10–12 minutes. Use tongs or two large spoons to turn the chicken.
3 Add the vinegar and use a wooden spoon to dislodge any browned bits stuck to the base of the pan. Cover the pan and cook the chicken over low heat for about 1 hour, turning it occasionally. It is essential to keep the pan tightly covered to prevent evaporation of the juices. However, should the chicken appear dry, add up to 4 tablespoons of water in the last 30 minutes of cooking.
4 Take the pan off the heat and sprinkle the chicken with salt, turning it so that it is seasoned evenly. Allow the chicken to settle in the pan, covered, for about 10 minutes. Carve the chicken and serve it hot with its pan juices.

KCal 370 P 40g C 0g S 352mg SFA 5g UFA 17g (4)

PETTI DI POLLO IMPANATI
Breaded chicken breast cutlets

This is a classic preparation of chicken breast cutlets that is light and elegant, but very easy to make. The cutlets can be served hot or at room temperature. Cold, they are excellent for the picnic basket.

INGREDIENTS

4 boneless chicken breast halves, partially frozen
1 tsp freshly grated Parmesan
pinch of freshly grated nutmeg
1 tsp grated onion
salt and freshly ground black pepper, to taste
2 eggs, beaten
1½ cups (90g) lightly toasted white bread crumbs
4 tbsp unsalted butter
2 tbsp olive oil
1 lemon, cut into wedges, to serve

PREPARATION

1 Slice each breast section horizontally into three slices to make very thin, even cutlets.
2 Beat the Parmesan, nutmeg, onion, salt, and pepper with the egg. Marinate the cutlets in the mixture for up to 3 hours.
3 Spread the bread crumbs on a piece of waxed paper or on a plate. Heat the butter and oil in a skillet until hot enough to make the chicken sizzle. Just before frying, dip each cutlet into the crumbs, making sure they are covered completely. Sauté the chicken over medium heat until golden on the outside but still tender and moist within, 2–3 minutes on each side. Drain on paper towels.
4 Serve the cutlets, squeezing a little lemon juice over them at the table.

KCal 465 P 29g C 28g S 775mg SFA 12g UFA 13g (4)

VARIATIONS

• Substitute turkey breasts for chicken breasts to make **Petti di Tacchino Impanati**.
• For a variation with fontina and ham **(Petti di Pollo Impanati alla Piemontese)**, prepare the chicken breasts according to the recipe, omitting lemon juice. Preheat the oven to 400°F (200°C). Arrange the cooked cutlets in a baking dish and top them with a layer of thinly sliced ham. Cover the ham with ⅓–½ cup (90–125g) of shredded fontina. Bake in the top of the oven until the cheese melts, about 5 minutes. Serve immediately.

POLLO ALLA MARENGO
Chicken Marengo

Pollo alla Marengo commemorates the Battle of Marengo, being the dish that was served to Napoleon on the eve of his victory over the Austrians on Lombard soil in June 1800. Some say that the general's cook created the dish from the few ingredients that were at hand; others claim the dish included crayfish, tomatoes, and eggs and was created by somebody else entirely. Whatever, this dish became Napoleon's preferred pre-battle dinner and he resisted all later attempts to dress it up with truffles and spirits. My version of this superb dish includes wine and mushrooms. Accompany with plenty of fresh bread or rice. Serves 4–6. Illustrated on page 121.

INGREDIENTS
3½lb (1.75kg) chicken, cut up
1 tbsp extra-virgin olive oil
2 tbsp unsalted butter
2 large garlic cloves, bruised
1 onion, chopped
1 carrot, chopped
1 celery rib with leaves, chopped
2 tbsp chopped fresh flat-leaf parsley
5oz (150g) mushrooms
2–3 tbsp olive oil
⅔ cup (150ml) dry white wine
2 tbsp flour
1½ cups (350ml) good chicken stock
salt and freshly ground white or black pepper, to taste

PREPARATION
1 Remove excess fat from the chicken. Use the blunt side of a chef's knife to break the bottom of the leg bone. Divide each breast piece in half.
2 Heat the extra-virgin olive oil and butter in a Dutch oven. Add the garlic and sauté gently for about 3 minutes, until it begins to color and release its juices. Add the onion, carrot, celery, and half the parsley. Sauté until softened, then set aside.
3 Meanwhile, clean the mushrooms with a soft brush or cloth; do not wash them. Trim their stems, discarding any that are woody. If they are large, cut the caps into quarters, then slice.
4 Heat the olive oil in a skillet. When it is hot enough to make the chicken sizzle, add the pieces (in batches, if necessary) and brown them on all sides, about 15 minutes. Transfer to the Dutch oven.
5 Drain the oil from the skillet, return it to the heat, and add the wine. Allow the alcohol to evaporate, about 3 minutes, using a wooden spoon to dislodge any bits of meat stuck to the pan. Meanwhile, mix the flour with just enough water to make a paste, then stir it into the skillet. Add the

stock and stir to make a smooth sauce.
6 Pour the liquid mixture into the pot and season with salt, stirring thoroughly. Cover the pot, leaving the lid slightly askew. Cook over medium-low heat for 20 minutes, stirring occasionally. Finally, stir in the remaining parsley and plenty of pepper.
KCal 495 P 44g C 11g S 625mg SFA 9g UFA 17g (4)

CONIGLIO ALLA VENETA
Rabbit in the style of the Veneto

Here is a way to cook rabbit that is also successful with chicken. A great deal of flavor is derived from the liver, heart, and kidneys of the animal, which are chopped and added to the sauce, but you can make do with just the liver. Plenty of rich sauce is produced. In the Veneto, such gamy dishes are typically served with Polenta (see page 169), but buttered noodles, plain rice, or Purè di Patate (see page 129) are also good.

INGREDIENTS
3lb (1.5kg) rabbit, including liver,
heart, and kidneys, cut up
½ cup (60g) flour for dredging
2 tsp chopped fresh rosemary, or ¾ tsp dried
freshly ground black pepper, to taste
2 tbsp unsalted butter
1 tbsp olive oil
1 large garlic clove, bruised
½ tsp salt
zest of 1 lemon
½ cup (125ml) dry white wine

PREPARATION
1 Wash and dry the rabbit pieces. Remove any excess fat. Chop the liver, heart, and kidneys.
2 Spread the flour on a plate and mix in half the rosemary and plenty of pepper.
3 Place the butter, oil, and garlic in a large skillet and sauté the garlic until golden. Remove it and set aside. Just before you are ready to fry the rabbit, dredge each piece lightly in flour. Slip the pieces immediately into the pan and cook them for 10–12 minutes. Fry them in batches if necessary. Transfer the browned rabbit pieces to a dish.
4 Add the liver, heart, and kidneys to the pan and sauté for 30 seconds. Return the rabbit to the pan, add the salt, remaining rosemary, lemon zest, and wine. Allow the wine to evaporate, about 3 minutes. Pour in ½ cup (125ml) of water, bring to a boil, then reduce the heat to low. Simmer gently, partially covered, until the rabbit is cooked through but still moist, about 15 minutes, then serve.
KCal 450 P 52g C 12g S 353mg SFA 8g UFA 10g (4)

ANATRA ALL'ARANCIA
Roasted duck with orange
sauce, Tuscan style
(page 124)

POLPETTONE FARCITO
Meat loaf stuffed with
ham and frittatine
(page 110)

POLLO ALLA MARENGO
Chicken Marengo
(page 119)

STUFATO DI CERVO
Venison stew

Anna Amedolara Nurse is a legend in New York food circles. She cooks with great gusto, and her friends have many an anecdote to tell about her food. One such story is told by a relative who was at Anna's home when her husband, Gene, returned from a hunting trip with a prize deer. Anna lost no time. She moved her guests to the sidelines, covered the floor with a cloth, and butchered the animal on the spot while her company looked on in amazement. With this story in mind, I decided that Anna's venison recipe must be shared. Here it is.

INGREDIENTS

½ cup (125ml) olive oil
2lb (1kg) boneless venison leg or shoulder, cut into 1⅓in (3.5cm) cubes
4oz (125g) pancetta or blanched back bacon, diced
1 onion, chopped
2 garlic cloves, finely chopped
1 celery rib, diced, plus 2 tbsp chopped celery leaves
1 carrot, diced
½ cup (30g) chopped fresh flat-leaf parsley
1 bay leaf
½ tsp chopped fresh thyme, or ¼ tsp dried
pinch of hot red pepper flakes
3 fresh ripe tomatoes, or ½lb (250g) canned drained tomatoes, peeled, seeded, and chopped
½ cup (125ml) dry white wine
1 cup (250ml) Meat Broth (see page 72) or good stock
salt and freshly ground black pepper, to taste

PREPARATION

1 Heat the olive oil in a deep skillet or Dutch oven until hot enough to sear the meat. Add the venison to the pan in batches and allow it to brown, about 10 minutes. Transfer the meat to a plate, then drain off all but 3 tablespoons of the oil.
2 Reheat the oil and add the pancetta, onion, garlic, celery, carrot, herbs, and pepper flakes to the pan, using a wooden spoon to loosen any bits of meat stuck to the bottom. Cover and cook over low heat until the vegetables are translucent, 8–10 minutes.
3 Stir in the tomatoes. Sauté for 2 minutes, then add the wine and broth and raise the heat. Bring to a boil, then quickly reduce the heat to medium-low.
4 Return the venison to the pan, cover, and cook until tender, about 40 minutes, stirring occasionally. Stir in the salt and pepper. Transfer the venison to a warm platter. Return the pan to the heat and simmer the gravy until reduced and thickened slightly, 4–8 minutes. Pour the gravy over the venison and serve.

KCal 645 P 65g C 7g S 981mg SFA 7g UFA 29g (4)

QUAGLIE SAPORITE
Savory braised quail

Small game birds are an immensely popular food in Italy. They are cooked in many ways — larded and spit-roasted, pan-roasted with wine, wrapped in aromatic leaves and boiled, cooked in parchment, and even baked whole into pies. Quail are prized for their delicate meat; unlike many game birds, their tender flesh makes them ideal for sautéing. Serves 2.

INGREDIENTS

2 tbsp unsalted butter
1 tbsp sunflower or vegetable oil
1oz (30g) pancetta or back bacon, finely chopped
⅓ cup (45g) flour for dredging
freshly ground black pepper, to taste
2 quail, each about 6oz (175g), split into quarters
livers and gizzards from the quail, if available, chopped
1 small onion, grated
6 fresh sage leaves, chopped, or ¾ tsp dried crumbled sage
salt, to taste
½ cup (125ml) dry white wine
¾ cup (175ml) Chicken Broth (see page 73) or good stock

PREPARATION

1 Heat the butter and oil in a wide, preferably nonstick skillet. Add the pancetta and sauté until lightly colored, 1–2 minutes.
2 Meanwhile, place the flour and pepper on a plate and dredge the quail sections in the flour. Transfer them to the skillet and sauté until browned all over, about 10 minutes. Transfer them to a dish.
3 Add the liver and gizzards, the onion and sage to the pan. Sauté just until the onion softens.
4 Stir in a little salt and the wine, using a wooden spoon to dislodge any bits of meat stuck to the pan. Allow the alcohol to evaporate, about 4 minutes. Pour in the broth and bring it to a simmer.
5 Return the quail sections to the pan. Braise, partially covered, until cooked through, 20–25 minutes, turning them once. Serve hot, perhaps accompanied by sautéed mushrooms and loose Polenta (see page 169).

KCal 445 P 24g C 22g S 800mg SFA 11g UFA 13g (2)

FARAONA RIPIENA

*Pan-roasted guinea fowl with bread and
sun-dried tomato stuffing, Sardinian style*

*Guinea fowl are very popular in central Italy and
Sardinia. These birds cannot be raised in cages because
they roost in trees, and their meat has a great deal
more flavor than chicken. Because of their low fat
content, guinea fowl are best cooked with moisture —
either pot-roasted, or in the oven al cartoccio, sealed in
paper or foil. This Sardinian stuffing is also used for
boiled chicken. Serves 6.*

INGREDIENTS

*2 guinea fowl, each about 2lb (1kg)
freshly ground black pepper, to taste
4 tbsp extra-virgin olive oil
½ cup (125ml) dry red or white wine
3 carrots, quartered
2 onions, quartered
½ tsp salt
1 cup (250ml) Chicken Broth (see page 73)
or good stock*

Stuffing

*6 sun-dried tomatoes preserved in oil or dry
2 cups (250g) packed 2-day-old very thinly sliced Italian
or French bread, crusts removed
2 tbsp chopped fresh flat-leaf parsley
⅛ tsp saffron strands, or 1 envelope (130mg)
saffron powder
½ cup (125ml) Chicken Broth (see page 73)
1 egg
½ tsp salt, or to taste
freshly ground black pepper, to taste
1 tbsp oil from sun-dried tomatoes
or extra-virgin olive oil*

PREPARATION

1 Make the stuffing. If using tomatoes preserved in
oil, drain and chop them. If using the dry variety,
first soak them in hot water until they are tender,
about 20 minutes. Combine the chopped tomatoes
with the bread and parsley.
2 Heat the saffron strands, if using, in a small
skillet until they start to color and release their
aroma, about 15 seconds. Remove from the heat
and pulverize them with the back of a spoon.
3 Lightly beat together the broth, egg, saffron
strands or powder, salt, pepper, and oil. Pour this
mixture over the tomato, bread, and parsley, then
toss everything together.
4 Wash the guinea fowl inside and out with cold
water, then sprinkle pepper into the cavities. Fill
the birds with the stuffing mixture and close the
cavities securely using a needle and thread. Pat the
skin dry with paper towels.
5 Heat the olive oil in a large heavy-bottomed pot
over medium-high heat, then add the birds. Sauté
until the birds are nicely browned on all sides,
about 10 minutes. Use tongs to turn them so you
avoid puncturing the skin. Add the wine to the pot
and let the alcohol evaporate, about 3 minutes.
Remove the guinea fowl and set them aside.
6 Add the vegetables, stirring to coat them with
the juices. Return the birds to the pan, setting
them on their backs. Add the salt and half the broth
to the pan and partially cover.
7 When the broth begins to simmer, reduce the
heat to low and cook the guinea fowl until tender,
approximately 1¼ hours. Stir occasionally and add
more liquid, if necessary, to keep the birds and
vegetables moist. Do not turn the guinea fowl.
Make a cut in the leg joint to see if the juices run
clear. If not, continue to cook, partially covered,
for 10–15 minutes longer. Do not overcook or the
flesh will be dry. Remove the pot from the heat.
8 Allow the guinea fowl to settle for 15 minutes.
Meanwhile, skim the fat from the juices, remove
the trussing thread, and serve the birds split down
the middle, with the stuffing left intact. Surround
with the vegetables and pour over the pan juices.
KCal 610 P 31g C 24g S 1011mg SFA 7g UFA 32g (4)

ANATRA ALL'ARANCIA

Roasted duck with orange sauce, Tuscan style

This is one of many dishes taken to France by Caterina de' Medici's cooks. Traditional recipes call for aquavit, but brandy may be used. Basting with orange and honey gives the duck a deep golden brown skin. Serves 4–6.
Illustrated on page 120.

INGREDIENTS

1 duck, about 6lb (3kg)
salt, to taste
5 oranges
15 cloves
½ cup (125ml) brandy
3 tbsp honey or sugar
1½ tbsp flour

PREPARATION

1 Preheat the oven to 400°F (200°C).
2 Wash the duck inside and out, then cut out excess fat from the cavity. Wipe dry the cavity and sprinkle it with salt. Keep the skin wet.
3 Press two of the oranges against the work surface to soften them. Using a small knife, puncture the oranges and insert the cloves. Place the oranges in the cavity of the duck. Puncture the skin of the duck, then close the cavity with small skewers.
4 Place the duck on a rack in a roasting pan, breast side down, and roast for 30 minutes.
5 Meanwhile, remove the zest from two of the remaining oranges, then squeeze their juice – there should be about 1 cup (250ml) – and strain. Mix it with the brandy, honey or sugar, and ½ teaspoon of salt. Cut the zest into matchstick strips, soak in boiling water for 1 minute, then drain and set aside.
6 Remove the duck from the oven and lower the temperature to 350°F (180°C). Drain all the fat from the pan and pierce the duck skin again to release fat. Baste the duck with some of the orange juice mixture. Return to the oven and cook for 1 hour, basting every 20 minutes or so.
7 Turn the duck breast side up so that it browns nicely on both sides. Cook for a final 30 minutes.
8 Remove the duck from the oven and make an incision in the leg joint. If the juices do not run clear, cook the duck for 10–15 minutes longer. Lift the duck from the pan and allow it to stand.
9 Skim the fat from the pan juices. In a small pan, combine the flour with a little orange juice mixture, then stir in the remaining juice mixture, the zest, and pan juices. Heat until thickened, 8–10 minutes, stirring frequently. Serve the duck with the sauce, surrounded by slices of the remaining orange.

KCal 455 P 46g C 27g S 454mg SFA 3g UFA 7g (4)

ROGNONCINI CON PISELLI

Sautéed kidneys with peas and shallots

Here is a delicate and simple dish in which kidneys are at their best. I like to serve it with rice, or simply with plenty of good bread to soak up the sauce.

INGREDIENTS

1lb (500g) fresh lamb or veal kidneys
salt, to taste
1 cup (125g) frozen peas, thawed, or fresh shelled peas
2 tbsp unsalted butter
1 tbsp olive oil
2 shallots, chopped
1 tbsp chopped fresh flat-leaf parsley
½ tsp chopped fresh marjoram, or ¼ tsp dried
2 tbsp dry white wine
freshly ground white or black pepper, to taste

PREPARATION

1 Soak the kidneys for 30 minutes in cold water to which 1 teaspoon of salt has been added. Meanwhile, if using fresh peas, blanch them in salted boiling water for 1½ minutes. Drain and rinse in cold water, then set aside.
2 Remove any membranes from the kidneys and trim any fat. Cut them into ¼in (5mm) slices.
3 Heat the butter and oil with the chopped shallots. When the shallots are soft, add the kidneys and sauté them over high heat for several minutes, just until they lose their pinkness. Take care not to overcook them, or they will lose their delicacy.
4 Reduce the heat and add the parsley, marjoram, wine, and salt to taste. Continue to sauté, allowing the wine to evaporate, 2–3 minutes. Stir in the peas. Sauté for 3 minutes, add plenty of pepper, and serve.

KCal 235 P 23g C 4g S 669mg SFA 6g UFA 6g (4)

FEGATO ALLA VENEZIANA
Venetian-style sautéed calf's liver

The Venetians are famous for this dish, which is no ordinary treatment of liver and onions. The secret to its success lies in sweating the onions until they are almost melted, and in sautéing the paper-thin liver so rapidly that its tenderness and delicacy are retained. Choose very fresh, light pink liver from a young calf. While it is not traditional to do so, and may be considered heresy by Venetians, I sometimes add a drop of balsamic vinegar to each slice of liver at the table. Serve with polenta crostini or plain Polenta with butter (see page 169).

INGREDIENTS

4 tbsp corn or sunflower oil
2lb (1kg) onions, halved and sliced as thinly as possible
1½lb (750g) calf's liver, partially frozen
salt and freshly ground black or white pepper, to taste

PREPARATION

1 Heat 3 tablespoons of oil in a large nonstick skillet. Add the onions, turn the heat to medium-low, stir, then cover the pan. Cook the onions until very soft, about 30 minutes, stirring occasionally.
2 Meanwhile, use a very sharp knife to cut away the tough outer skin of the liver. Slice the liver on the diagonal into paper-thin strips. Cut out any hard tubes you may find. Set the pieces aside.
3 Transfer the onions to a dish. Warm the rest of the oil in the pan over medium-high heat. Place as many pieces of liver as possible in the pan without crowding. Sauté the liver quickly on both sides, just until it changes color (less than half a minute); do not allow it to brown. Transfer it to a dish and return the onions to the pan just to heat through.
4 Pile the onions onto a warm serving dish, arrange the liver on top, season well, and serve.

KCal 510 P 41g C 23g S 570mg SFA 6g UFA 19g (4)

TRIPPA IN UMIDO
Stewed honeycomb tripe

This is the first dish I ever cooked without help. I was nine when dinner responsibilities were left to me due to the unusual absence of my mother, who gave me the instructions for this recipe, probably because she knew it was one of my favorites. We served it with Polenta (see page 169) scattered with Parmesan. I recommend you do the same.

INGREDIENTS

2lb (1kg) honeycomb tripe, washed and trimmed of fat
salt, to taste
3 tbsp olive oil
2 large garlic cloves, finely chopped
1 onion, chopped
1 large celery rib with leaves, chopped
1 large carrot, chopped
2 fresh bay leaves, bruised but left whole
6 tbsp (90g) tomato paste
½ cup (125ml) dry white wine
freshly ground black pepper, to taste

PREPARATION

1 Slice the tripe into strips about 2in (5cm) long and 1in (2.5cm) wide and rub salt into each piece. Wash the strips in cold water, rinse, and pat dry.
2 Heat the oil in a large pot and add the garlic, onion, celery, carrot, and bay leaves. Sauté gently until the vegetables soften, about 7 minutes.
3 Add the tripe and sauté over medium heat for 5–10 minutes, stirring occasionally. Lower the heat and stir in the tomato paste. Add the wine and the pepper and cook for 2–3 minutes.
4 Add 1½ cups (350ml) of water and a teaspoon of salt. Partially cover the pot and simmer gently until the tripe is tender, 1–1¼ hours. There should be abundant, thick gravy. Taste for salt before serving.

KCal 240 P 25g C 8g S 574mg SFA 3g UFA 5g (4)

SALSICCIE CON CIME DI RAPA
Sausages with broccoli rape, Apulian style

Few things are as contentedly mated as sweet Italian sausages and peppery cime di rapa. Kale can be used successfully, though it is inauthentic.

INGREDIENTS

1lb (500g) fresh sweet Italian pork sausages
2lb (1kg) broccoli rape or kale, trimmed and stems peeled
⅓ cup (90ml) extra-virgin olive oil
4 large garlic cloves, finely chopped
½ tsp salt, or to taste

PREPARATION

1 Cook the sausages as described on page 164. Cover them and take off the heat.
2 Cut the leaves and stems across into 3in (7cm) pieces and wash well. Bring a pan of water to a boil and parboil the greens for 5 minutes. Drain well.
3 Warm the oil and garlic together in a large skillet until the garlic has softened, about 2 minutes.
4 Add the greens and the salt to the frying pan. Cover and cook gently, stirring occasionally, until tender but not mushy, about 5 minutes. Serve the greens immediately alongside the sausages.

KCal 745 P 21g C 20g S 1194mg SFA 19g UFA 43g (4)

VEGETABLE DISHES

The traditional Italian diet is based on products from the local landscape. The heart of every village, town, and city is the market, where the opulent red of tomatoes and peppers, the vibrant greens of herbs, and the stunning colors of golden squashes and purple cabbages dazzle the eye. The Italian way of cooking vegetables is straightforward, aiming to make food taste of itself, so the raw ingredients must be absolutely fresh. The Italian for vegetable dishes, *contorni*, means "surroundings," but vegetables are never relegated to side-dish status. Some of the recipes in this chapter are simple in composition. The more complex dishes, prepared in larger quantities, might be served as main courses.

INVOLTINI DI CAVOLO

Stuffed cabbage

When I think back to my childhood and the dishes I loved the most, many come to mind. But the ones for which I have a particular fondness are the fortifying winter dishes. My mother always served stuffed cabbage as a main course, but the tartness given the dish by sour pickles makes it a good appetizer for 8. Balsamic vinegar, my own touch, rounds out all the flavors nicely.

INGREDIENTS

24 leaves from a green cabbage
salt, to taste
10 small gherkin pickles, thinly sliced lengthwise
2 bay leaves
2 tbsp balsamic vinegar
Filling
½ cup (100g) long-grain rice
¾lb (375g) lean ground beef
¾lb (375g) lean ground pork
1 egg
1 small onion, grated
2 tbsp chopped fresh flat-leaf parsley
1 tsp ground allspice
1 tsp salt
½ tsp freshly ground black pepper
Sauce
2 tbsp extra-virgin olive oil
1 small celery rib with leaves, finely chopped
1 small onion, grated
1 large garlic clove, finely chopped
2½ cups (625g) canned drained tomatoes, chopped

PREPARATION

1 Slice off the protruding tip of the central rib of each cabbage leaf so that each will lie flat. Prepare a large bowl half-full of cold water.

2 Bring 8 cups (2 liters) of water to a boil in a large pot. Add 2 teaspoons of salt. Drop in the leaves a few at a time and cook until just tender, 3–4 minutes. Transfer them to the cold water. Reserve the cooking water. Remove the leaves from the water and dry them with a clean dish towel.

3 Thoroughly combine the filling ingredients with 2 tablespoons of water. Place 2 teaspoons of filling in a cylindrical shape at the base of each leaf, across the spine. Begin to roll up the leaf, folding in the sides as you work to make a neat package. Use any leftover stuffing to make small meatballs.

4 Secure each bundle with a toothpick. Place the bundles side by side in a heavy-bottomed pot, slipping the sliced gherkins in between. Tuck the bay leaves into the pot.

5 In a bowl, combine the ingredients for the sauce. Stir in 2 cups (500ml) of cabbage cooking water. Pour the sauce over the cabbage bundles and simmer over low heat, partially covered, until the sauce is thickened and the rice is tender (make a cut in one of the bundles to test), about 1½ hours.

6 Use a slotted spoon to transfer the bundles to a serving plate. Reheat the sauce, moistening it with cabbage water if necessary. If it is runny, simmer it uncovered until reduced. Taste for salt, sprinkle in the vinegar, and simmer for another 2 minutes. Spoon the sauce over the cabbage and serve hot or at room temperature, with additional rice if desired.

KCal 255 P 23g C 18g S 528mg SFA 3g UFA 7g (8)

CAVOLO ALLA PARMIGIANA

Stewed cabbage with pancetta and vinegar, Parma style

This recipe was given to me by Paola Rinaldini, who with her husband runs a small farm and winery in the Parma countryside. The cabbage, flavored with pancetta and vinegar, is stewed very slowly so that the flavors become concentrated as the cabbage cooks down to a creamy consistency. Signora Rinaldini serves this dish with the famous cotechino sausage, and it is indeed a splendid match for any pork or game dish. Serves 6.

INGREDIENTS

2 tbsp vegetable oil or olive oil
3oz (90g) pancetta, sliced and finely diced
1 onion, quartered and thinly sliced
1 tbsp tomato paste
3 tbsp red wine vinegar
2lb (1kg) cabbage, shredded
1 tsp salt

PREPARATION

1 Heat the oil, add the pancetta, and sauté until it begins to color. Add the onion and sauté over low heat until softened, about 4 minutes.
2 Dissolve the tomato paste in 4 tablespoons of water, stir it into the pan, then pour in the vinegar. Add the cabbage and salt, and toss with a wooden spoon. Pour in 1 cup (250ml) of water and stir.
3 Turn the heat to medium-high and cook until the cabbage begins to sweat, about 6 minutes, tossing frequently. Reduce the heat to low, cover, and cook until the cabbage has an almost creamy consistency, about 1½ hours, stirring occasionally. If it seems dry, add a teaspoon or two of water. Serve hot.
KCal 120 P 6g C 9g S 556mg SFA 1g UFA 5g (6)

PATATE FRITTE

Fried potatoes

On the Italian table, fried potatoes are something special – nothing like the greasy, mass-produced french fries of some fast food restaurants. Part of the secret lies in using good potatoes and olive oil. The method is crucial, too – slice the potatoes thin, dry them well, and salt them before frying to ensure crispness. Illustrated on page 107.

INGREDIENTS

1lb (500g) boiling potatoes, peeled and washed
freshly ground sea salt, to taste
olive oil
4 large garlic cloves, unpeeled and cut in half
freshly ground white or black pepper, to taste

PREPARATION

1 Dry the potatoes well. If they are large, halve them. Using a chef's knife, cut the potatoes into very thin slices. Blot them between two cotton dish towels to absorb moisture. Transfer to dry towels and sprinkle lightly with salt. When they begin to produce more moisture, blot them again.
2 Pour olive oil into a skillet to a depth of ¾in (1.5cm) and heat. Add the garlic, fry until golden, then remove. Slip the potatoes in rapidly, one by one, to prevent the slices from sticking to each other. Fry them in batches to avoid crowding the pan. Sauté until they are golden brown on both sides, then drain on paper towels. Transfer to a warm platter and sprinkle with pepper. Serve hot.
KCal 145 P 2g C 17g S 396mg SFA 1g UFA 6g (4)

GÂTEAU DI PATATE

Potato cake

This Neapolitan treatment of potatoes produces a layered "cake" of sorts. The mozzarella creates a generous middle layer, which serves as a nice oozy contrast to the potatoes.

INGREDIENTS

3lb (1.5kg) boiling potatoes, scrubbed but unpeeled
8 tbsp (125g) unsalted butter, plus butter for greasing
1 cup (250ml) warm milk
2 eggs, lightly beaten
3 tbsp freshly grated pecorino or Parmesan
5 tbsp bread crumbs, lightly toasted
8oz (250g) mozzarella, diced
4oz (125g) prosciutto or Italian salami, finely diced
large pinch of paprika

PREPARATION

1 Preheat the oven to 350°F (180°C).
2 Boil the potatoes until tender, then drain. When they have cooled slightly, peel them and pass them through a potato ricer, or use a masher. Mix in the butter, milk, eggs, and 1 tablespoon of grated cheese.
3 Butter a baking dish and sprinkle in half of the bread crumbs, making sure they coat the surface entirely. Tap out any excess crumbs.
4 Spoon half of the potato mixture into the dish, spreading it evenly. Top with the mozzarella, 1 tablespoon of grated cheese, and the prosciutto or salami, then cover with the rest of the potato.
5 Sprinkle the top with the leftover bread crumbs, the final tablespoon of grated cheese, and a little paprika. Bake for 30 minutes. If the top isn't golden brown, place the dish under the broiler for a few minutes. Let rest for 10 minutes, then serve.
KCal 855 P 40g C 59g S 1408mg SFA 32g UFA 17g (4)

PATATE AL FORNO
Scalloped potatoes baked in milk

Serves 6.

INGREDIENTS

2¾lb (1.25kg) potatoes, scrubbed but kept whole
3 tbsp unsalted butter, plus butter for greasing
1 cup (250g) sour cream blended with 2–3 tbsp milk
½ tsp salt
½ cup (45g) freshly grated Parmesan
1 cup (250ml) milk

PREPARATION

1 Boil or steam the potatoes until they are half-cooked, 20–30 minutes, according to size. Drain them thoroughly and let cool completely. Peel them and cut them into ¼in (5mm) slices.
2 Preheat the oven to 400°F (200°C).

3 Butter a baking dish that will comfortably hold the potatoes. Arrange a layer of potatoes in the dish, then dot with butter and spread with some of the thinned sour cream. Sprinkle with some of the salt, then scatter a little of the Parmesan on top.
4 Repeat the process, layering until all of the potatoes are used. Distribute butter, cheese, and salt evenly between the layers (leave a little butter and Parmesan for scattering on the top). Pour the milk over all, and finish with little pieces of the remaining butter and a sprinkling of Parmesan. Cover the dish tightly with foil.
5 Bake the dish on the top rack of the oven for 20 minutes. Take off the foil and continue baking until the potatoes are golden brown on top, another 5–10 minutes.
6 Remove the dish from the oven and let it rest for 10–15 minutes before serving.
KCal 350 P 10g C 35g S 268mg SFA 12g UFA 6g (6)

PURE DI PATATE
Puréed potatoes

The Italian version of puréed potatoes goes one step beyond what is called mashed potatoes. Once the potatoes are mashed, they are returned to the pan while first butter and then hot milk — as much as the potatoes will absorb — are beaten into them. The result is creamy, light, and fluffy. Include Parmesan only if it is compatible with the main dish. Serves 6.

INGREDIENTS

1½lb (750g) boiling potatoes, scrubbed but kept whole
4 tbsp unsalted butter, cut into thin slices
salt, to taste
¾ cup (175ml) hot milk
¼ cup (30g) freshly grated Parmesan, optional
freshly ground white pepper, to taste

PREPARATION

1 Boil the potatoes until tender, about 30 minutes, then drain. Take care not to puncture the skins too often during cooking or the potatoes will absorb too much water. Rinse the pan.
2 When the potatoes have cooled just enough to handle, peel them and pass them through a potato ricer into the pan, or use a potato masher, pressing out all lumps.
3 Place the pan over a heat-diffusing mat, if available, or over the lowest possible heat. Add the butter and salt, stirring constantly to prevent any scorching. Using an electric beater or whisk, beat in the hot milk a little at a time.
4 Remove the pan from the heat, adjust for salt, and beat in the Parmesan, if using, and pepper.
KCal 190 P 5g C 19g S 338mg SFA 7g UFA 3g (6)

FAGIOLINI E PATATE ALL' ISTRIANA
Green beans and potatoes, Istrian style

This dish was made for me by Lidia Bastianich after one of our vegetable-hunting trips in the Lecce market. Among our finds were creamy-fleshed baby yellow potatoes and freshly picked buttery green beans. They complement each other beautifully in this earthy and tasty dish. Serves 6.

INGREDIENTS

1lb (500g) baby yellow new potatoes, unpeeled
1½lb (750g) green beans, trimmed
salt, to taste
⅓ cup (90ml) extra-virgin olive oil
6 large garlic cloves, thinly sliced
freshly ground black pepper, to taste

PREPARATION

1 Scrub the potatoes well and cut the green beans in half. Bring a large pan of water to a boil and cook the potatoes until three-quarters tender, 15–20 minutes (test them with a skewer).
2 Add the green beans and 2 teaspoons of salt to the pan. Cook until the beans are just tender, 8–10 minutes, then drain. When the potatoes are cool enough to handle, peel them and set aside.
3 Warm all but 1 tablespoon of the olive oil in a skillet with the garlic. Fry the garlic until it begins to color, but do not let it brown. Add the potatoes and green beans, using a wooden spoon to mix them thoroughly and pressing down to mash them slightly. Continue to sauté until the potatoes begin to acquire a golden crispness, 5–7 minutes.
4 Remove the pan from the heat and stir in the remaining oil. Check the seasoning and sprinkle with plenty of pepper. Serve hot or warm.
KCal 210 P 3g C 15g S 267mg SFA 2g UFA 13g (6)

VARIATION

Sprinkle the finished dish with 1 tablespoon of chopped fresh flat-leaf parsley and ¼lb (125g) of bacon, cut into julienne strips and fried until crisp.

FAGIOLINI AL POMODORO
Green beans with tomato and garlic

Illustrated on page 56.

INGREDIENTS

1lb (500g) green beans, trimmed
salt, to taste
3 tbsp extra-virgin olive oil
2 large garlic cloves, chopped
1lb (500g) fresh or canned drained tomatoes, peeled, seeded, and chopped
3–4 large fresh basil leaves, torn into small pieces, or 1 tbsp chopped fresh flat-leaf parsley
freshly ground black or white pepper, to taste

PREPARATION

1 Bring a large pan of water to a rolling boil. Add the beans and 2 teaspoons of salt. Cook the beans until almost tender, 7–9 minutes, then drain.
2 Meanwhile, heat the olive oil in a skillet and add the garlic. When the garlic begins to color, stir in the tomatoes and basil, or parsley. Simmer the sauce for 5 minutes, then check the seasoning.
3 Add the beans to the sauce and simmer until they are thoroughly tender, 10–15 minutes, then sprinkle with pepper. Serve warm or at room temperature.
KCal 45 P 3g C 7g S 437mg SFA neg UFA neg (4)

FINOCCHI GRATINATI
Baked fennel
Illustrated on page 57.

INGREDIENTS

6 fennel bulbs
salt, to taste
2 tsp unsalted butter
3 tbsp freshly grated Parmesan
3oz (90g) fontina cheese, shredded

PREPARATION

1 Trim the tough bases of the fennel bulbs. Cut off the tough stalks and feathery leaves, reserving them for some other dish, and cut away any blemished parts. Quarter the bulbs lengthwise.
2 Place the fennel bulbs in a pan with just enough water to cover them and add salt – 1 teaspoon per 1 quart (1.25 liters). Bring the water to a boil and cook the fennel until almost tender, about 7 minutes, then drain thoroughly.
3 Preheat the oven to 425°F (220°C).
4 Arrange the fennel wedges in a baking dish. Scatter the butter and cheeses on top. Bake in the middle of the oven until the cheese melts and forms a golden crust, about 25 minutes. Serve hot.
KCal 165 P 11g C 3g S 338mg SFA 8g UFA 3g (4)

VARIATION

Prepare the fennel as described in steps 1 and 2. Place the boiled fennel in a baking dish and cover lightly with Besciamella (see page 136). Sprinkle with the butter and cheeses and bake as directed. This method is used for many cooked vegetables, particularly asparagus, onions, and cauliflower.

SCAROLA IN PADELLA CON FAGIOLI
Sautéed escarole with beans

The origins of this dish are in hearty southern Italian peasant cooking, which makes use of a great variety of leafy greens. Escarole, chicory, or broccoli rape can be used. Rape is often hard to find outside Italian markets, but its agreeable bitter taste is especially complemented by the creaminess of the beans. Boiling rather than steaming the greens not only sweetens them, but sets their vibrant color. This makes a good vegetarian meal, or a side dish for sausage or pork. Serves 6.

INGREDIENTS

1½lb (750g) escarole, chicory, or broccoli rape
salt, to taste
3 tbsp extra-virgin olive oil
2 garlic cloves, chopped
pinch of hot red pepper flakes
1 cup (300g) dried cannellini beans, soaked
and cooked (see page 161)

PREPARATION

1 If using escarole or chicory, slice off the bottom of the stalk. Place the leaves in a large bowl of water and soak for 15–20 minutes. If using broccoli rape, trim the ends of the stalks, then peel the skin from the tough lower stalks. Rinse thoroughly in cold water, then drain. Cut or tear the greens into pieces about 3in (7cm) long.
2 Bring a large pan of water to a rolling boil. Add the greens and 1 tablespoon of salt to the pan. Bring back to a boil, cover partially, and cook for 5 minutes longer.
3 Meanwhile, place the olive oil, garlic, and pepper flakes in a skillet. Turn the heat to low and sauté gently until the garlic just starts to color (do not let it brown), about 5 minutes.
4 Drain the cooked greens, leaving some water still clinging to the leaves, and transfer them and the drained beans to the skillet. Toss them over medium heat until heated through. Check for salt, stir, cover, and cook gently until tender, about 5 minutes, before serving.
KCal 210 P 10g C 24g S 307mg SFA 1g UFA 7g (6)

VARIATION

Friarelli (Greens with pancetta, garlic, onion, and hot red pepper, Campanian style). Cook the greens as above. Warm the oil, then add the garlic, pepper flakes, 1oz (30g) sliced, finely diced pancetta, and a small onion to the pan. Sauté until the garlic, onion, and pancetta begin to color. Add the greens and beans and proceed as above. Illustrated on page 57.

ASPARAGI ALLA PARMIGIANA

Asparagus, Parma style

Serves 8.

INGREDIENTS

2lb (1kg) tender asparagus
salt, to taste
4 tbsp unsalted butter
⅔ cup (60g) freshly grated Parmesan
freshly ground white pepper, to taste

PREPARATION

1 Preheat the oven to 425°F (220°C).
2 Trim the ends of the asparagus and peel away the skin at the end of each stalk (see page 161).

3 In a skillet large enough to accommodate the length of the asparagus, bring enough water to cover the asparagus to a boil. Add salt –
1 teaspoon per 1 quart (1.25 liters) of water. Lower the asparagus into the water and boil until tender but not mushy, about 6 minutes.
4 Drain the asparagus immediately and plunge it into ice water to stop the cooking.
5 Butter a baking dish that will hold the asparagus in two or three layers. Scatter pieces of butter over each layer of asparagus, sprinkle generously with Parmesan, and season with pepper.
6 Bake the dish in the middle of the oven until the Parmesan is just beginning to melt, approximately 15–20 minutes, then serve immediately.

KCal 115 P 6g C 2g S 181mg SFA 6g UFA 3g (8)

ZUCCHINI ALLA CASALINGA
Steamed zucchini with butter and onion

I often make this good and simple dish when young zucchini are in season. The natural sweetness of the zucchini, the large proportion of onion, and the creamy butter combine to create a delightfully sweet dish. It is best served warm or at room temperature, or even made a day ahead of serving. Serves 6.

INGREDIENTS

2lb (1kg) fresh, young zucchini, no more than 6–8oz (175–250g) each
1 large onion, finely diced
2 tbsp unsalted butter
2 tbsp extra-virgin olive oil
¾ tsp salt, or to taste
1 tsp chopped fresh thyme, or ½ tsp dried, or 1 tsp finely shredded fresh basil leaves

PREPARATION

1 Wash the zucchini and trim both ends. Slice them in half lengthwise and then crosswise into slices approximately ¾in (1.5cm) thick.
2 Place the zucchini, onion, butter, and olive oil in a heavy-bottomed covered pot, leaving a small opening for steam to escape. Cook over medium heat until the zucchini are tender but not falling apart, 15–20 minutes. Stir them frequently during cooking, and if there is excess water, remove the lid during the last 5 minutes. If the zucchini seem dry, cover the pot completely and reduce the heat.
3 When the zucchini are cooked, add the salt and herbs, and toss thoroughly. Let cool to room temperature before serving.
KCal 120 P 3g C 6g S 198mg SFA 4g UFA 6g (6)

MELANZANE AL FUNGHETTO
Eggplant with mushrooms, garlic, and herbs

This tasty dish is very straightforward to prepare. I like to serve it as an accompaniment to chicken or other fowl, or lamb.

INGREDIENTS

1½lb (750g) medium–small eggplants
salt, to taste
8oz (250g) cultivated mushrooms
4 tbsp extra-virgin olive oil
1 onion, chopped
2 large cloves garlic, finely chopped
½ tsp chopped fresh marjoram, or ¼ tsp dried
1 tbsp chopped fresh flat-leaf parsley
freshly ground black pepper, to taste

PREPARATION

1 Wash the eggplants and cut off the stems and navel ends; do not peel them. Cut into 1in (2.5cm) cubes. Sprinkle the cubes lightly with salt and place them in a colander. Set a weighted plate on top (a heavy can is ideal) and let drain for at least 40 minutes before rinsing. Pat dry with paper towels.
2 Meanwhile, clean the mushrooms with a brush or cloth; do not wash them. Trim the stems and slice the mushrooms lengthwise.
3 Warm the olive oil in a nonstick skillet. Add the onion and garlic and sauté over medium heat until they soften, about 4 minutes.
4 Transfer the eggplant to the pan and sauté for 10 minutes, stirring frequently. Add the sliced mushrooms and herbs and continue to cook, stirring constantly, until tender, 4–5 minutes. Sprinkle with salt and pepper and serve.
KCal 190 P 4g C 8g S 398mg SFA 2g UFA 13g (4)

CARCIOFI RITTI
Tuscan-style stuffed braised artichokes

This is a particularly good way to serve artichokes. It is substantial enough for an antipasto, but it is also an appealing accompaniment for pork or lamb. Serves 3.

INGREDIENTS

6 artichokes, about 8oz (250g) each
1 tbsp freshly grated Parmesan
3 tbsp extra-virgin olive oil
2 garlic cloves, finely chopped
2oz (60g) capocollo (see page 27) or prosciutto, finely chopped
3 tbsp chopped fresh flat-leaf parsley
2 tbsp lightly toasted bread crumbs
¼ tsp salt
good pinch of freshly ground pepper

PREPARATION

1 Prepare the artichokes for stuffing (see page 160).
2 Preheat the oven to 375°F (190°C).
3 Select a baking dish in which the artichokes will fit snugly. Combine the Parmesan, 2 tablespoons of oil, the garlic, capocollo or prosciutto, parsley, bread crumbs, salt, and pepper in a small bowl.
4 Use a teaspoon to fill each artichoke with the stuffing. Place the artichokes and their stems in the baking dish and pour ¾ cup (175ml) of water and the remaining oil into the bottom of the dish.
5 Cover the dish with foil. Bake until the artichokes are tender, about 40 minutes. Add more water if the dish gets dry. Let cool for 15 minutes, then serve.
KCal 265 P 15g C 11g S 694mg SFA 4g UFA 15g (3)

PISELLINI CON PROSCIUTTO

Baby peas with prosciutto, Roman style

INGREDIENTS

4 tbsp unsalted butter
1 small onion, finely chopped
2oz (60g) prosciutto in a thick slice, finely diced
3lb (1.5kg) fresh baby shell peas (unshelled weight), or
1lb (500g) frozen baby peas
1 tbsp chopped fresh flat-leaf parsley
½ cup (125ml) Chicken Broth (see page 73) or water
salt and freshly ground black pepper, to taste

PREPARATION

1 Melt the butter in a skillet. Add the onion and sauté until softened but not colored, 4–5 minutes.
2 Stir in the prosciutto and cook for 1–2 minutes to blend the flavors. Add the peas, parsley, and broth or water. Cover and cook gently until the peas are tender and most of the liquid has evaporated, about 15 minutes, stirring occasionally.
3 Season to taste and serve immediately.
KCal 240 P 13g C 14g S 523mg SFA 9g UFA 5g (4)

CONDIGGION

Summer vegetable salad, Ligurian style

Serves 6. Illustrated on page 56.

INGREDIENTS

4 yellow or red peppers, roasted, skinned, and seeded
(see page 160), and cut into ½in (1cm) wide strips
1 small seedless cucumber, peeled and thinly sliced
2 sweet vine-ripened tomatoes, cut into eighths
20 black or green olives, halved and pitted
10 anchovies in olive oil, drained and cut into small pieces
2 tbsp small capers, drained
1 tsp chopped fresh oregano, or ½ tsp dried
salt and freshly ground black pepper, to taste
4 hard-boiled eggs, quartered
extra-virgin olive oil

PREPARATION

1 In a salad bowl, combine the roasted peppers, cucumber, tomatoes, olives, anchovies, capers, oregano, and seasoning to taste.
2 Toss lightly, then lay the eggs over the salad and dress with the olive oil just before serving.
KCal 175 P 10g C 8g S 1025mg SFA 2g UFA 6g (6)

INSALATA RUSSA ALLA PIEMONTESE

Russian salad in the style of Piedmont

The Russian salad was assimilated into Italian cuisine long ago, though a simpler combination of vegetables is used in the Italian version of the true original. The hard-boiled eggs may be left out, but I think they add a great deal to the composition. Serves 6.

INGREDIENTS

1½lb (750g) boiling potatoes, scrubbed
2 carrots, scraped
2 medium beets
1 cup (150g) fresh or frozen peas
1 tbsp wine vinegar
1 hard-boiled egg
1 tbsp olive oil
1 quantity Maionese (see page 140)

PREPARATION

1 Place the potatoes in a pot, cover with cold water, and bring to a boil. Add the carrots to the pot. Cook the vegetables until tender (the carrots will cook more quickly and should be lifted out and set aside to cool). When the potatoes are cooked, drain and peel them, then set aside to cool.
2 Meanwhile, wash the beets and remove their stems but not the base of the stem. Avoid piercing the flesh. Place them in a pot and cover with cold water. Cook until a sharp knife inserted through a beet comes out easily, about 25 minutes.
3 Cook the peas in boiling salted water until tender but not mushy, 2–5 minutes, depending on type and size. Drain and rinse in cold water.
4 Drain the cooked beets and let cool completely. Peel them and remove the stems. Cut the flesh into dice, place in a bowl, and cover with cold water. Pour in the vinegar (this prevents the beets from "bleeding"). Let soak for 5 minutes, then drain.
5 Dice the potatoes and carrots, and cut the hard-boiled egg into slightly smaller dice.
6 Combine the vegetables and egg in a serving dish and mix with the olive oil. Add the mayonnaise, toss everything together, and serve.
KCal 455 P 7g C 27g S 211mg SFA 5g UFA 29g (6)

INSALATA DI PANE RAFFERMO E PEPERONI

Bread salad with roasted peppers

There are several famous Italian bread salads — such as Tuscan panzanella *and Apulian* cialed *— that should be made with only the best tomatoes. However, in this salad, the primary ingredients are excellent year-round. Its success depends on the quality of the bread: it should contain no sugar, eggs, or seeds, and must be chewy and substantial, not light and airy, in order to stand up to the dressing. An unsalted, sturdy peasant bread is perfect, but it must be firm — about 4 days old. Don't be afraid to add more pepper: a dressing with plenty of bite is a pleasant contrast to the sweetness of roasted peppers.*

INGREDIENTS

2 large red peppers, or a combination of
red and yellow peppers
1 lb (500g) sturdy white Italian bread or peasant bread
½ cup (125ml) extra-virgin olive oil
3 tbsp wine vinegar
1 small red or white onion, quartered and very finely sliced
1 scallion, including green top, finely sliced
2 tbsp pitted and sliced sharply flavored green olives
1 tbsp chopped fresh oregano, or 1 tsp dried
½ tsp salt
¼ tsp freshly ground black pepper, or more to taste

PREPARATION

1 Roast the peppers (see page 160). When they are cool enough to handle, cut them lengthwise in half. Remove the stem, lift off the skin, then scrape out all of the seeds.
2 Meanwhile, remove and discard all the crusts from the bread and cut it into bite-size cubes.
3 To make the dressing, combine the oil, vinegar, ½ cup (125ml) of water, onion, scallion, olives, herbs, salt, and pepper in a small bowl. Marinate for 10 minutes to allow the flavors to blend.
4 Cut the peppers into 2in (5cm) strips. Transfer the bread cubes and pepper strips to a salad bowl. Pour over the dressing, toss well, and check the seasoning. It is best served within several hours.
KCal 570 P 9g C 60g S 821mg SFA 5g UFA 27g (4)

VARIATION

To make a summer version of this salad, substitute firm Italian-style whole-wheat bread for white bread. Omit the red peppers and olives, and replace with two diced vine-ripened tomatoes, 1 teaspoon of chopped fresh oregano (or half a teaspoon of dried oregano), and 2 tablespoons of torn fresh basil leaves. Adjust the quantities of oil and vinegar according to taste.

Wine vinegar

Extra-virgin olive oil

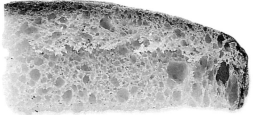

Italian bread

Red and yellow peppers

Red onion

Scallion

Green olives

Oregano

Salt

Black pepper

SAUCES

Italian *salse* are a simple affair in comparison to those of the classic French kitchen, which require lengthy simmering, straining, and reduction. The foundation of many sauces is the cooking liquid from the dish, often enriched by wine. Few sauces that are made separately are butter based, and cream is rarely used. The basic ingredient is often olive oil, to which pounded nuts, herbs, cheese, or bread crumbs are added for body and flavor. As for tomato sauces, I have no doubt that there are as many varieties as there are cooks in Italy. Quickly cooked, they preserve the inherent flavor of the tomatoes. Some are not cooked at all, but combine sun-ripened tomatoes with fruity olive oil, thickened with herbs, capers, or olives. The sauces in this chapter have a multitude of purposes.

BESCIAMELLA
Béchamel sauce

The origins of this white sauce have long been disputed between the Italians and the French. Its name is supposed to derive from the Marquis de Béchamel, maître d'hôtel to Louis XIV, but its place in northern Italian cuisine predates its appellation. Béchamel is as fundamental to Italian cooking as tomato sauce. It acts as a binder for fillings and croquettes; it is indispensable in baked lasagne; it moistens vegetable gratins and is a foundation for other sauces. If it is to be used as a binder, the consistency should be made thicker by long simmering. The recipe below is for a pouring sauce.

INGREDIENTS

2¼ cups (550ml) milk
4 tbsp unsalted butter
3 tbsp all-purpose flour
¼ tsp salt

PREPARATION

1 Heat the milk to just below the boiling point; keep it warm.
2 Melt the butter in a heavy-bottomed saucepan over low heat. Add the flour and stir with a wooden spoon or whisk to remove lumps. Heat the flour and butter paste through, stirring constantly, for about 2 minutes. Do not allow it to brown.
3 Add the warm milk 1 tablespoon at a time, stirring constantly. Begin to add several tablespoons at a time, still stirring, then slowly trickle in the remaining milk. If lumps appear, you may be adding the milk too quickly, or the heat may be too high. Should this occur, turn off the heat and stir vigorously, pressing the lumps against the side of the pan.
4 When all the milk has been added, simmer the sauce gently for 15 minutes longer, until it is thick enough to coat the back of a spoon. Add salt during the last 10 minutes of cooking. The sauce may be kept covered in the refrigerator for up to 4 days.

KCal 960 P 22g C 61g S 699mg SFA 46g UFA 20g (whole quantity)

VARIATIONS

For pasta dishes, add a pinch of nutmeg with the salt. For vegetable casseroles and other dishes, add 1 bay leaf to the milk before heating it and remove it when the sauce is finished.

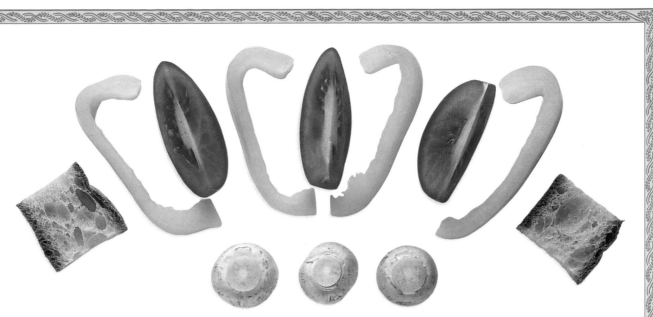

BAGNA CAÔDA

Hot anchovy sauce in the style of Piedmont

This garlicky sauce, literally "hot bath" in the regional dialect, is served straight from the cooking pot and used for dipping vegetables — particularly cardoons, peppers, and celery — or thin slices of sturdy bread. It also makes a good sauce for thin spaghetti, or if there is a little bit of leftover sauce in the pan, you can scramble eggs in it. It is usually made with an equal proportion of butter to olive oil, but you can vary the quantities. Makes about 1 cup (250ml), enough for ½lb (250g) of pasta.

INGREDIENTS

6 large garlic cloves, finely chopped
milk
⅓ cup (90ml) extra-virgin olive oil
4oz (125g) anchovy fillets in olive oil
½ cup (125g) unsalted butter
shavings of white or black truffle, or
¼ tsp truffle oil, optional

PREPARATION

1 Place the garlic in a small bowl and cover with milk. Set aside for about 2 hours to soften the garlic's strong flavor, then drain off the milk and rinse the garlic under cold water.
2 In a small saucepan over very low heat, combine the oil, the anchovies in their oil, and the garlic. Use a wooden spoon to mash the anchovies.
3 When the anchovies have dissolved into the oil, stir in the butter and truffle or truffle oil, if desired. Melt, then pour the sauce into a fondue pot; keep the heat under the sauce very low. Serve with a selection of vegetables and robust country-style bread for dipping.

KCal 2085 P 33g C 1g S 4927mg SFA 80g UFA 101g (whole quantity)

SUGO DI POMODORI FRESCHI

Fresh tomato sauce

Authentic Italian tomato sauces, with their pungent sweetness and depth of flavor, are impossible to replicate without vine-ripened Mediterranean plum tomatoes, and it is far better to use good canned plum tomatoes than the ubiquitous artificially ripened variety. This simple sauce makes the most of good, fresh summer tomatoes. It can be used with pasta and is particularly good with seafood.

INGREDIENTS

5 cups (1.25kg) fresh, sweet, mature vine-ripened plum tomatoes, peeled, seeded, and chopped
5 tbsp (75ml) extra-virgin olive oil
4 garlic cloves, bruised
½ small onion, sliced into fine half-moons
1 tbsp chopped fresh flat-leaf parsley
½ tsp sea salt
6 large fresh basil leaves, shredded
freshly ground black pepper, to taste

PREPARATION

1 Place the tomatoes in a colander over a bowl and let drain for about 5 minutes.
2 Warm the olive oil and garlic together in a pan, pressing on the bruised garlic to release its juices. When the oil is hot, add the onion and parsley and sauté just until the garlic begins to color lightly and the onion is softened, about 2 minutes.
3 Discard the tomato juice and add the tomatoes and salt. Use a potato masher to crush the tomatoes finely. Bring the sauce to a simmer, then reduce the heat and continue to simmer, stirring occasionally, until thickened, about 20 minutes.
4 Add the basil and pepper and check for salt.

KCal 915 P 10g C 45g S 896mg SFA 12g UFA 65g (whole quantity)

SALSETTA ROSSA ALLA LIGURE
Uncooked tomato sauce with black olives

This tomato sauce is particularly suitable for fish. The best tomatoes to use here are the sweet, vine-ripened Italian plum variety. The next best are other tasty vine-ripened tomato varieties that are available during the summer when farm stands sell fresh produce. Cherry tomatoes are often good, and widely available, although they require a little more work to prepare.

INGREDIENTS

1½lb (750g) fresh vine-ripened tomatoes,
peeled, seeded, and chopped
1 small garlic clove, finely chopped
1 anchovy, mashed, optional
½ cup (60g) pitted black olives, sliced
1 tbsp torn or chopped fresh basil
4 tbsp extra-virgin olive oil
½ tsp salt, or to taste
freshly ground black pepper, to taste

PREPARATION

1 Place the tomatoes in a colander over a bowl and let drain for about 30 minutes.
2 Discard the tomato juice and mix together the tomatoes with all the other ingredients, adding pepper to taste. Allow to stand for 1–3 hours before using to give the flavors time to develop.

KCal 690 P 10g C 24g S 2785mg SFA 9g UFA 47g (whole quantity)

SUGO DI POMODORO
Tomato sauce

A basic cooked tomato sauce with countless possibilities, this is ideal with pasta. For use in baked dishes or as a foundation for other sauces, it is best to pass the sauce through a food mill (see page 159) or strainer, which produces a smooth purée. Makes enough for 2lb (1kg) of pasta.

INGREDIENTS

4 cups (1kg) canned plum tomatoes in juice
5 tbsp (75ml) extra-virgin olive oil, plus extra to serve
2 large garlic cloves, bruised
1 onion, finely chopped
1 small carrot, finely chopped
1 tbsp chopped fresh flat-leaf parsley
½ tsp salt, or to taste
4 large basil leaves, chopped

PREPARATION

1 Drain the tomatoes, reserving their juice for another use. If the sauce is not to be passed through a food mill or strainer, scoop out the excess seeds. Crush or mash the tomatoes and set aside.
2 Warm the oil and garlic together in a pan, heating gently until the garlic is golden, 1–2 minutes. Add the onion, carrot, and parsley and continue to sauté until softened but not colored, about 10 minutes.
3 Add the tomatoes, salt, and basil. Simmer gently until a uniformly thick sauce forms and the oil collects on the surface, 20–25 minutes. Remove the sauce from the heat.
4 If you are not straining the sauce, discard the garlic cloves. For added flavor, an additional tablespoon of extra-virgin olive oil may be stirred into the sauce before serving.
5 To strain the sauce, let it cool slightly, then place a food mill over a pan and pass the sauce through it, including the garlic cloves, if desired. Press out as much pulp as possible. Return to the heat just long enough for the sauce to warm through. Stir in an additional drizzle of extra-virgin olive oil for added flavor, if desired.

VARIATION

For a creamy tomato sauce, add 2 tablespoons of mascarpone, or 4 tablespoons of heavy cream to the strained tomato sauce. Return to the heat just to heat through, but do not allow to boil.

KCal 915 P 13g C 47g S 1196mg SFA 11g UFA 61g (whole quantity)

SALSETTA ROSSA CRUDA
Uncooked red sauce

This is one of the several traditional sauces that accompany the classic boiled dinner (meat or fish). It can also be used as a topping for pasta, but grated Parmesan should not be added. The sauce can only be as good as the tomatoes used, which must be sweet and flavorful. It is best made up to several hours before serving.

INGREDIENTS

1½lb (750g) mature, vine-ripened plum tomatoes, peeled, seeded, and chopped
6–8 large basil leaves, finely shredded
4 tbsp extra-virgin olive oil
1 small garlic clove, finely chopped
½ tsp salt
¼ tsp freshly ground black pepper

PREPARATION

1 Place the tomatoes in a colander over a bowl and let drain for about 30 minutes.
2 Discard the tomato juice and combine the tomato flesh with the basil, oil, garlic, salt, and pepper. Cover and leave for at least 1 hour, and up to 3 hours, before serving.

KCal 670 P 6g C 24g S 845mg SFA 9g UFA 51g (whole quantity)

VARIATION

Omit the garlic and add 1 tablespoon of grated red onion and 1 tablespoon of capers. Thicken with a tablespoon of dry bread crumbs, if desired.

SALSA VERDE
Green sauce

Salsa verde, "green sauce," a piquant olive oil-and-herb-based sauce, is the classic accompaniment to simple meat and fish dishes. It also goes well with grilled shrimp or chicken, or with potatoes of any kind. The addition of bread makes a thicker sauce for a variation in texture. Use only white Italian or French bread made without sugar.

INGREDIENTS

4 tbsp freshly squeezed lemon juice, or wine vinegar (if serving with meat)
1 small garlic clove, finely chopped
½ cup chopped fresh flat-leaf parsley
2 tbsp minced sweet white onion or scallion
3 tbsp small capers, drained and rinsed
1 tsp Dijon mustard
½ cup (125ml) extra-virgin olive oil
freshly ground salt and black pepper, to taste

PREPARATION

1 In a bowl, combine the lemon juice, garlic, parsley, onion, capers, and mustard. Gradually beat in the oil using a fork.
2 Season with salt and pepper to taste. Set aside at room temperature for 1–2 hours to marinate. Salsa verde can be made up to one day in advance and kept at room temperature until ready to serve.

KCal 1160 P 2g C 5g S 1518mg SFA 18g UFA 102g (whole quantity)

VARIATIONS

• **Salsa Verde con Peperoncini** (Green sauce with little green peppers). Add 1 finely chopped miniature pickled green Italian pepper and 1 mashed cooked egg yolk to the basic mixture.
• **Salsa Verde alla Mollica di Pane** (Green bread sauce). Add 1 teaspoon of mashed anchovy and 2 tablespoons of finely chopped pickled gherkins to the basic mixture. Soak 1 slice of white Italian or French bread, crusts removed, in a little water. Squeeze out as much water as possible, then chop the bread to a fine consistency in a food processor. Use a fork to blend it with the other ingredients. This sauce can be made up to one day in advance and kept at room temperature until ready to serve.
• **Salsa Verde al Rafano** (Green horseradish sauce). Subsitute red wine vinegar for the lemon juice; omit the garlic, onion, or scallion, and capers; reduce the parsley to 2 tablespoons and the olive oil to 4 tablespoons and add 4 tablespoons of grated fresh or prepared horseradish to the sauce.

PEPERONATA
Sweet pepper sauce

This cooked sauce, which includes sweet peppers, is especially compatible with beef and pork. Its flavor is improved if it is made in advance up to step 5. Let it cool, leaving out the remaining tablespoon of olive oil and the parsley until just ready to serve. It can be prepared 2–3 days in advance and stored, tightly covered, in the refrigerator.

INGREDIENTS

1½lb (750g) mature, vine-ripened plum tomatoes, or canned drained tomatoes, peeled, seeded, and chopped
1 red and 1 yellow pepper
4 tbsp extra-virgin olive oil
1 small onion, finely chopped
2 garlic cloves, finely chopped
pinch of hot red pepper flakes
2 tbsp chopped fresh flat-leaf parsley

PREPARATION

1 Place the tomatoes in a colander over a bowl and let drain for about 5 minutes.
2 Using a vegetable peeler, peel the skin off the peppers. Alternatively, place them under a hot broiler until blackened all over (see page 160). Let cool slightly, then lift off the skin. Cut them in half lengthwise and remove their cores and seeds. Cut the halves into ½in (1cm) wide strips, then cut the strips into small dice. Set aside.
3 Warm 3 tablespoons of oil in a skillet over medium-low heat. Sauté the onion and garlic until soft and translucent, stirring occasionally.
4 Add the pepper flakes and diced peppers and continue to sauté gently until the peppers begin to soften, 10–12 minutes. Add the tomatoes, discarding the juice, cover, and simmer gently, stirring occasionally, until the peppers are thoroughly tender, 5–8 minutes.
5 Remove from the heat and stir in the parsley and the remaining tablespoon of olive oil. Serve hot, warm, or at room temperature.

KCal 830 P 12g C 55g S 96mg SFA 9g UFA 52g (whole quantity)

VARIATION

Mandorlata di Peperoni (Pepper and almond sauce in the style of Basilicata). In this variation, which is particularly suited to fish, the sauce is embellished with ground almonds. Add 1 teaspoon of red wine vinegar to the tomatoes; omit the parsley and stir in ⅓ cup (45g) of blanched, ground, untoasted almonds just before serving.

MAIONESE
Mayonnaise

Mayonnaise has a great many uses in the Italian kitchen. Homemade mayonnaise using fresh eggs and good olive oil is a far cry from the commercial product. The procedure for making mayonnaise with a food processor is simple, as long as all the utensils and ingredients are at room temperature before you begin. Classic mayonnaise is made with only the yolk of the egg, but I use the whole egg, which produces lighter mayonnaise with a higher protein content (the yolk is nearly pure fat, while the white is pure protein). Makes about 1 cup (250g).

INGREDIENTS

½ cup (125ml) vegetable oil
4 tbsp extra-virgin olive oil
1 egg, at room temperature
½ tsp salt, or to taste
1 tsp Dijon mustard
2 tbsp freshly squeezed lemon juice, or to taste
sprinkling of freshly ground white pepper

PREPARATION

1 Mix the oils together in a small pitcher.
2 Crack the egg into the blender container and add the salt. Beat lightly and briefly.
3 Drizzle in 2 tablespoons of the combined oils. Blend on high speed for 10 seconds. Pour in the remaining oil in a thin, steady stream. It is critical that the oil be added slowly and gradually in order for the mayonnaise to emulsify.
4 Stop the blender and scrape the inside of the container so that the ingredients can be mixed in thoroughly. Add the mustard, lemon juice, and pepper and blend again. Use immediately or cover tightly and refrigerate for up to a week.

KCal 1740 P 6g C 1g S 847mg SFA 23g UFA 156g (whole quantity)

VARIATIONS

• **Maionese Verde** (Green mayonnaise). Add 1 finely chopped small pickled green Italian pepper, 2 tablespoons of finely chopped flat-leaf parsley, 1 tablespoon of chopped capers, freshly ground black pepper, and half a small anchovy fillet, well mashed, to the basic mayonnaise. Mix with a wooden spoon. Serve with boiled beef (see page 110), boiled chicken (see page 73), boiled fish (see page 50), or on hard-boiled eggs.
• **Maionese Tonnata** (Tuna mayonnaise). Blend 1 tablespoon of freshly squeezed lemon juice and 3½oz (100g) drained canned tuna in olive oil into the basic mayonnaise. Use over cold boiled sliced veal, on hard-boiled eggs, or on sliced tomatoes. Sprinkle drained small capers over the sauce.

PESTO

Pounded basil and pine nut sauce

It is said that Genoa, where this sauce originated, produces the best pesto because of the superior fragrance of Italian Riviera basil. The flavor of the olive oil and the blend of cheeses used are at least as important: Parmesan provides depth and complexity, and can be used alone, while pecorino adds intensity and sharpness. The unctuous quality of pesto necessitates a sturdy pasta cut to support it; trenette and eggless fettuccine are used in Genoa. Suitable dried pastas are spaghetti, linguine, and bucatini. Makes enough for 1lb (500g) of pasta.

INGREDIENTS

2 cups (75g) fresh basil leaves, solidly packed
3 garlic cloves, roughly chopped
⅓ cup (45g) pine nuts, lightly toasted
½ cup (125ml) extra-virgin olive oil
½ tsp salt
pinch of freshly ground black or white pepper
½ cup (45g) freshly grated Parmesan
¼ cup (20g) freshly grated pecorino
2 tbsp unsalted butter, at room temperature

PREPARATION

1 Put the basil, garlic, pine nuts, oil, salt, and pepper in a food processor and blend for about 20 seconds to make a smooth, even purée.
2 Transfer to a bowl and, using a wooden spoon, beat in the grated cheeses and butter (you can use the food processor, engaging the motor for 10 seconds, but the texture will not be as good).
3 If using the pesto as a pasta sauce, place it in the serving bowl. Add 2 tablespoons of the cooking water from the pasta to the pesto and blend. Toss the drained pasta with the pesto sauce.

Note: Pesto can be stored in a glass jar, topped with a little olive oil, and covered with plastic wrap (press the wrap directly onto the surface to prevent discoloration). It will keep refrigerated for several months, or frozen for up to 3 months. The flavor will be better if the grated cheeses and the butter are omitted until the pesto is needed. Beat them in up to several hours before serving.

KCal 1965 P 32g C 6g S 1656mg SFA 48g UFA 140g (whole quantity)

Black pepper

Parmesan   Pecorino   Butter

Salt

Olive oil

Pine nuts

Garlic

Basil

DESSERTS

Italians usually reserve desserts for celebrations. An exception to this custom is the consumption of little pastries or *biscotti* with espresso at breakfast or at midday. Religious feasts bring confections that invariably have symbolic meaning, and in every region the diversity of sweet dishes is astonishing. They are often bestowed with charming, whimsical names, such as *coscie di monache*, "nun's thighs," *chiacchiere di monache*, "nun's chatter," and *suspirus*, "sighs." The desserts in this chapter represent the types of sweets more usually made in the home.

CRESPELLE DOLCI CON LE MELE

Sweet apple crepes

Delicate crespelle (see page 89) can have sweet and savory stuffings. This apple filling is very good. Makes 20 crepes.

INGREDIENTS

3lb (1.5kg) apples
½ cup (125g) sugar
⅓ tsp ground cinnamon
4 tbsp unsalted butter, plus butter to grease
4 tbsp Cognac or brandy
1 quantity Crespelle (see page 89), with the zest of 1 lemon added to the batter, optional confectioners' sugar, to dust

PREPARATION

1 Peel, halve, and core the apples. Cut them into thin slices and place in a large bowl. Add the sugar and cinnamon and toss well.
2 Heat the butter in a large shallow skillet. Add the sliced apples and sauté until they are a rich golden color, about 10 minutes. Pour in the Cognac and toss everything together. Cook over medium heat until the alcohol is evaporated, the apples are tender, and the juices have reduced slightly. Allow to cool while making the crepes.
3 Preheat the oven to 375°F (190°C).
4 Lightly butter two large baking dishes. Place a rounded tablespoonful of filling at one end of each crepe. Brush a little apple liquid along the inside edge of the crepe, fold it over, then press to seal. Repeat with the remaining crepes, then place them in the dishes, leaving a little space around each one.
5 Bake the crepes for about 15 minutes, then remove them from the oven and let rest for 10 minutes. Sprinkle with sugar and serve.
KCal 850 P 16g C 108g S 351mg SFA 16g UFA 20g (4)

ZUPPA INGLESE

Italian trifle ("English soup")

Zuppa inglese is one of Italy's most popular desserts. This is the version I grew up with. It is best made a day ahead, up to step 4. Serves 6. Illustrated on page 150.

INGREDIENTS

12 ladyfingers or savoiardi biscuits, split
3–4 tbsp raspberry jam
4 tbsp dry sherry or rum
2 egg yolks
3 tbsp sugar
1 heaping tbsp cornstarch
pinch of salt
1in (2.5cm) strip of lemon zest
1½ cups (350ml) milk
14 strawberries, 8 sliced and 6 left whole
2 cups (500ml) heavy or whipping cream
dash of vanilla extract
small piece of frozen bittersweet chocolate, to decorate

PREPARATION

1 Select a wide glass bowl. Spread the insides of the ladyfingers with jam and arrange them in the bowl. Sprinkle with sherry or rum and set aside.
2 In a small pan off the heat, beat the yolks with 2 tablespoons of sugar. Mix in the cornstarch. Stir in the salt, lemon zest, and milk. Place over very low heat and stir constantly until the custard is thick enough to coat the spoon, about 7 minutes.
3 Pour the custard over the ladyfingers and arrange a layer of sliced strawberries on top.
4 Whip the cream, adding the remaining sugar and a dash of vanilla, then spread it over the fruit.
5 Pare chocolate shavings onto the cream. Decorate with whole strawberries and chill before serving.
KCal 590 P 6g C 36g S 228mg SFA 28g UFA 16g (6)

ZABAIONE
Zabaione with Marsala

While zabaione has become a popular dessert, it is also considered a restorative in Italy. I remember my uncle Aldo, a serious athlete, whipping up and then downing straight zabaione for an energy boost. It can be eaten as it is or combined with whipped cream, and it is excellent with baked fruit desserts or fresh strawberries.

INGREDIENTS

3 egg yolks
3 tbsp sugar
3 tbsp dry Marsala or Vin Santo, if available
1 cup (250ml) chilled heavy cream, whipped with
1½ tbsp confectioners' sugar, optional

PREPARATION

1 Bring water to a boil in the bottom of a double boiler or pan, then reduce the heat to let the water simmer.
2 Meanwhile, place the eggs, sugar, and Marsala in the top of the double boiler, or in a large, shallow heatproof bowl, and whisk thoroughly.
3 Position the bowl over the water, making sure it does not touch. Beat until light, pale, and velvety. The mixture is ready when it is thick enough to coat the back of a spoon. Do not allow it to overheat.
4 Remove the zabaione from the heat. It can be eaten as it is, or left to cool, then folded into the chilled cream. Pour it into glasses and serve at once.

KCal 345 P 3g C 20g S 26mg SFA 16g UFA 10g (4)

COPPA ORESTE
"Oreste's goblet" mascarpone dessert

This wonderful dessert originated in the Oreste restaurant in Modena.

INGREDIENTS

12 large amaretti cookies
3 tbsp brandy
2 eggs
¼ cup (60g) sugar
1 cup (250g) softened mascarpone cheese
½oz (15g) plain chocolate shavings, to decorate

PREPARATION

1 Put three amaretti in each of four wide goblets. Sprinkle the brandy over the cookies.
2 Beat together the eggs and sugar until pale, then beat in the mascarpone until smooth and creamy. Spoon the mixture into the glasses, then chill until firm, 2 hours. Sprinkle with chocolate and serve.

KCal 520 P 8g C 45g S 681mg SFA 21g UFA 10g (4)

MONTE BIANCO
Chestnut and chocolate "white mountain"

This dessert is named after Mont Blanc, whose frosty white peaks are within view of Lombardy, where the dish originates. It is often made without chocolate, but I prefer this version, which was taught me by my friend Flavia Destefanis. Use fresh chestnuts if available; canned ones don't have the same depth of flavor.

INGREDIENTS

1lb (500g) fresh chestnuts or drained canned chestnuts
2 cups (500ml) milk
pinch of salt
⅔ cup (150g) sugar
2in (5cm) piece of vanilla pod, or ½ tsp vanilla extract
1 tbsp unsalted butter
4 tbsp cocoa powder, or 6oz (175g) semisweet chocolate, melted
2 tbsp Cognac or rum, optional
2 cups (500ml) chilled heavy cream
4 tbsp confectioners' sugar, plus extra if necessary
2oz (60g) candied violets, or 2 tbsp chopped toasted almonds, optional

PREPARATION

1 Chill the bowl and whisk for whipping the cream.
2 If using fresh chestnuts, soak them in warm water for 30 minutes. Score an X-shape on the flat side of each chestnut (avoid piercing the flesh), then put them in a pot, cover with water, and bring to a boil. Reduce the heat and simmer, partially covered, until tender, about 40 minutes. Drain, cover with warm water to keep them soft, and begin to peel them.
3 Place the peeled or canned chestnuts in a pan with the milk. Add the salt, sugar, and vanilla. Bring to a boil, then lower the heat to medium and cook the chestnuts until they are starting to fall apart, 20–30 minutes. If the milk becomes syrupy, add a little more. Drain the chestnuts, discard the vanilla pod, and reserve the milk.
4 Purée the chestnuts, butter, cocoa or chocolate and Cognac or rum in a food processor, or pass the mixture through a potato ricer or food mill, adding up to 4 tablespoons of reserved milk to moisten.
5 Taste the purée and add a little confectioners' sugar if required. Chill for at least an hour.
6 Pass the mixture through a ricer or food mill again directly onto a serving plate, spiraling inward to create an airy mound of purée.
7 Place the cream in the chilled bowl with the confectioners' sugar and whip into soft peaks. Spoon some cream over the mound and scatter the violets or almonds on top. Serve with the remaining cream.

KCal 1140 P 13g C 98g S 464mg SFA 45g UFA 28g (4)

LATTE ALLA PORTOGHESE
Orange flan

This dessert takes its name from the typical Portuguese custard flan. Custards are popular in Italy, too. I especially like this delicate, orange-flavored version. Serves 12.

INGREDIENTS

8 extra-large eggs
2 tsp vanilla extract
finely grated zest and the juice of 1 small orange, about 4 tbsp total
2¾ cups (560g) sugar
4 cups (1 liter) milk
pinch of salt
candied orange peel to decorate, optional

PREPARATION

1 Preheat the oven to 350°F (180°C).
2 Prepare twelve 6oz (175g) ovenproof custard cups or a 12in (30cm) ring mold.
3 Beat the eggs. In a separate bowl, combine the vanilla, orange zest and juice, ¾ cup (175g) of sugar, the milk, and the salt. Combine this mixture with the eggs, then put it through a sieve.
4 Heat the remaining sugar in a large pan over medium-low heat until it melts and caramelizes.
5 Carefully pour the caramelized sugar into the individual cups or the ring mold, coating the bottom and sides evenly. Work quickly while the caramel remains liquid (if it starts to set, reheat it). Let the caramel cool and harden.
6 Pour the custard into the cups or ring mold, over the caramel. Place the cups or mold in a 2in (5cm) deep baking dish. Pour boiling water into the dish to within ½in (1cm) of the top of the cups or mold. Slide it into the oven. Bake the large flan for about 1 hour, and the individual ones for 45 minutes–1 hour, or until a skewer comes out clean (test during the last 15 minutes of cooking).
7 Let the flan cool for 10 minutes, then refrigerate until cold (3–4 hours). Invert the flan(s) onto a plate. The caramel will form an amber sauce around the firm custard. Decorate the top with pieces of candied orange peel, if desired.

KCal 300 P 8g C 54g S 168mg SFA 3g UFA 3g (12)

CROSTATA DI CREMA DI LIMONE
Nick Malgieri's Ligurian lemon tart

My friend Nick Malgieri, a master pastry chef and cookery writer, found this recipe during his travels. Pasta frolla, the classic sweet Italian pastry, forms the crust. Like the lemon tart of Nice, it has a distinctive dark top. Serves 12.

INGREDIENTS

Pasta frolla
2 cups (250g) all-purpose flour
1/3 cup (75g) sugar
1/2 tsp baking powder
1/4 tsp salt
1/2 cup (125g) unsalted butter, cut into small pieces
2 large eggs

Filling
1 cup (250g) sugar
1/3 cup (45g) flour
8 eggs
2 tsp lemon zest
1/2 cup (125ml) lemon juice
2 cups (500ml) heavy cream

PREPARATION

1 Combine the flour, sugar, baking powder, and salt. Rub in the butter to make a fine, crumblike mixture.
2 Add the eggs and beat everything together until the mixture forms a ball of dough. Wrap the dough in plastic wrap and chill in the refrigerator.
3 Preheat the oven to 325°F (160°C).
4 Grease a 10 x 2in (25 x 5cm) round layer pan. Roll the dough to a thickness of 1/4in (5mm), keeping it approximately the size of the pan, and line the pan.
5 Beat the sugar and flour together in a mixing bowl, then whisk in the eggs, two at a time. Next, whisk in the lemon zest, juice, and heavy cream.
6 Pour the filling into the pan and bake on the lowest rack of the oven for about 1 hour, or until the crust is golden and the filling has set. Let it cool, then cover and refrigerate before unmolding.

KCal 505 P 9g C 45g S 130mg SFA 20g UFA 12g (12)

PIZZA DOLCE PASQUALE
Neapolitan sweet Easter pizza

This traditional Easter sweet is really cheesecake in a cookie-like crust. Serves 6–8. Illustrated on page 151.

INGREDIENTS

Pastry
1/2 cup (125g) unsalted butter, at room temperature
4 tbsp sugar
1 small egg
1 1/2 cups (175g) cake flour, or more if necessary

Filling
3 tbsp golden raisins, or chopped candied peel
1 tbsp Grand Marnier or Anisette
2 1/2lb (1.25kg) whole-milk ricotta
2 extra-large eggs
4 tbsp heavy cream
1/2 cup (125g) sugar
good pinch of salt
grated zest of 1 orange
slices of candied fruit, optional, to decorate

PREPARATION

1 Cream the butter and sugar until very light in color and texture. Gradually beat in the egg until the mixture is creamy and smooth.
2 Sift in the flour. Stir by hand, just until the flour is absorbed. Shape the dough into a thick disk, adding up to 1/2 cup (60g) more flour if needed to make a workable dough. Wrap it and chill for at least 5 hours.
3 Roll out the dough, fit it into a 9 10in (23–25cm) tart pan and chill for another hour.
4 Soak the golden raisins in liqueur for 30 minutes.
5 Preheat the oven to 375°F (190°C).
6 Beat the ricotta with the eggs until you have a smooth, even mixture. Beat in the cream, then the sugar, salt, orange zest, raisins, and the liqueur.
7 Pour the filling into the crust. Bake for 1 hour and 15 minutes, or until a skewer comes out clean. Decorate with candied fruit, and serve chilled.

KCal 590 P 20g C 48g S 349mg SFA 22g UFA 11g (8)

PESCHE RIPIENE
Baked stuffed peaches from the Piedmont

INGREDIENTS

6 large fresh, sweet, ripe peaches, halved and pitted
18 amaretti, crushed, about 1 1/2 cups (150g), or more to bind
1 tbsp unsalted butter, melted, plus butter to grease
1 egg yolk
1 tsp sugar, or to taste
1 tsp Cognac or brandy

PREPARATION

1 Preheat the oven to 375°F (190°C).
2 Scoop out the pulp from each peach half, leaving 1/4in (5mm) of the peach shell intact. Chop the pulp.
3 Combine the amaretti, 2 teaspoons of butter, the egg yolk, sugar, and Cognac with the peach pulp.
4 Fill the peach halves with the mixture. Place them in a buttered baking dish and brush the edges of the peaches with butter. Bake, uncovered, until thoroughly cooked, about 30 minutes.

KCal 260 P 4g C 42g S 128mg SFA 3g UFA 5g (4)

PERE RIPIENE CON CREMA PASTICCIERA

Stuffed poached pears with custard sauce

This is one of my mother's tried and true dessert recipes, her own "fantasia." Ginger is not commonly used in Italian cooking and baking, but it is a splendid flavor match with the pears. For 2 people.

INGREDIENTS

3 green pears (not too ripe)
juice of half a lemon
½ cup (125ml) dry sherry
1 slice of fresh ginger
1 tbsp honey or sugar

Custard
5 tsp sugar
1 egg yolk
1 heaping tbsp cornstarch
1 cup (250ml) milk
small pinch of salt
1in (2.5cm) strip of lemon zest

Filling
8 amaretti or macaroons, crushed, about ⅔ cup (60g)
1 tbsp raisins, chilled and chopped
pinch of ground cinnamon

PREPARATION

1 Peel and halve the pears. Carefully remove the seeds and surrounding membrane. Leave the stems intact. Sprinkle the pear halves with lemon juice to preserve their color and place them in a pan, hollow part down, without overlapping them.

2 Pour 1 cup (250ml) of water and the sherry over the pears. Add the ginger, and honey or sugar. Cover the pan, bring to a boil, then lower the heat and cook the pears until they are firm but not mushy, about 5 minutes. With a slotted spoon, transfer them to a baking dish, reserving 1 tablespoon of liquid, and let cool.

3 Meanwhile, make the custard. Place the sugar and egg yolk in a saucepan and beat for a few minutes until creamy. Beat in the cornstarch and 2 tablespoons of milk using a wooden spoon.

4 Place the pan over low heat and gradually add the rest of the milk, salt, and lemon zest. Stir constantly until the mixture is simmering gently and is thick enough to coat a spoon. Remove from the heat, cover, and keep warm.

5 Combine the amaretti, raisins, cinnamon, 2 tablespoons of custard, and the reserved pear liquid. Stuff the pears and turn them onto a serving plate. Drizzle with warm custard, sprinkle with cinnamon, and serve immediately.

KCal 550 P 8g C 94g S 390mg SFA 4g UFA 5g (2)

Sugar

Honey

Fresh ginger

Dry sherry

Lemon juice

Pears

Egg yolk

Cornstarch

Milk

Salt

Lemon
zest

Amaretti

Raisins

Cinnamon

FRAPPE
Sweet fried pastry ribbons

There are many versions of these light, ribbonlike pastries that are typically made for celebrations. In Tuscany they are called cenci, "tatters"; in Perugia, frappe, "fringe"; and in Liguria, bugie, "lies." A variation is even mentioned in a 13th-century Emilian manuscript. In my grandmother's Apulian version, the dough includes olive oil, and the pastries are soaked in a honey syrup. I prefer this, my mother's version. Serve with confectioners' sugar, or with Salsetta d'Uva Passa (right) and make plenty, because once you start eating them, you can't stop. Serves 10–15. Illustrated on page 150.

INGREDIENTS

*4 cups (500g) flour
2 tbsp chilled unsalted butter, cut into small pieces
1 whole egg and 2 yolks, beaten together
⅔ cup (150g) sugar
¼ tsp salt
1 cup (250ml) dry sherry or dry vermouth
corn or other vegetable oil for shallow frying
confectioners' sugar, to dust*

PREPARATION

1 Sift the flour and rub in the butter, either by hand or in a food processor fitted with a metal blade, until the mixture has become fine and crumbly. Transfer the mixture to a large pastry board.
2 Make a well in the center of the mound. Beat together the eggs, sugar, salt, and sherry in a separate bowl, and pour the mixture into the well.
3 Using a fork, draw the dry ingredients into the liquid, always beating in the same direction. When the dough becomes pliable, begin to work it with your hands. If it is too soft, sprinkle in more flour, but do not make it too stiff. Divide it into four parts.
4 Work with one piece at a time, keeping the rest covered with a damp dish towel. Roll out the dough until it is paper-thin, or use a hand-cranked pasta machine to do so, working through all the settings.
5 Using a fluted pastry wheel or a knife, cut the dough into 1in x 5in (2.5cm x 12cm) strips. Tie the strips into loose knots or pinch short pieces in the middle to form bows. Spread them out on dry dish towels and cover them while you make the rest.
6 Heat the oil in a skillet. When it is hot enough to make the dough sizzle, add the first batch of frappe and fry until golden on both sides. There should be space around each one so they cook quickly and evenly. Transfer them to paper towels and let drain.
7 Sprinkle the cooled pastries with confectioners' sugar or drizzle with raisin sauce and serve.

KCal 350 P 5g C 49g S 43mg SFA 3g UFA 10g (12)

SALSETTA D'UVA PASSA
Raisin sauce with port wine

My paternal grandmother made this syrup for lacing over cartadatte, Apulia's counterpart of frappe. Some of my friends like to serve it with their Christmas ham. The port, which is my innovation, adds depth to the flavor.

INGREDIENTS

*1 lb (500g) raisins
1 cup (250ml) port wine
½ tsp cloves
½ tsp cinnamon
½ cup (125g) honey*

PREPARATION

1 Place the raisins in a pan with 3 cups (750ml) of water, cover, and simmer gently for 1 hour, lowering the heat once the liquid starts to bubble.
2 Strain the cooked raisins through a food mill or strainer. Return the syrup to the pan and add the port, spices, and honey. Simmer for another 30 minutes, then let cool before serving.

KCal 1400 P 1g C 300g S 170mg SFA neg UFA neg (total amount)

FICHI MANDORLATI
Dried stuffed figs, Apulian style

Stuffed figs are a specialty of Apulia. This variation, typical of Bari, is my favorite. The filling includes chocolate, which goes exceedingly well with almonds and figs, and bay leaves impart a beguiling aroma. Store them in sealed glass jars to let the scents and flavors marry. Eat these little jewels with espresso or sweet dessert wine.

INGREDIENTS

*50 soft, moist, unstrung dried figs, preferably Barese
50 whole unblanched almonds, roasted for 15 minutes
2 tbsp fennel seeds
6oz (175g) bittersweet chocolate, broken into small pieces
25 bay leaves*

PREPARATION

1 Preheat the oven to 350°F (180°C).
2 Make a slit in each fig. Place an almond, a pinch of fennel seeds, and a sliver of chocolate in the center of each fig, then press the opening closed.
3 Place the figs on a baking sheet and bake until heated through and lightly colored, about 20 minutes. Remove from the oven and let cool.
4 Place the figs in a glass jar, between layers of bay leaves. Sprinke in any remaining fennel seeds. Seal and store in a cool place for 1–2 weeks before using.

KCal 65 P 1g C 11g S 12mg SFA 1g UFA 1g (per fig)

BISCOTTI DELLA NONNA
Italian sesame biscuits

Because these biscotti are traditionally dunked into sweetened espresso, they are meant to be firm. Two versions of these popular biscuits are included. The first recipe produces a hard dunking biscuit. The variation, made with more butter, is richer and more cookielike. Both versions will keep for 3 months or more in a sealed container, stored in a cool, dry place. Makes 5 dozen.

INGREDIENTS

1 cup (250g) sugar
4 tbsp unsalted butter
3 large eggs
1 tsp vanilla extract
3½ cups (425g) all-purpose flour
¼ tsp salt
3 tsp baking powder
1 cup (150g) sesame seeds (toasted or untoasted)
4 tbsp milk

PREPARATION

1 Preheat the oven to 350°F (180°C).
2 Beat together the sugar and butter until very creamy – the more you beat, the better. Add the eggs and continue to beat for a few minutes by hand, or for a minute with an electric mixer.
3 Beat in the vanilla. Sift in the flour, salt, and baking powder, and beat again for several minutes by hand until you have a firm, well-mixed dough. Wrap the dough in plastic wrap and chill for 1 hour.
4 Spread the sesame seeds on a plate. Dust your hands with flour and shape the dough into long ropes about 1in (2.5cm) across. Cut the ropes into 1in (2.5cm) pieces.
5 Brush the dough pieces with milk and roll them in the sesame seeds. Place them on greased baking sheets, leaving plenty of space between each one. Bake until golden, 15–20 minutes.

KCal 60 P 2g C 9g S 30mg SFA 1g UFA 2g (per biscuit)

VARIATION

For a softer, crumblier biscuit, preheat the oven to 375°F (190°C). Sift 4 cups (500g) of flour, 1 cup (250g) of sugar, 1 tablespoon of baking powder, and ½ teaspoon of salt into a mixing bowl. Cut in 1 cup (250g) of butter until the mixture resembles fine crumbs. Mix 2 beaten eggs with ½ cup (125ml) of milk and 1 teaspoon of vanilla extract. Stir them into the dry ingredients to make a soft dough. Wrap the dough in plastic wrap and chill for 1 hour. Shape the dough into pieces as decribed above. Brush with milk and roll them in the sesame seeds. Bake for 12–15 minutes, or until golden.

BISCOTTI CON PINOLI
Pine nut cookies, Piedmontese style

Elisa De Rogatis gave me this recipe, which has been in her family for years. The lack of flour and butter may strike one as odd, but the almond paste makes them really light. Makes 4–5 dozen. Illustrated on page 150.

INGREDIENTS

1lb (500g) almond paste
2 cups (500g) sugar, plus 2 tbsp
¾ cup (45g) fairly dry white bread crumbs
5 large egg whites
1 tsp vanilla extract
12oz (375g) pine nuts

PREPARATION

1 Preheat the oven to 375°F (190°C).
2 Combine the almond paste, sugar, and bread crumbs using two knives or a pastry cutter. Work the mixture until it is fine and crumbly.
3 Add the egg whites and vanilla, and beat by hand just until the mixture is smooth and sticky.
4 Spread the pine nuts on a plate. Break off a walnut-sized piece of dough and roll it into an oval shape. Roll it in the pine nuts. Place the cookies on baking sheets lined with baking parchment, leaving about 1½in (3.5cm) between each one.
5 Bake the cookies until lightly golden, 12–15 minutes. Slip the parchment off the sheet and leave for 2 minutes before peeling off the cookies.

KCal 120 P 2g C 16g S 11mg SFA neg UFA 5g (per cookie)

CROCCANTE DI MANDORLE
Sardinian almond brittle

This rustic sweet can be eaten with coffee, or crushed and used as an ice cream topping. Illustrated on page 150.

INGREDIENTS

1 cup (250g) sugar
½lb (250g) blanched almonds, lightly toasted and chopped
grated zest of 1 lemon, and 1 lemon to spread brittle

PREPARATION

1 Lightly oil a marble or wooden pastry board.
2 Place a heavy nonstick skillet over medium heat. Add the sugar and stir occasionally until caramelized. Stir in the almonds and lemon zest.
3 Working quickly, pour the mixture onto the board. Use the whole lemon to spread it out to about ⅓in (1cm) thick. Allow it to harden and cool, then break it into pieces and store in a sealed jar.

KCal 2515 P 53g C 280g S 35mg SFA 12g UFA 122g (total)

ZUPPA INGLESE
Italian trifle ("English soup")
(page 142)

BISCOTTI CON PINOLI
Pine nut biscuits,
Piedmontese style
(page 149)

CROCCANTE DI MANDORLE
Sardinian almond brittle
(page 149)

FRAPPE
Sweet fried pastry ribbons
(page 148)

PIZZA DOLCE PASQUALE
Neapolitan sweet Easter pizza
(page 145)

MENU PLANNER

Here are menus that draw from eight regions of Italy. Each course is meant to be served separately, never on the same plate. The *antipasto*, if there is one (this course is often reserved for Sunday or feast days), arrives first. The *primo* follows. It may consist of a soup, a pasta or a risotto dish, but never more than one (soup and pasta would not be eaten at the same meal, for example). The *secondo*, "second course," is one of meat or fish. The *contorno*, "side dish," or *contorni*, may appear alongside the *secondo* or afterward, as vegetables are never an afterthought, but instead a highlight in the whole menu scheme. There may be cheese to savor after the side dishes, but if not, there's always fruit to end the meal. Certain fruit are specialties of particular regions, and I have therefore included fruit of note in each menu. *Dolci*, "desserts," are rarely a part of everyday meals, but are included here to represent what might be prepared for a celebratory occasion. While this book does not concern itself with bread or wines, it should be remembered that both of these sacred foods are essential parts of the Italian meal.

·

LAZIO

ANTIPASTO
Involtini di Cavolo (see page 126)
Stuffed cabbage

·

PRIMO
Bucatini all'Amatriciana (see page 85)
Bucatini with tomato and bacon sauce

·

SECONDO
Uccelletti Scappati (see page 115)
Veal rolls stuffed with prosciutto and fontina

·

CONTORNO
Pisellini con Prosciutto (see page 133)
Baby peas with prosciutto, Roman style

·

FORMAGGIO
Mozzarella di bufala,
caciocavallo, provolone

·

FRUTTA
Fruit in season (melon, plums,
pears, peaches, figs)

·

DOLCE
Tiramisù (see page 58)
Chocolate and mascarpone "pick me up"

LIGURIA

ANTIPASTO
Melanzane Ripiene (see page 64)
Stuffed eggplant

·

PRIMO
Riso Arrosto (see page 95)
Roasted rice with sausage and artichokes

·

SECONDO
Costolette d'Agnello Impanate (see page 114)
Pan-fried breaded lamb chops

·

CONTORNO
Condiggion (see page 133)
Summer vegetable salad

·

FRUTTA
Fruit in season (figs, tangerines, oranges, grapes)

·

DOLCE
Crostata di Crema di Limone (see page 145)
Nick Malgieri's Ligurian lemon tart

APULIA

ANTIPASTO
Cozze Arracanati (see page 66)
Baked mussels

•

PRIMO
Ciceri e Tria (see page 86)
Salentine fettuccine with
chickpeas and onions

•

SECONDO
Taiedda (see page 108)
Baked fish fillets with vegetables,
potatoes, and white wine

•

CONTORNO
Fagiolini al Pomodoro (see page 129)
Green beans with tomato and garlic

•

FORMAGGIO
Ricotta forte, pecorino, caciocavallo,
scamorza, provòle

•

FRUTTA
Fruit in season (loquats, pears,
quinces, figs, apricots)

•

DOLCE
Fichi Mandorlati (see page 148)
Dried figs stuffed with roasted almonds,
chocolate, and fennel

Biscotti della Nonna (see page 149)
Italian sesame cookies

Ciceri e Tria

EMILIA

ANTIPASTO
Salumi
Cured meats – prosciutto, salame, culatello

•

PRIMO
Cappelletti in Brodo (see page 80)
Little pasta dumplings with meat and
cheese filling, cooked in broth

•

SECONDO
Petti di Pollo Impanati (see page 118)
Breaded fried chicken breast cutlets served
hot with wedges of lemon

•

CONTORNO
Asparagi alla Parmigiana (see page 131)
Asparagus, Parma style

•

FORMAGGIO
Parmigiano-reggiano
(A two-year-old Parmesan)

FRUTTA
Fruit in season (cherries, plums, pears,
apples, strawberries, raspberries)

•

DOLCE
Coppa Oreste (see page 143)
"Oreste's goblet" mascarpone dessert

Asparagi alla Parmigiana

PIEDMONT

ANTIPASTO
Castellana di Peperoni (see page 63)
Stuffed roasted pepper "sandwiches,"
grissini (breadsticks)

•

PRIMO
Brodo di Manzo (see Manzo Lesso, page 110)
Beef broth

•

SECONDO
Gallinelle e Polenta (see page 52)
Fricassee of game hen with wild mushrooms
and polenta

•

CONTORNO
Finocchi Gratinati (see page 130)
Baked fennel

•

FORMAGGIO
Toma, robiola, Gorgonzola

•

FRUTTA
Castagne Arrosto (see page 161)
Roasted chestnuts

•

DOLCE
Zabaione (see page 143)
Zabaione cream with Marsala

TUSCANY

ANTIPASTO
*Crostini con Fegatini di Pollo alla Salvia
(see page 70)*
Sautéed chicken livers with
sage on crostini

Carciofi Ritti (see page 132)
Stuffed braised artichokes

•

PRIMO
Minestrone Invernale (see page 42)
Winter vegetable soup

•

SECONDO
Arista Fiorentina con Patate (see page 113)
Florentine loin of pork with rosemary and
garlic, and pan-roasted potatoes

•

CONTORNO
Fagioli in Stufa (see page 90)
Beans stewed with garlic and herbs

•

FORMAGGIO
Caciotta
(Young sheep's cheese with extra-virgin
olive oil and freshly ground black pepper)

•

FRUTTA
Fruit in season (grapes, quinces, plums,
peaches, strawberries)

•

DOLCE
Zuppa Inglese (see page 142)
Italian trifle ("English soup")

Gallinelle e Polenta

Zuppa Inglese

LOMBARDY

ANTIPASTO
Peperoni Ripieni (see page 64)
Peppers stuffed with rice and Gorgonzola

•

SECONDO
Risotto alla Milanese (see page 92)
Saffron risotto, Milanese style

Osso Buco alla Milanese (see page 54)
Braised veal shanks, Milanese style

•

CONTORNO
Insalata Mista
Mixed green salad

•

FORMAGGIO
Grana, Gorgonzola (spread on bread with
unsalted butter), stracchino,
bel paese, taleggio

FRUTTA
Fruit in season (grapes, apples, pears)

•

DOLCE
Monte Bianco (see page 143)
Chestnut and chocolate "white mountain"

SARDINIA

ANTIPASTO
Funghi Fritti alla Sarda (see page 63)
Crispy fried mushrooms

•

PRIMO
Polenta Pasticciata di Mia Nonna (see page 96)
My grandmother's baked polenta

•

SECONDO
Agnello alla Sarda (see page 113)
Roast leg of lamb with rosemary and garlic,
my mother's way

•

CONTORNI
Fagiolini
Boiled green beans dressed with
extra-virgin olive oil and lemon

Pinzimonio
Fresh radishes and sliced raw artichoke hearts
with an extra-virgin olive oil, salt, and
black pepper dip

•

FORMAGGIO
Fior di Sardegna
(Semisoft Sardinian pecorino cheese)

•

FRUTTA
Fruit in season (loquats, apricots, pears,
figs, pomegranates, cactus fruit)

•

DOLCE
Croccante di Mandorle (see page 149)
Almond brittle

Osso Buco

Polenta Pasticciata di Mia Nonna

155

TECHNIQUES

Italian cooking is, for the most part, informal and straightforward. There are practically no complicated culinary techniques, no lengthy preparation of reductions and stocks. The only real necessity for the cook is to know how to handle the raw ingredients. These photographic step-by-step sequences are designed to demonstrate the fundamental preparation techniques and to offer some useful guidance on making the most of the ingredients that are typically found in the Italian kitchen. The basic recipes for fresh pasta, polenta, and pizza and focaccia dough may also be found in this chapter.

EQUIPMENT

There is little sophisticated equipment in the Italian kitchen. Most tasks are accomplished with a good knife or *mezzaluna,* and a cutting board. Pots and pans are simple, too. The traditional vessel is earthenware, which is superbly versatile. Copper or cast-iron cookware is also invaluable because it allows even cooking.

OTHER TYPICAL EQUIPMENT
Vegetable peeler, long-handled wooden spoons, sifters, wire whisk, baking stone and baker's peel, ladle, pastry brushes, blender, pepper mill, mortar and pestle, stove-to-oven pan, and covered skillet.

KNIVES
The best types of blades are made of carbon steel, as they have a cleaner edge and can be sharpened more easily than those made of stainless steel. A large chef's knife with a straight edge for slicing and a paring knife for smaller tasks are essentials. A mezzaluna with a 10in (25cm) blade is indispensable for chopping.

Straight-edged chef's knife

Small paring knife

Straight-edged cutting wheel

Fluted cutting wheel

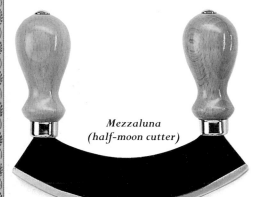

*Mezzaluna
(half-moon cutter)*

PASTRY WHEELS
Sheets of fresh pasta and pastry dough can be cut with pastry wheels. Straight-edged wheels are used primarily for cutting pizza and focaccia. Flute-edged wheels make attractive edges on ribbon-style fresh pasta and stuffed pasta.

MEAT MALLET
A meat mallet with a blunt end and a textured metal end is used to tenderize meat and to flatten cutlets, chicken breasts, and beef slices for stuffed meat rolls.

COLANDER
A sturdy, freestanding metal colander with large round holes is needed to drain pasta quickly (rapid draining is necessary to prevent pasta from continuing to cook after being removed from the heat).

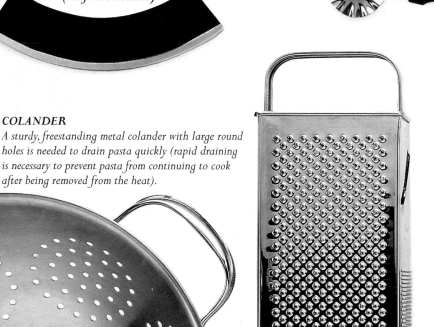

BOX GRATER
Choose a stainless steel grater. Use the smallest holes for grating nutmeg, the medium holes for hard cheese or to make bread crumbs, and the larger holes for shredding softer cheese or vegetables.

PASTA MACHINE

The roller-type pasta machine is the only equipment that produces good homemade pasta as it both kneads the dough and rolls it into very thin sheets. Extrusion machines do not successfully accomplish these tasks. The heaviest, most sturdy roller machines are best because their rollers are better calibrated for rolling out the dough thinly and evenly. These machines are cranked by hand, or may have electric motors attached for automatic rolling.

Pasta machine

Separate cutting attachment

POTATO RICER

This is the best piece of kitchen equipment for transforming cooked potatoes into a smooth purée. It can also be used for other cooked ingredients, such as chestnuts. The ricer works like a garlic press, extruding the ingredient in very fine shreds.

DOUGH SCRAPER

A scraper is used for clearing the work surface of flour and dried dough that has stuck to it and would otherwise find its way into a ball of dough. Scrapers may also be made of plastic or metal.

FOOD MILL (Passatutto)

No piece of modern electric equipment can replace the food mill. It pushes through food, such as cooked tomatoes, and purées as it strains. (Blenders and food processors can purée well, but they do not hold back seeds or skin.)

WIRE MESH SPOON
This is a useful tool for retrieving food from a deep-fryer or from boiling water. It allows liquid to drain off quickly before the food is transferred to absorbent paper or served.

SPATULA
Use a rubber spatula to scrape clean the inside of a bowl while blending or mixing.

Three disks can be inserted into the mill for varying degrees of fineness

Long-handled mesh spoon

PREPARING VEGETABLES

V egetables are best eaten fresh, not
frozen or canned, and this necessitates
some preparation. Wilted or yellow leaves
should be removed from greens. Bruises
should be cut from fennel bulbs or celery.
Carrots must be scraped and, if very
large, cored; eggplant should be salted
and drained to leach out bitter juices.

PEELING TOMATOES

*Blanch the tomatoes in rapidly boiling
water for 30–45 seconds. Drain, then
plunge them into cold water. Score the
skin with a paring knife, then lift it off
with your fingers.*

SEEDING TOMATOES

*Using a small sharp knife, cut out the
tough core portion. Slice the tomatoes in
half lengthwise. Push out the seeds with
your finger. The tomatoes may then be
left in a colander to drain.*

PEELING PEPPERS

*Place the peppers under a hot broiler,
turning them until the surface is
blackened all over. Lift off the charred
skin. Cut the peppers as described and
scrape out the ribs and seeds.*

PREPARING ARTICHOKES FOR STUFFING

*1 Slice off the stem of the artichoke.
Using a paring knife, tear off the
tough outer leaves. Cut across the head
of the artichoke with a serrated knife,
leaving about 1½in (3.5cm) of the base.*

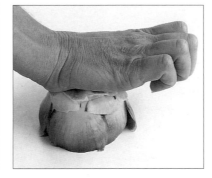

*2 Trim the top of the base with
kitchen shears. Turn the artichoke
upside down on the work surface and
bang it with the heel of your hand,
forcing the leaves to spread open.*

*3 Reach into the center of the
artichoke to pull out the hairy
choke (use a teaspoon if necessary).
Spread the leaves open farther to make
room for the stuffing.*

CLEANING MUSHROOMS

*Use a soft cloth, brush, or paper towels
to remove any dirt. Do not immerse them
in water — that ruins their texture.
Remove their stems and trim off any
woody parts. Wild mushrooms, such as
porcini, may have to be washed quickly
to rid them of earth or grit. They should
be dried immediately and thoroughly.*

USING A POTATO RICER

To mash potatoes after cooking, peel them and pass through the potato ricer, one at a time, while they are still warm. This method gives a light, even-textured mass; a hand masher does not remove lumps, while a food processor makes cooked potatoes gluey.

SHAPING GNOCCHI

Take each piece of gnocchi dough between the thumb and forefinger and drag it down the face of the grater with the medium-sized holes, pushing your thumb into it as you do so to make a small, concave dumpling.

SOAKING & COOKING DRIED BEANS

To prepare beans, place in a bowl, covering with cold water by 3in (7cm). Let stand for at least 4 hours, or overnight. (Or place in a pan with cold water to cover by 3in (7cm). Bring to a boil, cover, and remove from the heat. Let stand for 1 hour. Drain and rinse.) Place in a pan with water to cover by 3in (7cm). Bring to a boil, then reduce the heat. Simmer until tender, about 1 hour. Season only after cooking and drain well.

To prepare chickpeas, rinse well, then place in a pan. Add 5 cups (1.25 liters) of cold water and ⅛ teaspoon of baking soda per 1 cup (200g) of chickpeas. Cover and leave in a cool place for 12–15 hours. Drain and rinse. Place in a pan with 6 cups (1.5 liters) of water. Bring to a boil, then reduce the heat. Simmer until tender, 1–1½ hours. Add 1 teaspoon of salt. Let stand for 15 minutes.

TRIMMING ASPARAGUS

Cut the hard ends off the asparagus. Using a vegetable peeler, pare the thicker skin at the base end of each stalk to reveal the tender stalk underneath.

ROASTING CHESTNUTS

Wash the chestnuts and place them in a bowl with warm water to cover, soaking them for about 30 minutes. Score an X shape on the flat side of each chestnut, without penetrating the flesh (this prevents the chestnuts from exploding in the oven). Place the chestnuts in a roasting pan, scored side up. Roast until tender, 20–30 minutes depending on their size and freshness. Peel while still hot or warm; otherwise, it will be difficult to remove the thin membrane that surrounds the nut.

PREPARING FISH AND SHELLFISH

Most Italian fish and seafood dishes are quite simple to prepare. Fish is generally kept whole as a great deal of flavor permeates the flesh from the head, bones, and skin: scaling and gutting are therefore the only techniques usually needed. It is very important to rinse the cavity of the fish completely after gutting in order to remove any traces of entrails, which have a very bitter taste. Shellfish, too, must be scrupulously fresh and cleaned thoroughly before cooking.

SCALING AND GUTTING FISH

1 *Draw the blunt side of a chef's knife along the body of the fish, working toward the head. Be careful not to tear the delicate flesh underneath.*

Keep the knife at a right angle to the fish

2 *Using a sharp chef's knife, make a slit up along the belly toward the gills, taking care not to insert the blade too far into the body.*

3 *Ease out the innards with the point of the knife. Wash the fish well inside and out, making sure that it is free of blood and any membranes.*

CHOOSING AND PREPARING SALT COD

When buying salt cod, or *baccalà*, select meaty, white fillets, not thin dark pieces. The skinless and boneless variety eliminates tedious preparation techniques. Traditionally preserved salt cod has a high salt content and is very dry. It should be soaked for two days, and the water must be changed twice a day. Today, salt cod is often preserved with less salt than in traditional methods, and the flesh is still somewhat soft. This greatly reduces the soaking time.

1 To rehydrate "soft" salt cod, soak it in cold water for 24 hours (see note left). Keep the bowl covered in the refrigerator and change the water twice.

2 Drain the salt cod and rinse it thoroughly in fresh, cool water. Pull off any skin and remove any remaining bones before cooking.

PEELING AND BUTTERFLYING SHRIMP

1 Remove the head of the shrimp behind the gills, then peel off the shell from the body (you may need to use a small, sharp knife for larger shrimp, which have thicker shells).

2 Make a deep cut along the shrimp's back, then use the point of a knife to lift out the dark intestinal vein. Rinse the shrimp under cold water to remove any traces of intestinal matter.

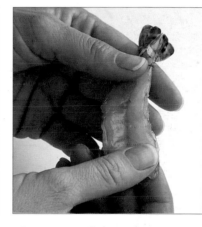

3 Using your fingers, open up the shrimp along the cut so that it can be spread flat like a book. Transfer the butterflied shrimp to a bowl of salted ice water and let stand for 15 minutes.

SOAKING MUSSELS AND CLAMS

Mussels and clams must be purged of any sand or grit before cooking. Place them in a large bowl and let soak. Cover with a plate and refrigerate for several hours, or up to 48 hours, changing the water several times and adding flour or cornmeal with each change. After soaking, carefully sort through the shellfish. Discard any that have broken shells or that feel much too heavy for their size (these are full of sand), then clean the shells thoroughly.

1 Cover the mussels and clams with cold water and add a handful or two of flour or cornmeal to plump them.

2 Scrub the shells to remove surface dirt. To debeard mussels, pull out any strands protruding from the shells.

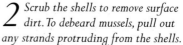

PREPARING MEAT

If possible, try to procure organic or free-range meat that has been raised as naturally as possible. A good butcher will advise on choosing cuts of meat, but as a general rule, it is best to buy tender meat from young animals. Certain cuts, such as the fillet and small rib chops, are tender enough not to require any preparation. For traditional Italian-style veal cutlets (*costolette*), choose chops from the small end of the rack as this is the most succulent cut. There are typical Italian-style meat cuts that require specific treatment. Veal escalopes (*scaloppini*), for example, require flattening to even out the thickness and tenderize them. If you are boning meat, save the bones to make meat broths or stocks.

TENDERIZING MEAT

Place the escalope or cutlet on a cutting board. Pound it lightly with the blunt side of a meat mallet to tenderize and flatten it, being careful not to "break" it.

TYING OSSO BUCO

Tie a length of kitchen string around the circumference of the shank piece to prevent the meat from falling off the bone during cooking.

ROLLING UP MEAT LOAF

Working from the long edge of the mixture, very carefully roll the meat loaf, jelly-roll fashion, to make a long, narrow sausagelike loaf.

COOKING SAUSAGES

Fresh sausages are best eaten within 3 days of being made. The following technique of steaming and then browning fresh sausages, rather than frying them in oil, was taught me by an Italian sausage-maker, Ignacious Bonanno. It ensures that the sausages will stay moist and tender.

Select a large skillet. Pour in water to reach ¼in (5mm) up the sides of the sausages and bring to a boil. Add the sausages and cover. When the water has evaporated and the sausages have browned on one side, turn them. If necessary, add a little more water in order to brown the sausages on all sides. Do not cut or pierce them. Cook until done on the inside and nicely browned, about 20 minutes.

APPLYING A RUB TO A ROAST

Using your hands, press the rub into the incisions on the roast, then work the remaining mixture into the surface flesh.

CUTTING UP A CHICKEN

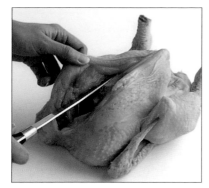

1 Using a very sharp chef's knife, cut along the breastbone toward the tail end. Work down the side of the breastbone to loosen the flesh.

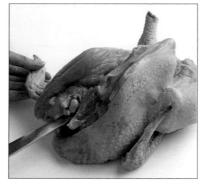

2 Continue cutting down until the wing joint is reached. Slice through it, then place the knife point in the wing socket and pry away the breast.

3 Cut downward through the skin and flesh, then, using your hands, pull away the whole side of the chicken from the carcass.

4 Slice down through the leg joint and break it away from the main carcass. Cut away the whole side of the chicken.

5 Cut around the drumstick and thigh joint to separate it from the breast and wing. Chop off and discard the wing tips.

6 Divide the wing and breast piece, leaving a small piece of breast attached to the wing. Cut the drumstick from the thigh.

7 Repeat this process with the other side of the chicken. You will have 8 separate portions that can be used in a variety of dishes.

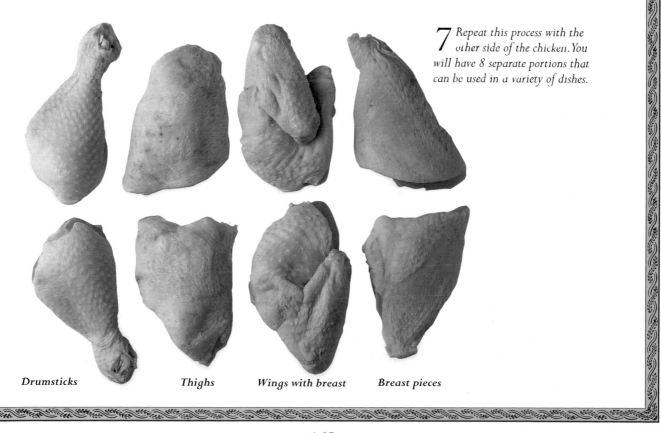

Drumsticks   *Thighs*   *Wings with breast*   *Breast pieces*

MAKING FRESH PASTA

Pasta is still made by hand throughout Italy, but it takes a great deal of practice and experience to achieve light, delicate pasta. Hand-cranked or motorized roller-type pasta machines produce excellent results and are very easy to use. Pasta attachments on food processors do not knead the dough thoroughly enough. Below is a basic recipe for fresh pasta. The dough can be cut by machine or by hand into different shapes for loose or stuffed pasta.

PASTA FRESCA
Fresh egg pasta

Makes about 1½lb (750g), enough for 4 standard servings.

INGREDIENTS

2¼ cups (300g) unbleached all-purpose flour
⅛ tsp salt
3 large eggs
1 tbsp vegetable oil

1 Combine the flour and salt on a large pastry board or work surface. Make a well in the center of the flour. In a small bowl, lightly beat the eggs with the oil and pour the mixture into the well of the flour.

2 Gradually draw in the flour from the inside wall of the well with a fork, beating in the same direction. Use your free hand to protect the outside wall of flour until the wet mixture is well integrated with the flour.

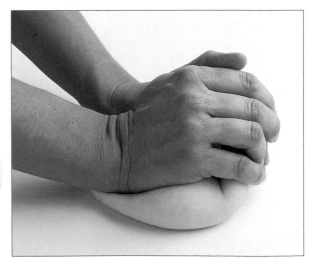

3 When the mixture becomes too stiff to work with a fork, use your hands to form it into a soft ball. With a pastry scraper, sweep up the flour left on the board and sift it, discarding any dried-out dough pieces. Add enough of the flour to form a firm but very pliable dough.

4 Using the heels of your hands, flatten the dough ball and knead it from the middle outward, folding it in half after working it each time. Knead both sides, keeping a round shape; do not let it rest. Cover the dough with an inverted bowl or slightly damp dish towel. Let rest for 15 minutes–3 hours.

ROLLING PASTA BY MACHINE

1 Attach the pasta machine to the work surface. Divide the dough into six equal portions. Use your hands or a rolling pin to flatten one piece of dough; keep the others covered.

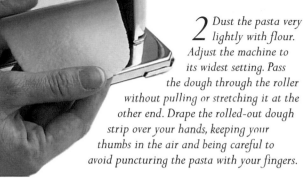

2 Dust the pasta very lightly with flour. Adjust the machine to its widest setting. Pass the dough through the roller without pulling or stretching it at the other end. Drape the rolled-out dough strip over your hands, keeping your thumbs in the air and being careful to avoid puncturing the pasta with your fingers.

3 Fold the dough strip into thirds as you would a letter, overlapping the top third, then the bottom third over the middle portion to make a rectangular shape. Dust the dough strip very lightly with flour on one side.

4 Set the rollers at the next notch. Feed the dough through. Repeat the process of folding the dough into thirds, pressing out the air, flouring it lightly on one side, and passing it through the second notch three times.

5 Feed the flattened piece of dough, narrow end first, through the machine's rollers at each of the remaining settings (see step 6). If the dough begins to stick at any point, dust it lightly with flour on both sides.

6 For all shapes except fettuccine, pass the dough through every notch. For fettuccine, pass the dough through to the next-to-last notch. When the sheet has passed through the rollers for the last time, collect it carefully in your hands and unfold to its full length, keeping your thumbs out of the way. Roll out each portion of dough in the same manner and lay on dry dish towels. Cover with dry dish towels until ready to cut.

The dough must dry slightly, for 10–15 minutes, before being cut

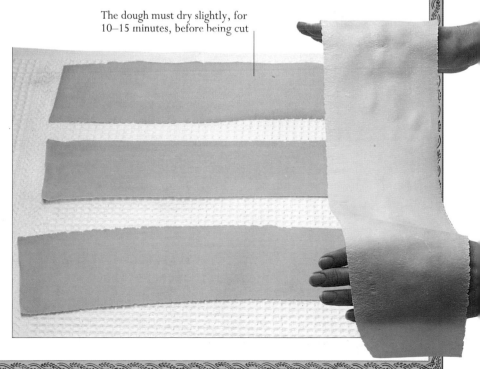

TIPS

• *Keep any dough that is not being worked with covered at all times.*

• *Pinch the pasta together to mend any breaks.*

CUTTING TAGLIATELLE

2 Collect the cut noodles at the base of the cutting attachment. Line four baking sheets with dry dish towels. Lay the noodles out to dry flat for 10–15 minutes, or for up to 3 hours.

1 Attach the cutting attachment to the machine. Take a strip of pasta dough (see page 167). It should now have a slight patina on the surface, but should

not be too dry as this makes cutting difficult. Cut the strips of dough in half across to shorten the strands. Pass each strip through the attachment.

3 To make pasta nests, wrap a few strands loosely around your fingers, lay them flat, and let dry. Store for up to 2–3 weeks in a clean container.

MAKING RAVIOLI

1 Roll out the pasta into 4in (10cm) wide strips (see page 167), passing the dough through every notch of the machine. Work with two strips at a time and set them side by side; keep the rest covered with a dry dish towel.

2 Place 1 teaspoon of filling at 2in (5cm) intervals along one strip of pasta. Use a clean brush to paint thin lines of egg white between the mounds of filling, so that each mound is surrounded by a square of egg white.

3 Cover the strip of pasta with the second strip. Using a pastry wheel or knife, cut the pasta into squares along the egg white lines. Press around each bundle to seal the edges. Repeat with the remaining pasta strips.

MAKING POLENTA

Do not confuse ordinary cornmeal with polenta cornmeal. Italian "instant" polenta cooks in five minutes, but thickens so quickly that lumps easily form before it can be stirred properly. In the traditional method, the polenta is added to boiling water in a steady trickle. The following cold water method is just as effective and less tricky. Use a heavy-based pan that will conduct the heat evenly, and stir the polenta continuously with a long-handled spoon as it tends to bubble and splutter.

POLENTA

Basic polenta

This quantity serves 6 as an accompaniment.

INGREDIENTS

7 cups (1.75 liters) cold water
1 tbsp coarse salt
2 cups (300g) coarse yellow polenta cornmeal

PREPARATION

1 Combine the water and salt in a deep pan. Pour in the cornmeal, stirring constantly with a wooden spoon or whisk.
2 Place the pot over medium heat. Continue to stir the polenta without interruption in the same direction (this prevents lumps from forming and keeps the boiling temperature constant, which is important if the polenta is to be soft and creamy).

3 Continue to stir until the polenta is so thick that it begins to resist stirring and pulls away easily from the sides of the pan with the spoon or whisk, about 30 minutes.
4 Pour the polenta directly into a serving dish if eating immediately. Top with a generous lump of unsalted butter and the grated cheese of your choice (pecorino, Parmesan, ricotta salata, or Gorgonzola are good choices). Loose polenta is also excellent served with Sugo di Pomodoro (see page 138) or Salsa Bolognese (see page 88). Alternatively, make polenta crostini (see below).

VARIATION

To make ***Patùgoi a la Bàita*** (milk polenta with smoked goat cheese, Veneto style), substitute milk for water. Pour the cooked polenta into a serving dish and top with a large lump of unsalted butter and crumbled smoked goat cheese.

MAKING POLENTA CROSTINI

1 *Pour the cooked polenta into a lightly oiled baking sheet or mold, or onto an oiled scratch-proof cutting board or work surface. Dip a narrow spatula in water and spread out the polenta. Let set for about 20 minutes.*

2 *Cut the cooled polenta into diamonds or squares, according to the recipe directions, and lift the pieces off the sheet with a spatula. Proceed with the recipe, or broil or fry the pieces (see step 3).*

3 *To broil, brush the polenta pieces with oil, place on a baking sheet under a hot broiler, and brown on both sides, 8–10 minutes. Alternatively, dredge the pieces in flour and fry in hot olive oil until golden. Drain on paper towels.*

PIZZA AND FOCACCIA DOUGH

The same basic recipe is used for pizza bases and focaccia. The initial mixing of the ingredients can be done by hand or in a food processor. See pages 68–70 for recipes for the different toppings and fillings. Probably no pizza in the world can match the famed pizzas of Naples. What makes the Neapolitan pizza crust so exceptional is the flavorful wheat used in the flour, which is typically a high-gluten "00" flour that produces a chewy but light and tender crust. Unbleached all-purpose flour, preferably stone-ground, is a good substitute. The bases may be cooked on a traditional baking stone, but a baking sheet will also produce excellent, crisp dough.

PIZZA AND FOCACCIA DOUGH

INGREDIENTS

1 cake (10g) fresh yeast, or 1 envelope active dry yeast
½ cup (125ml) warm water
4 cups (500g) all-purpose flour, plus flour to dust
1½ tsp salt
1 cup (250ml) cold water
2 tbsp extra-virgin olive oil, plus extra for brushing

PREPARATION

1 Combine the yeast and half the warm water. Let stand in a warm place for about 10 minutes, or until foamy.
2 Sift together 1 cup (125g) of flour and the salt. Make a well in the center of the flour. Add the remaining warm water, the cold water, and oil to the yeast mixture, then pour the liquid into the well.

3 Gradually stir the flour into the liquid until it is absorbed. Sift in another 2 cups (250g) of flour. When the dough becomes too stiff to stir, shape it into a ball. Proceed as shown opposite.

VARIATION

To make the dough in a food processor, prepare the yeast mixture as described in step 1. Place 3 cups (375g) of flour and the salt in a food processor bowl and process for 30 seconds. Stir the remaining warm water, the cold water, and oil into the yeast mixture, then pour onto the flour. Process until a sticky ball of dough has formed, about 40 seconds. Transfer the dough to a lightly floured board and knead it with your knuckles for 3–4 minutes, sifting onto it as much of the remaining flour as is necessary to make a silky and elastic dough. Proceed as shown opposite, beginning with step 2.

PIZZA QUANTITIES AND BAKING TIMES

Pizza and focaccia should be cooked at 400°F (200°C).
One quantity of pizza dough yields the following amounts:

Pizza type	Quantity	Cooking time
Roman-style pizza base – *thickness: ⅛in (2mm)*	*2 x 14in (35cm) crusts* *4 x 12in (30cm) crusts* *8 x 8in (20cm) crusts*	*7 minutes* *5 minutes* *3–4 minutes*
Neapolitan-style pizza base – *thickness: ¼in (5mm)*	*2 x 12in (30cm) crusts* *4 x 8in (20cm) crusts* *8 x 6in (15cm) crusts*	*9–10 minutes* *5 minutes* *4 minutes*
Focaccia base – *thickness: ½in (1cm)*	*1 x 14in (35cm) x 18in (45cm) rectangular focaccia, or 1 x 12in (30cm) round focaccia*	*10–11 minutes*

KNEADING AND SHAPING THE DOUGH

1 Transfer the dough to a lightly floured board. Knead it with your knuckles for 8–10 minutes, sifting on to it as much of the remaining flour as is needed to make a silky and elastic dough.

2 Place the dough in a lightly oiled bowl and brush it with oil. Cover the bowl with plastic wrap or a clean dish towel. Let rise at room temperature until doubled in size, 1–2 hours.

3 Punch down the dough with your knuckles to expel the air. Lightly oil the baking sheet(s), or if using a pizza baking stone, place it in a hot oven and allow it to preheat.

4 Knead the dough for several minutes until it is elastic. If making more than one pizza, divide the dough into the number of portions desired. Keep covered until ready to shape.

5 Using the palms of your hands, flatten the dough into a disk. Working from the center outward and turning the dough, press and stretch it with your fingers to make the base.

6 Transfer to the baking sheet(s), or a baker's peel or flour-dusted baking sheet if using a stone. Cover with clean dish towels. Leave to rise for 30 minutes then bake (see baking times opposite).

SHAPING FOCACCIA DOUGH

Proceed with the method above up to step 3, then turn to the main recipe (see page 70). The base may be dimpled before the topping is added.

Using your fingers, make indentations all over the focaccia base, creating little dimples to trap olive oil.

INDEX

Figures in **bold** refer to pages with illustrations

———— A ————

Abruzzo, 11
Agnello alla Sarda, 113
almonds, **37**
  almond brittle, 149, **151**
  dried stuffed figs, 148
  pepper and almond sauce, 140
amaretti cookies, **37**
  baked stuffed peaches, 145
  "Oreste's goblet" mascarpone
    dessert, 143
  stuffed poached pears with
    custard sauce, **146-7**
Anatra all'Arancia, **120**, 124
anchovies, **22**
  green bread sauce, 139
  green mayonnaise, 140
  hot anchovy sauce, 137
  in olive oil, **34**
  summer vegetable salad, **8, 14,
    56**, 133
  uncooked tomato sauce with
    black olives, **138**
apples:
  sweet apple crepes, 142
apricots, **36**
Apulia, 13
  menu, 153
Arista Fiorentina con Patate,
  113
artichokes, **21**
  preparing for stuffing, **160**
  roasted rice with sausage and
    artichokes, 95
  stuffed braised, 132
arugula, **20**
  veal chops with fresh tomato
    and arugula sauce, 114
Asparagi alla Parmigiana, **57,131,
  153**
asparagus, **20**
  asparagus and mushroom
    frittata, **41**, 66
  Parma style, **57, 131, 153**
  trimming, **161**

———— B ————

baby peas with prosciutto, 133
Baccalà al Forno, **104**, 109
Baccalà Stufato con Olive e
  Patate, 109
bacon:
  bucatini with tomato and
    bacon sauce, 85
  green beans and potatoes, 129
  spaghetti with eggs and bacon,
    85
  venison casserole, 122
Bagna Caôda, 137
baked:
  fennel, **57**, 130

fish fillets with vegetables,
  potatoes, and wine, 108
mussels, 66
my grandmother's baked
  polenta, **8, 96, 97, 155**
polenta casserole, 95
potato gnocchi with fontina, 79
salt cod with potatoes and
  tomatoes, **104**, 109
shrimp with garlic and parsley,
  101, **105**
stuffed peaches, 145
barley:
  beef soup with barley and
    vegetables, 73
basil, **32**
  pizza with tomato, mozzarella,
    and basil sauce, **44**, 68
  pounded basil and pine nut
    sauce, **141**
  risotto with tomato and basil, 94
Basilicata, 12
bay, **33**
beans, **30**
  sautéed escarole with beans,
    57, 130
  soaking and cooking dried
    beans, **161**
  stewed with garlic and herbs, 90
  winter minestrone, **9, 10, 42-3**
  see also cannellini, green beans
béchamel sauce, 130, 136
beef, **27**
  boiled with various sauces, 110
  chargrilled steak, 111
  lasagne, 84
  little meatballs, **9, 10, 40, 67**
  meat broth, 72
  meat loaf stuffed with ham and
    frittatine, 110, **121**
  my grandmother's baked
    polenta, **8, 96, 97, 155**
  soup with barley and
    vegetables, 73
  sour pan-roasted, 111
  stuffed cabbage, 126
  tagliatelle with bolognese
    sauce, **82, 88**
Besciamella, **57**, 136
Biscotti della Nonna, 149
Biscotti con Pinoli, 149, **151**
Bistecca alla Fiorentina, 111
boiled:
  beef with various sauces, 110
braised:
  savory quails, 122
  stuffed artichokes, 132
  veal shanks, **8, 16, 54-5**
  veal with wine, lemon, and
    pine nuts, 114
brandy:
  baked stuffed peaches, 145
  "Oreste's goblet" mascarpone
    dessert, 143
  roasted duck with orange
    sauce, 124
  sweet apple crepes, 142
bread, **30-1**

bread dumplings in broth, 76
bread salad with roasted
  peppers, **134-5**
breaded chicken breast cutlets,
  118
green bread sauce, 139
pan-roasted guinea fowl with
  bread and sun-dried tomato
  stuffing, 123
potato bread turnovers stuffed
  with pork, 71
sautéed chicken livers with
  sage on crostini toasts, 70
sweet, 16, **31**
bresaola, 16, **26**
broccoli rape, see cime di rapa
Brodo di Carne, 72
Bucatini all' Amatriciana, 85
bucatini with tomato and bacon
  sauce, 85
butter:
  lentils with butter and parsley,
    90
  puréed potatoes, 129
  steamed zucchni with butter
    and onion, 132

———— C ————

cabbage:
  beef soup with barley and
    vegetables, 73
  stewed with pancetta and
    vinegar, 127
  stuffed, 126
  winter minestrone, **9, 10, 42-3**
Caciocavallo, **28**
cactus fruit, **36**
Calabria, 13
Calamari in Zimino alla
  Livornese, 101
Campania, 12
candied fruit and flowers, **37**
cannellini, **30**
  beans stewed with garlic and
    herbs, 90
  sautéed escarole with beans,
    57, 130
capers, **34**
  green mayonnaise, 140
  green sauce, 139
  summer vegetable salad, **8, 14,
    56**, 133
  tuna with onion, olives and
    capers, 103
Cappelletti, **8, 14, 31**, 80, **81**
Carciofi Ritti, 132
Casseruola di Lenticchie con
  Salsicce, **91**
Castellana di Peperoni, 63
cauliflower, **21**
  penne with cauliflower and
    onions, 88
Cavolo alla Parmigiana, 127
chargrilled steak, 111
cheeses, 12, 14, 15, **28-9**
chestnut mushrooms, **21**

chestnuts, **37**
  chestnut and chocolate "white
    mountain," 143
  roasting, **161**
chicken:
  breaded chicken breast cutlets,
    118
  broth with pastina, 73
  cutting up, **165**
  game hen fricassee with
    polenta, **52-3, 154**
  hunter's style, **116-17**
  livers and mushrooms with
    polenta, 96
  Marengo, 119, **121**
  meat broth, 72
  pan-roasted with rosemary and
    garlic, 118
  rice with chicken livers, 94
  sautéed chicken livers with
    sage on crostini toasts, 70
chickpeas, **30**
  fettuccine with chickpeas and
    onions, **9, 13, 86-7, 153**
chicory, **21**
chocolate, **37**
  chestnut and chocolate "white
    mountain," 143
  dried stuffed figs, 148
  Tiramisù, 58
Ciceri e Tria, **8, 13, 86-7, 153**
cime di rapa (broccoli rape), 21
  Italian sausages with broccoli
    rape, 125
  orecchiette with sausage and
    broccoli rape, 84
cinnamon, **33**
Cipolline all'Agrodolce, **40**, 63
citrus fruit, **36**
clams, **24**
  baked, 66
  linguine with clam sauce, **46-7**
  seafood "soup," 98, **99**
  soaking, **163**
cloves, **33**
cod:
  baked salt cod with potatoes
    and tomatoes, **104**, 109
  mixed fish fry, 100
  poached fillets with fresh
    herbs, 108
  salt, **23**
  salt cod stewed with olives and
    potatoes, 109
coffee, **36**
  Tiramisù, **58-9**
conchiglie, **31**
  with harlot's sauce, **83**, 85
Conchiglie alla Puttanesca, **83**, 85
Condiggion, **8, 14, 56**, 133
Coniglio alla Veneta, 119
coppa, **27**
Coppa Oreste, 143
Costolette d'Agnello Impanate,
  114
Costolette di Vitello alla Salsa di
  Pomodoro Crudo e Rucola,
  114

Cozze Arracanati, 66
crabs, **25**
cream:
   cappelletti in a cream sauce, 80-1
   chestnut and chocolate "white mountain," 143
   Italian trifle, 142, **150**, **154**
   lemon tart, 145
   scalloped potatoes baked in milk, **56**, **128**
   sweet Easter pizza, 145, **150**
   zabaione with Marsala, 143
creamy tomato sauce, 138
crepes, 89
   stuffed with ricotta, 89
   sweet apple, 142
Crespelle, 89
Crespelle Dolci con le Mele, 142
Crispelle, **45**, **69**
crispy fried mushrooms, **41**, 63
Croccante di Mandorle, 149, **151**
Crostata di Crema di Limone, 145
crostini, polenta, **169**
Crostini con Fegatini di Pollo alla Salvia, 70
cutlets:
   breaded chicken breast cutlets, 118
   veal rolls stuffed with prosciutto and fontina, **115**
cuttlefish, **24**

D·E

dates, **37**
dried fruit, **37**
   dried stuffed figs, 148
   raisin sauce with port wine, 148
duck, **26**
   roasted with orange sauce, **120**, 124
dumplings:
   bread dumplings in broth, 76
   little pasta dumplings with meat and cheese, **8**, **14**, **31**, 80, **81**
eggplant, **20**
   fritters, 62
   stuffed, 64
   with mushrooms, garlic, and herbs, 132
eggs:
   asparagus and mushroom frittata, **41**, 66
   Italian trifle, 142, **150**, **154**
   lemon tart, 145
   orange flan, **144**
   "Oreste's goblet" mascarpone dessert, 143
   Russian salad, 133
   spaghetti with eggs and bacon, 85
   summer vegetable salad, **8**, **14**, **56**, 133
   sweet Easter pizza, 145, **150**
   Tiramisù, **58**
   zabaione with Marsala, 143
Emilia menu, 153
Emilia-Romagna, 14
equipment, **158-9**
escalopes, pounding, **164**
escarole, **21**

pizza with wilted escarole and olives, **44**, 68
sautéed with beans and ham, **57**, 130
soup, 76

F

Fagioli in Stufa, 90
Fagiolini con Patate all'Istriana, 129
Fagiolini al Pomodoro, **56**, 129
Faraona Ripieno, 123
farfalle, **31**
Fegatini di Pollo con Funghi e Polenta, 96
Fegato alla Veneziana, 125
fennel, **21**, **32**, **33**
   baked, **57**, 130
   pizza with ricotta and fennel seeds, **44**, 68
fettuccine with chickpeas and onions, **9**, **13**, **86-7**, **153**
Fichi Mandorlati, 148
figs, **37**
   dried stuffed, 148
Finocchi Gratinati, **57**, 130
fish, scaling and gutting, **162**
flounder:
   baked fish fillets with vegetables, potatoes, and white wine, 108
   with garlic, lemon, and olives, 103
   mixed fish fry, 100
   in parchment, 102
   poached fillets with fresh herbs, 108
focaccia, **44-5**, 70
   dough, **170-1**
Focaccia Aglio e Olio, 70
Focaccia di Gorgonzola, 70
Focaccia alle Olive, **45**, 70
Focaccia al Rosmarino, **45**, 70
Focaccia alla Sarda, **45**, 70
fonduta, 15
fontina, 15, **28**
   breaded chicken breast cutlets, 118
   potato gnocchi with fontina, 79
   stuffed roasted pepper "sandwiches," 63
   veal rolls stuffed with prosciutto and fontina, **115**
Frappe, 148, **151**
fresh egg pasta, **166-8**
fresh tomato sauce, 137
Friarelli, **57**, 130
fried potatoes, **106-7**, 127
Frittata agli Asparagi, **41**, 66
Frittelle di Zucchini, 62
fritters, 62
Fritto Misto di Mare, 100
Friuli-Venezia Giulia, 16
Funghi Fritti alla Sarda, **41**, 63

G

Gallinelle e Polenta, **52-3**, **154**
game hen fricassee with polenta, **52-3**, **154**
garlic, 15, **32**
   baked shrimp with garlic and parsley, 101, **105**
   beans stewed with garlic and herbs, 90
   eggplant with mushrooms, garlic, and herbs, 132
   green beans with tomato and garlic, **56**, 129
   grilled porgy with garlic, 103
   hot anchovy sauce, 137
   pan-roasted chicken with rosemary and garlic, 118
   pounded basil and pine nut sauce, 141
   sole with garlic, lemon, and olives, 103, **104**
"Gateau" di Patate, 127
gnocchi:
   potato gnocchi, 78, **83**
   potato gnocchi with fontina, 79
   shaping, **161**
Gnocchi alla Fontina Valdostana, 79
Gnocchi di Patate, 78, **83**
Gorgonzola, **28**
   focaccia topping, 70
   peppers stuffed with rice and Gorgonzola, **41**, 64, **155**
grana, **29**
grapes, **37**
green beans, **21**
   and potatoes, 129
   with tomato and garlic, **56**, 129
green bread sauce, 139
green horseradish sauce, 139
green mayonnaise, 140
green sauce, **50-1**, **139**
   with little green peppers, 139
gremolata, **54-5**
grilled:
   porgy with garlic, 103
   shrimp with sage, 100
guinea fowl, **26**
   pan-roasted with bread and sun-dried tomato stuffing, 123

H·I·K

hake:
   mixed fish fry, 100
   poached fillets with fresh herbs, 108
ham:
   breaded chicken breast cutlets, 118
   meat loaf stuffed with ham and frittatine, 110, **121**
   sautéed escarole with beans and ham, **57**, 130
   see also pancetta, prosciutto
haricot beans:
   beans stewed with garlic and herbs, 90
   winter minestrone, **9**, **10**, **42-3**

herbs and spices, **32-3**
honey, **36**
   raisin sauce with port wine, 148
   stuffed poached pears, **146-7**
horseradish:
   green horseradish sauce, 139
hot anchovy sauce, 137
Insalata di Pane Raffermato e Peperoni, **134-5**
Insalata Russa alla Piemontese, 133
Involtini di Cavolo, 126
Italian sausages with bitter broccoli, 125
Italian sesame biscuits, 149
Italian trifle, 142, **150**, **154**
kidneys sautéed with peas and shallots, 124
Knödl alla Tirolese in Brod, 76

L

lamb, **27**
   pan-fried breaded lamb chops, 114
   roast leg of lamb, 113
langoustine, **25**
Lasagne Imbottite, 84
Latte alla Portoghese, **144**
Lazio, 11
   menu, 152
lemon, **36**
   almond brittle, 149, **151**
   braised veal with wine, lemon, and pine nuts, 114
   sole with garlic, lemon, and olives, 103, **104**
   swordfish with lemon sauce, **9**, **17**, **106-7**
   tart, 145
Lenticchie alla Casalinga, 90
lentils, **30**
   lentil stew with sausages, **91**
   with butter and parsley, 90
Liguria, 14
   menu, 152
linguine, **31**
   with clam sauce, **46-7**
Linguine alle Vongole, **46-7**
liver:
   sautéed calves' liver, 125
   see also chicken
lollo rosso, **20**
Lombardy, 16
   menu, 155

M·N

Maccheroni alla Barese con Cavolfiore, 88
Maionese, 140
Maionese Tonnata, 140
Maionese Verde, 140
Mandorlata di Peperoni, 140
Manicotti, 89
Manzo Lesso con Salse Varie, 110
Marche, 11
marjoram, **32**
Marsala, **36**
   zabaione with Marsala, 143

mascarpone, **29**
  creamy tomato sauce, 138
  "Oreste's goblet" dessert, 143
  Tiramisù, **58-9**
mayonnaise, 140
meat, preparing, **164**
meatballs:
  lasagne, 84
  Umbrian style, **9, 10, 40,** 67
meat broth, 72
meat loaf:
  rolling up, **164**
  stuffed with ham and frittatine, 110, **121**
Melanzane al Funghetto, 132
Melanzane Ripiene, 64
Merluzzo all' Erbe, 108
milk:
  milk polenta with smoked goat cheese, 169
  scalloped potatoes baked in milk, **56,** 128
Minestra di Gamberetti e Bietola, **74-5**
Minestra di Manzo e Verdura con Orzo, 73
Minestra di Zucca, **77**
Minestrina di Zucchine, 76
Minestrone Invernale, **8, 10, 42-3**
mint, **33**
  rice with chicken livers, 94
mixed fish fry, 100
Molise, 12
monkfish, **23**
Monte Bianco, 143
mortadella, **26**
  little pasta dumplings with meat and cheese, **8, 14, 31,** 80, **81**
  tagliatelle with bolognese sauce, **82,** 88
mozzarella, **29**
  baked polenta casserole, 95
  crepes stuffed with ricotta, 89
  crispelle, **45, 69**
  lasagne, 84
  pizza with tomato, mozzarella, and basil sauce, **44,** 68
  potato "cake," 127
  risotto with tomato and basil, 94
  Roman-style pizza, 68
mushrooms, 10, 11, **21**
  asparagus and mushroom frittata, **41,** 66
  chicken hunter's style, **116-17**
  chicken livers and mushrooms with polenta, 96
  cleaning, **160**
  crispy fried, **41,** 63
  eggplant with mushrooms, garlic, and herbs, 132
  game hen fricassee with polenta, **52-3, 154**
  vegetable risotto, **8, 15, 48-9**
mussels, **24**
  baked, 66
  in white wine, **40, 65**
  seafood "soup," 98, **99**
  soaking, **163**
my grandmother's baked polenta, **8, 96, 97, 155**
nutmeg, **33**
nuts, **37**

O

olive oil, 14, **35**
olives, **34**
  bread salad with roasted peppers, **134-5**
  focaccia with sliced black olives, **45,** 70
  pizza with wilted escarole and olives, **44,** 68
  salt cod stewed with olives and potatoes, 109
  sole with garlic, lemon, and olives, 103, **104**
  summer vegetable salad, **8, 14, 56,** 133
  tuna with onion, olives, and capers, 103
  uncooked tomato sauce with black olives, **138**
onions:
  bread salad with roasted peppers, **134-5**
  fettuccine with chickpeas and onions, **9, 13, 86-7, 153**
  penne with cauliflower and onions, 88
  sautéed calves' liver, 125
  sautéed kidneys with peas and shallots, 124
  steamed zucchini with butter and onion, 132
  sweet and sour onions, **40,** 63
  tuna with onion, olives, and capers, 103
orange, **36**
  flan, **144**
  roasted duck with orange sauce, **120,** 124
orecchiette, **31**
  with sausage and broccoli rape, 84
Orecchiette con Salsiccia e Cime di Rapa, 84
oregano, **32**
"Oreste's goblet" mascarpone dessert, 143
organ meats, **27**
Osso Buco alla Milanese, **8, 16, 54-5**
osso buco, tying, **164**

P · Q

Pagro alla Griglia, 103
pancetta, **26**
  bucatini with tomato and bacon sauce, 85
  focaccia with pancetta and sage, **45,** 70
  sautéed escarole with beans and ham, **57,** 130
  spaghetti with eggs and bacon, 85
  stewed cabbage with pancetta and vinegar, 127
panettone, 16, **31**
pan-fried breaded lamb chops, 114
pan-roasted:
  chicken with rosemary and garlic, 118
  guinea fowl with bread and sun-dried tomato stuffing, 123

Panzerotti alla Pugliese, 71
Parmesan, 14, **29**
  asparagus, Parma style, **57, 131, 153**
  baked potato gnocchi with fontina, **15,** 79
  eggplant fritters, 62
  little pasta dumplings with meat and cheese, **8, 14, 31,** 80, **81**
  pizza with sweet Italian sausage, **44,** 68
  scalloped potatoes baked in milk, **56, 128**
  zucchini fritters, 62
parsley, **33**
  baked shrimp with garlic and parsley, 101, **105**
  green mayonnaise, 140
  lentils with butter and parsley, 90
  meat loaf stuffed with ham and frittatine, 110, **121**
pasta, **31,** 78-89, **166-8**
  making fresh egg, **166**
  rolling and cutting by machine, **167-8**
Pasta Fresca, **166**
pasta frolla, 145
Pastina in Brodo di Pollo, 73
Patate al Forno, **56, 128**
Patate Fritte, **106-7,** 127
Patùgoi a la Bàita, 169
peaches, **36**
  baked stuffed, 145
pears, **37**
  stuffed poached with custard sauce, **146-7**
peas:
  baby peas with prosciutto, 133
  Russian salad, 133
  sautéed kidneys with peas and shallots, 124
pecorino, **28**
  pizza with ricotta and fennel seeds, **44,** 68
  pizza with sweet Italian sausage, **44,** 68
  ravioli with ricotta, prosciutto, and pecorino, 79
penne, **31**
  with cauliflower and onions, 88
Peperonata, 140
Peperonata con Carne di Maiale, **9, 12, 112**
Peperoni Ripieni, **41,** 64, **155**
pepper, **32**
peppers, **20**
  bread salad with roasted peppers, **134-5**
  green mayonnaise, 140
  green sauce with little green peppers, 139
  peeling, **160**
  pepper and almond sauce, 140
  pork and peppers, **9, 12, 112**
  stuffed with rice and Gorgonzola, **41,** 64, **155**
  stuffed roasted pepper "sandwiches," 63
  summer vegetable salad, **8, 14, 56,** 133
  sweet pepper sauce, 140
Pere Imbottite con Crema Pasticciera, **146-7**
Pesce Lesso con Due Salse, **50-1**

Pesce Spada al Salmoriglio, **8, 17, 106-7**
Pesche Ripiene, 145
Pesto, **141**
Petti di Pollo Impanati, 118
Petti di Pollo Impanati alla Piemontese, 118
Petti di Tacchino Impanati, 118
Piemonte, 15
  menu, 154
pine nuts, **34**
  braised veal with wine, lemon, and pine nuts, 114
  pine nut cookies, 149, **151**
  pounded basil and pine nut sauce, **141**
Pisellini con Prosciutto, 133
pistachios, **35**
pizza, **44-5,** 68-9
  dough, **170-1**
Pizza Dolce Pasquale, 145, **150**
Pizza Napoletana, **12,** 68
Pizza con Ricotta, **44,** 68
Pizza con Salsiccia, **44,** 68
Pizza con Scarola, **44,** 68
Pizzetta Margherita, **44,** 68
poached:
  fish with two sauces, **50-1**
  hake fillets with fresh herbs, 108
  stuffed pears with custard sauce, **146-7**
polenta, **30, 169**
  baked polenta casserole, 95
  chicken livers and mushrooms with polenta, 96
  crostini, **169**
  game hen fricassee with polenta, **52-3, 154**
  milk polenta with smoked goat cheese, 169
  my grandmother's baked polenta, **8, 96, 97, 155**
Polenta Maritata, 95
Polenta Pasticciata di Mia Nonna, **8, 96, 97, 155**
Pollo alla Cacciatora, **116-17**
Pollo alla Marengo, 119, **121**
Pollo in Tegame, 118
Polpettine alla Toscana, 67
Polpettine all'Umbra, **9, 10, 40,** 67
Polpettone Farcito, 110, **121**
porcini mushrooms, **21, 34,** 160
  baked polenta, 96
  game hen fricassee with polenta, **52-3, 154**
  vegetable risotto, **8, 15, 48-9**
porgy:
  grilled porgy with garlic, 103
pork, **27**
  lasagne, 84
  little meatballs, **9, 10, 40,** 67
  little pasta dumplings with meat and cheese, **8, 14, 31,** 80, **81**
  loin of pork with pan-roasted potatoes, 113
  meat loaf stuffed with ham and frittatine, 110, **121**
  pork and peppers, **9, 12, 112**
  potato bread turnovers stuffed with pork, 71
  stuffed cabbage, 126
  tagliatelle with bolognese sauce, **82,** 88

port wine:
  raisin sauce with port wine, 148
potatoes:
  baked fish fillets with vegetables, potatoes, and white wine, 108
  baked salt cod with potatoes and tomatoes, **104**, 109
  fried potatoes, **106-7**, 127
  green beans and potatoes, 129
  loin of pork with pan-roasted potatoes, 113
  potato bread turnovers stuffed with pork, 71
  potato "cake," 127
  potato gnocchi, 78, **83**, **161**
  puréed, 129
  Russian salad, 133
  salt cod stewed with olives and potatoes, 109
  scalloped potatoes baked in milk, **56**, **128**
  winter minestrone, 8, **10**, 42-3
prosciutto, 27
  baby peas with prosciutto, 133
  crispella stuffed with prosciutto, **45**, **69**
  little meatballs, 9, 10, **40**, 67
  little pasta dumplings with meat and cheese, 8, **14**, **31**, 80, **81**
  potato "cake," 127
  ravioli with ricotta, prosciutto, and Pecorino, 79
  stuffed braised artichokes, 132
  stuffed roasted pepper "sandwiches," 63
  veal rolls stuffed with prosciutto and fontina, **115**
provolone, 28
  pizza with ricotta and fennel seeds, 44, 68
Puglie, 13
pumpkin soup, **77**
puréed potatoes, 129
Purè di Patate, 129
puttanesca sauce, **82**, 85
Quaglie Saporite, 122
quail, **26**
  savory braised, 122

R

rabbit, 26
  in the style of Veneto, 119
radicchio, **20**
raisins, **37**
  raisin sauce with port wine, 148
ravioli, 79
  making, **168**
  with ricotta, prosciutto, and pecorino, 79
Ravioli alla Potentina, 79
red mullet, 22
  seafood risotto, 92, **93**
red sauce, uncooked, **50-1**, 139
rice, **30**
  peppers stuffed with rice and Gorgonzola, 41, 64, **155**
  risotto with tomato and basil, 94
  roasted with sausage and artichokes, 95
  saffron risotto, 92

seafood risotto, 92, **93**
stuffed cabbage, 126
Swiss chard and shrimp soup with rice, **74-5**
vegetable risotto, 8, **15**, 48-9
with chicken livers, 94
ricotta, **29**
  crepes stuffed with ricotta, 89
  lasagne, 84
  pizza with ricotta and fennel seeds, 44, 68
  ravioli with ricotta, prosciutto, and pecorino, 79
  sweet Easter pizza, 145, **150**
Riso Arrosto, 95
Riso in Peverada, 94
risotto:
  saffron, 92
  seafood, 92, **93**
  with tomato and basil, 94
  vegetable, 8, **15**, 48-9
Risotto alla Marinara, 92, **93**
Risotto alla Milanese, 92
Risotto alle Verdure, 8, **15**, **48-9**
Risotto con Pomodoro e Basilico, 94
roasted:
  duck with orange sauce, **120**, 124
  leg of lamb, 113
  rice with sausage and artichokes, 95
Rognoncini con Piselli, 124
rosemary, **33**
  focaccia with rosemary, **45**, 70
  game hen fricassee with polenta, 52-3, **154**
  loin of pork with pan-roasted potatoes, 113
  pan-roasted chicken with rosemary and garlic, 118
rum:
  Italian trifle, 142, **150**, **154**
  Tiramisù, **58-9**
Russian salad, 133

S

saffron, 17, **33**
  risotto, 92
sage, **33**
  focaccia with pancetta and sage, **45**, 70
  grilled shrimp with sage, 100
  sautéed chicken livers with sage on toast, 70
  sole in parchment, **102**
  veal rolls stuffed with prosciutto and fontina, **115**
salads:
  bread salad with roasted peppers, **134-5**
  Russian salad, 133
  summer vegetable salad, 8, **14**, **56**, **133**
salami, 27
  crispella stuffed with salami, **45**, 69
  little pasta dumplings with meat and cheese, 8, **14**, **31**, 80, **81**
  potato "cake," 127
Salmoriglio sauce, **106-7**

Salsa Verde, 50-**1**, **139**
Salsa Verde alla Mollica di Pane, 139
Salsa Verde con Peperoncini, 139
Salsa Verde al Rafano, 139
Salsetta Rossa Cruda, **50-1**, 139
Salsetta Rossa alla Ligure, **138**
Salsetta d'Uva Passa, 148
Salsiccie con Cime di Rapa, 125
salt, **32**
salt cod, **23**
  baked salt cod and potatoes with tomatoes, 109
  choosing and preparing, **163**
  salt cod stewed with olives and potatoes, 109
sardines, **23**
Sardinia, 17
  menu, 155
sauces:
  béchamel, 136
  fresh tomato, 137
  green, 50-1, 139
  hot anchovy, 137
  mayonnaise, 140
  pounded basil and pine nut, **141**
  sweet pepper, 140
  tomato, 138
  uncooked red, **50-1**, 139
  uncooked tomato sauce with black olives, **138**
sausage:
  cooking, **164**
  Italian sausages with broccoli rape, 125
  lasagne, 84
  lentil stew with sausages, **91**
  orecchiette with sausage and broccoli rape, 84
  peppers stuffed with rice and Gorgonzola, 41, 64, **155**
  pizza with sweet Italian sausage, 44, 68
  roasted rice with sausage and artichokes, 95
sautéed:
  chicken livers with sage on crostini toasts, 70
  escarole with beans, **57**, 130
  kidneys with peas and shallots, 124
savory braised quails, 122
scalloped potatoes baked in milk, **56**, **128**
scamorza, **29**
  crispella stuffed with scamorza cheese, **45**, **69**
Scampi al Forno, 101, **105**
Scampi con Salvia alla Griglia, 100
Scarola in Padella con Fagioli, 130
Scarpassa, 62
Schmorbraten, 111
sea bass, 22
  poached fish with two sauces, **50-1**
  seafood risotto, 92, **93**
  seafood "soup," 98, **99**
sea bream, **23**
  seafood risotto, 92, **93**
  seafood "soup," 98, **99**
seafood:
  risotto, 92, **93**
  "soup," 98, **99**

sesame seeds:
  Italian sesame cookies, 149
sherry:
  Italian trifle, 142, **150**, **154**
  stuffed poached pears with custard sauce, **146-7**
  sweet fried pastry ribbons, 148, **151**
shrimp, **25**
  baked with garlic and parsley, 101, **105**
  grilled with sage, 100
  mixed fish fry, 100
  peeling and butterflying, **163**
  seafood risotto, 92, **93**
  seafood "soup," 98, **99**
  Swiss chard and shrimp soup with rice, **74-5**
Sicilia, 17
snapper:
  mixed fish fry, 100
  seafood risotto, 92, **93**
  seafood "soup", 98, **99**
Sogliole all' Abruzzese, 103, **104**
Sogliole al Cartoccio, **102**
sole:
  with garlic, lemon, and olives, 103, **104**
  mixed fish fry, 100
  in parchment, **102**
  poached fillets with fresh herbs, 108
  stewed squid with spinach, 101
soups:
  beef broth, 110
  beef soup with barley and vegetable, 73
  bread dumplings in broth, 76
  chicken broth with pastina, 73
  escarole, 76
  meat broth, 72
  pumpkin, 77
  Swiss chard and shrimp soup with rice, **74-5**
  zucchini, 76
sour pan-roasted beef, 111
spaghetti, **31**
  with eggs and bacon, 85
Spaghetti alla Carbonara, 85
Spezzatino di Vitello in Umido con Limone e Pinoli, 114
spider crab, **25**
spinach, **21**
  stewed squid with spinach, 101
squash:
  pumpkin soup, **77**
  winter minestrone, 8, **10**, 42-3
squid, **25**
  cleaning, **99**
  mixed fish fry, 100
  seafood risotto, 92, **93**
  seafood "soup," 98, **99**
  stewed with spinach, 101
steamed zucchini with butter and onion, 132
stelline, **31**
  chicken broth with pastina, 73
stewed:
  beans with garlic and herbs, 90
  cabbage with pancetta and vinegar, 127
  honeycomb tripe, 125
  salt cod with olives and potatoes, 109
  squid with spinach, 101

strawberries, **37**
  Italian trifle, 142, **150**, **154**
Stufato di Cervo, 122
stuffed:
  baked peaches, 145
  cabbage, 126
  crepes, 89
  crispelle, **45**, **69**
  dried figs, 148
  eggplant, 64
  lasagne in the style of Naples, 84
  meat loaf with ham and frittatine, 110, **121**
  peppers with rice and Gorgonzola, **41**, 64, **155**
  poached pears with custard sauce, **146-7**
  roasted pepper "sandwiches," 63
  veal rolls with prosciutto and fontina, **115**
Sugo di Pomodoro, 138
Sugo di Pomodoro Freschi, 137
summer vegetable salad, **8, 14, 56**, 133
sweet and sour onions, **40**, 63
sweet apple crepes, 142
sweet fried pastry ribbons, 148, **151**
sweet pepper sauce, 140
Swiss chard, 21
  stewed squid, 101
  Swiss chard and shrimp soup with rice, **74-5**
swordfish, 23
  with lemon sauce, **9, 17, 106-7**
  with onion, olives, and capers, 103

T

tagliatelle, 31, 168
  with bolognese sauce, **82**, 88
  making fresh, 168
Tagliatelle con Salsa Bolognese, **82**, 88
Taiedda, 108
taleggio, 29
Tiramisù, **58-9**
toma, 28
tomatoes, **20, 35**
  baked polenta casserole, 95
  baked salt cod with potatoes and tomatoes, **104**, 109
  bucatini with tomato and bacon sauce, 85
  canned peeled plum, 35
  chicken hunter's style, **116-17**
  creamy tomato sauce, 138
  fresh tomato sauce, 137
  green beans with tomato and garlic, **56**, 129
  linguine with clam sauce, **46-7**
  little meatballs in tomato sauce, **9, 10, 40**, 67
  my grandmother's baked polenta, **8, 96, 97, 155**
  pan-roasted guinea fowl with bread and sun-dried tomato stuffing, 123
  pasta with harlot's sauce, **83**, 85
  peeling, **160**
  Pizza Napoletana, **12**, 68
  Pizzetta Margherita, **44**, 68
  purée, 35
  risotto with tomato and basil, 94
  seeding, **160**
  summer vegetable salad, **8, 14, 56**, 133
  sun-dried, 35
  tomato sauce, 138

uncooked red sauce, **50-1**, 139
uncooked tomato sauce with black olives, **138**
veal chops with fresh tomato and arugula sauce, 114
Tonno alla Stemperata, 103
Trentino-Alto Adige, 16
tripe, stewed honeycomb, 125
Trippa in Umido, 125
tuna, 23
  canned, **34**
  mayonnaise, 140
  with lemon sauce, 106
  with onion, olives, and capers, 103
turkey:
  breaded breast cutlets, 118
  little pasta dumplings with meat and cheese, **8, 14, 31**, 80, **81**
Tuscany, 10
  menu, 154

U·V

Uccelletti Scappati, **115**
Umbria, 10
uncooked:
  red sauce, **50-1**, 139
  tomato sauce with black olives, **138**
Val d'Aosta, 15
vanilla, **37**
veal, **27**
  braised shank, **8, 16, 54-5**
  braised with wine, lemon, and pine nuts, 114
  chops with fresh tomato and arugula sauce, 114
  meat broth, 72
  rolls stuffed with prosciutto and fontina, **115**
  vegetable risotto, **8, 15, 48-9**

Veneto, 17
venison, **27**
  venison casserole, 122
vinegar, **35**
  green horseradish sauce, 139
  stewed cabbage with pancetta and vinegar, 127
  sweet and sour onions, **40**, 63

W·Z

whitebait, 22
wine, 11, 17, **35**
  baked fish fillets with vegetables, potatoes, and white wine, 108
  braised veal with wine, lemon, and pine nuts, 114
  linguine with clam sauce, **46-7**
  little meatballs in wine, 67
  mussels in white wine, **40, 65**
  poached fish with two sauces, **50-1**
  seafood "soup," 98, **99**
  vegetable risotto, **8, 15, 48-9**
winter minestrone, **8, 10, 42-3**
Zabaione, 143
zucchini:
  fritters, 62
  soup, 76
  steamed with butter and onion, 132
  winter minestrone, 9, 10, **42-3**
Zucchini alla Casalinga, 132
Zuppa Inglese, 142, **150, 154**
Zuppa di Mitili alla Pugliese, **40, 65**
Zuppa di Pesce alla Gallipolina, 98, **99**
Zuppa di Scarola, 76

AUTHOR'S ACKNOWLEDGMENTS
Above all, thanks to my mother, who was my first introduction to fine Italian cooking and style, and who is my constant inspiration, and to my tender, courageous, and remarkable children, Gabriella Leah and Celina Raffaella, for whom I labor with love; to Alex Barakov for helping me in every way and with every task; to my extraordinary editor, Lorna Damms, and the exceptional team at Dorling Kindersley; to my agent, Judith Weber, for her good work; to my generous friend Flavia Destefanis for her advice and contributions; to Anna Amendolara Nurse for her recipes and everpresent help; to Valerie Serra for her kindness with recipe contributions and assistance and to Elio Serra for help with text; to Nancy Q. Keefe, always, for leading me here; to Jack Ubaldi for his advice about meat and butchering; to Dun Gifford, Sara Baer-Sinnott, and Oldways for bringing me to Apulia; to Alice Fixx and the consortium of Parmigiano-Reggiano cheese, especially Dr. Leo Bertozzi and Renzo Cattabiani, for hosting me in Emilia-Romagna; to Lidia

Bastianich for her kindness in allowing me to reproduce her recipes; also to La Molisana Pasta, Anna Teresa Callen, Nick Malgieri, Anna Aldorisi, Paul DuPont of Quebec, Pintelle of Toronto; Anna Salerno, Gisella and Cristiano Isidori, Andrea and Cathy Baruffi, Professore Folco Portinari, Ignacious Bonanno, Madhur Jaffrey, Joanne Muir, Jenna Holst, Connie Lozito, Carole Walter, Annette della Croce Messina, Emily Balducci, and Nina and Andy Balducci for help with research and recipe contributions.
I would also like to acknowledge the following books, which were helpful in my research:
La Cucina delle murge by Maria Pignatelli Ferrante, *Puglia la tradizione in cucina* by Angelina Stanziano and Laura Santoro, *La cucina pugliese* by Luigi Sada, *Guida gastronomica d'Italia* by Felice Cùnsolo, *Guida all'Italia gastronomica* by Massimo Alberini and Giorgio Mistretta, *Treasures of the Italian Table* by Burton Anderson, *The Tuscan Cookbook* by Wilma Pezzini, *Italian Cuisine: Basic Cooking Techniques* by Tony May, *Ricette tradizionali della Liguria: La*

cucina onegliese by Lucetto Ramella, *L'antica cucinieru genovese e ligure, DOC Cheeses of Italy: A Great Heritage* by Franco Angeli, *The Complete Book of Fruits and Vegetables* by Franceso Bianchini, Franceso Corbetta and Marilena Pistoia, and *Healing with Whole Foods* by Paul Pitchford.

Dorling Kindersley would like to thank Clive Streeter for his photographs and Lyn Rutherford for preparing the food and for hand modeling. Patrick McLeavey for design work; Andy Whitfield for photographic assistance and Amanda Grant for assisting Lyn; Jo Brewer, Karen Ruane, Dean Hollowood, and Harvey de Roemer for DTP work; Sarah Ponder for the artworks; Jasmine Challis for the nutritional breakdowns; David Roberts for the map on pages 8–9; Sarah Ereira for the index; Flavia Destefanis for checking the Italian. Many thanks also to the Elizabeth David Cookshop, London, for loaning equipment.

Picture credits: Photography by Clive Streeter except photographs of Julia della Croce by Martin Merchant at Everett Studios, White Plains, New York.